Talk as Therapy

Trends in Applied Linguistics 7

Editors

Ulrike Jessner
Claire Kramsch

De Gruyter Mouton

Talk as Therapy

Psychotherapy in a Linguistic Perspective

By
Joanna Pawelczyk

De Gruyter Mouton

ISBN 978-1-934078-66-2
e-ISBN 978-1-934067-9
ISSN 1868-6362

Library of Congress Cataloging-in-Publication Data

Pawelczyk, Joanna.
  Talk as therapy : psychotherapy in a linguistic perspective / by
Joanna Pawelczyk.
    p. cm. − (Trends in applied linguistics ; 7)
  Includes bibliographical references and index.
  ISBN 978-1-934078-66-2 (hardcover : alk. paper)
  1. Psychotherapy.   2. Psychotherapist and patient.   I. Title.
  RC475.P39   2011
  616.89'14−dc23
                                                                2011019777

Bibliographic information published by the Deutsche Nationalbibliothek

The Deutsche Nationalbibliothek lists this publication in the Deutsche Nationalbibliografie;
detailed bibliographic data are available in the Internet at http://dnb.d-nb.de.

Cover image: Roswitha Schacht/morguefile.com
Printing: Hubert & Co. GmbH & Co. KG, Göttingen
∞ Printed on acid-free paper

Printed in Germany

www.degruyter.com

Acknowledgements

I am deeply indebted to Dr Richard Erskine, the founder and director of the Institute of Integrative Psychotherapy, New York, for making this project possible in the first place. His enthusiasm, encouragement, and interest in my work enabled me to observe how 'psychotherapy' becomes a unique encounter between two people and to collect unique data.

I also extend my deepest gratitude to the participants of the Institute of Integrative Psychotherapy workshops, who kindly gave me permission to listen to their stories and who fully understood that only real-life data, collected by the researcher who is present at the site, can improve our understanding as to how and why psychotherapy is curative. The long and sometimes emotionally difficult hours spent at the two psychotherapy workshops provided me with enough examples of the power of the spoken word, which combined with the caring presence of another person truly enables one to overcome even the gravest difficulties and traumas of everyday existence.

My ideas and thinking on the topic of the discourse of psychotherapy and the therapeutic functioning of communication extensively benefited from my participation in annual Conversation Analysis & Psychotherapy conferences and the lively and insightful discussions following the presentations.

I would also like to acknowledge the ideas of Professor Srikant Sarangi which I fully share and which clearly underline the necessity of developing interprofessional dialogue between discourse analysts and professional practitioners.

I want to thank two anonymous reviewers for their insightful comments that helped to improve the final version of the manuscript.

I would like to express my gratitude to my colleagues at the School of English at Adam Mickiewicz University. I thank Professor Katarzyna Dziubalska-Kołaczyk, the Head of the School of English for her support and encouragement. I am indebted to Professor Agnieszka Kiełkiewicz-Janowiak for her critical and insightful comments on this manuscript at various stages of the project and her continuous interest in my work. I also thank Professor Małgorzata Fabiszak who read the whole manuscript and provided many useful comments and suggestions.

Special thanks are also due to my friend Eva Graf for her support and belief in this book and to Krystyna Golkowska for enabling me to use the library resources of the Cornell University.

Contents

Transcription Conventions

(based on the standard conventions of Conversation Analysis, cf. Jefferson 2004; Hutchby 2007)

C	Client
T	Therapist
[ ]	Square brackets indicate the start and end of the overlapping speech.
=	Equal signs indicate 'latching' stretch of talk, i.e., no discernible gap between the utterances.
//	Double slashes indicate an interruption, i.e. a point in the interaction where another interlocutor takes over the conversational floor before the current speaker has finished his/her utterance, i.e., prior to a possible transition place.
(1.0)	A number in parenthesis indicates the time, in seconds, of a gap in speech.
(.)	A 'micropause', i.e., a pause of less than one tenth of a second is indicated by a dot in parenthesis.
(( ))	Double parentheses indicate a nonverbal activity, e.g., crying which usually accompanies a stretch of talk.
( )	Empty parenthesis indicates the occurrence of an unclear utterance; or a removal of a part of the utterance due to privacy policy.
.hhh	H's preceded by a dot indicate audible inward breathing.
hhh	H's with no preceding dot indicate outward breathing.
ba:d	Colon(s) indicate(s) that the speaker has stretched the preceding sound; the more colons the greater the extent of the stretching.
. , ? !	Punctuation symbols are used to mark intonation, not grammar.
↓	Downward arrow indicates falling pitch or intonation.
↑	Upward arrow indicates rising pitch or intonation.
<u>Bad</u>	Underlined words/sounds are emphasized and typically louder.

BAD   Capitals indicate even greater loudness than underlined words/ sounds.

°bad°   Degree signs indicate that the material between them is quieter than the surrounding talk.

<bad>   Outward arrows indicate slower speech.

>bad<   Inward arrows indicate faster speech.

X Y Z   These capitals letters are used instead of the real names of people or places appearing in the clients' talk. This is a due to privacy policy.

→   Arrows in the left margin indicate analyst's significant line; alternatively the word/phrase is in bold face.

Introduction: Talk as therapy

> *The psychotherapeutic situation forces the patient*
> *to confront new conventions, new possibilities of*
> *understanding, multiple meanings in the simplest*
> *exchanges, and by being exposed to these frighten-*
> *ing possibilities in safe surroundings, to become*
> *willing to discover that all of the conventions we*
> *are used to can be altered or terminated if they be-*
> *come stagnating.* (Lakoff 1982: 145)

Psychotherapy has the potential to help people live more fulfilling and satisfying lives. Psychotherapists' waiting rooms brim with clients who share
a desire to overcome complicated life experiences, horrifying traumas, and
have actively sought out assistance in discovering ways to relieve their agony. While most undergo psychotherapy for help in dealing with the present via the past, some embark on a psychotherapeutic trajectory in the
hope of learning strategies that will protect them from potential future problems or assist them in coping with life's tribulations. In either case, there is
a common aim: to live a happier, more contactful existence. Psychotherapy
is increasingly attractive as a means through which people become aware of
their needs and make sense of their experience. It also provides guidance on
discovering the meaning of one's life as well as suggesting ways to sur-
mount everyday difficulties (cf. Czabała 2006).

    Since the time of Breuer and Freud, psychotherapy has been commonly
referred to as the 'talking cure',[1] as talk, in this context, functions as the
tool that is used to improve the mental health of the client,[2] or as a "process
which may most profitably be viewed in terms of communicative expression" (Russell 1987: 4). In psychotherapy, relief is brought about in talk
and through talk, yet does not take place in a social vacuum; the power of
therapeutic talk derives from the relationship that the participants of this
social event position each other to: "the very relationship that develops between therapist and client ... is the central constituent of the therapeutic
enterprise" (Spinelli 2006: 1). The 'talking cure' – just as any other social
encounter – underlines the centrality of the relational function of talk (cf.
Scollon 1998; Candlin, S. 2000). For many clients, an evolving interpersonal contact enables them to grow and heal. Although the actual positive
results that the talking cure produces have been called into question (Szasz

1978; cf. Czabała 2006), the effectiveness of psychotherapy has been measured.[3] A client gains inner strength to improve his/her life when the psychotherapist creates the necessary conditions for the client to take full responsibility for the way he/she lives. Thus successful psychotherapy empowers the client to dare initiate the desired change.

The interaction transpiring between the psychotherapist and client during a speech event referred to as a psychotherapy session can be more generally subsumed under the discourse of medical encounters (cf. Ainsworth-Vaughn 2001) or the discourses of health (cf. Candlin, C. N. 2000). According to Ainsworth-Vaughn (2001), the studies on talk in medical encounters can be divided into two types of literature: 'praxis' and 'discourse'. In the former, talk-as-data is removed from the initial steps of the research, and language is assumed to be the transparent vehicle of meaning. Consequently, a single functional meaning is attributed to each utterance, which is then coded and finally quantified. The latter, on the other hand, offers analyses of talk itself. As Ainsworth-Vaughn (2001) explains, these analyses grow out of contemporary theories about sequential, situated discourse, thus reflecting conversation-analytic, interactional-sociolinguistic as well as the ethnographic theoretical assumptions about communication.[4] A crucial difference between these two types of research lies in their respective orientation toward the balance of power between the two involved parties (viz.: the physician and the patient). While the praxis literature concerns itself with the power over future action (i.e., what are the outcomes of talk?), the discourse literature focuses on control over the emerging discourse. The psychotherapy session is regarded as an outgrowth of medical encounters as in this context discourse itself is not only central to psychotherapeutic practice but in fact constitutes the very practice (cf. Ainsworth-Vaughn 2001: 458), and as such is a unique social and interactional context and a fascinating research site both for praxis-oriented and discourse-oriented analysts.[5]

C. N. Candlin (2000) conceives of discourses of health[6] as subsuming three interrelated discourses referred to as: the discourse of health care, the discourse of health measurement and the discourse of health experience. Psychotherapy may entail all three of the discourse types, but for a speech event to be labeled psychotherapy it needs to involve at least the first and the last discourses entailing among others: treatment goals and decisions, hypotheses, and inferences (mainly offered by the psychotherapist), as well as the personal, subjective experiences (primarily supplied by the client) (cf. Candlin, C. N. 2000).

More specifically, the discourse of psychotherapy belongs to the genre of intimate discourse, together with, among others, discourse of 'troubles talk among friends' (Jefferson 1988), 'painful self-disclosure' between acquaintances (Coupland et al. 1988) and 'conversations of intimate friendship' (Lakoff 1990). Gerhardt and Stinson (1995: 635) frame therapeutic discourse as "another type of autobiographic narrative activity in which one part of the self not only narrates other parts of the self but observes, reflects on, evaluates, criticizes, censors and reveals other parts of the self for the purpose of achieving some kind of self-transformation".

The current model of healthcare communication (cf. Candlin, C. N. 2000; Candlin, S. 2000; Ragan 2000) places a significant emphasis on the importance of building and maintaining a therapeutic relationship – an alliance – both in the physician-patient[7] dyad as well as in the interactions between the psychotherapist and the client (cf. Horvath and Greenberg 1994; Moursund and Erskine 2004; Czabała 2006). The fundamental premise of such a relationship is the quality of the communication between the professional and the patient/client. Thus talk emerges as central to the effectiveness of a therapeutic relationship. This effectiveness consists in the patients/clients being relatively free to explore and express their feelings, free of the inevitable concerns that characterize normal, social interaction (cf. Kahn 1991). Since discourse constitutes the process of psychotherapy, the unique relationship that (ideally) characterizes the psychotherapist-client dyad can be regarded as a model for other healthcare professionals to pursue: "in successful therapy the therapist provides for the client a relationship unlike any the client has had before" (Kahn 1991: xi).

More importantly, psychotherapists use language to the therapeutic effect in skilled and often artful ways, which differ from ordinary conversations. Lambert and Hill (1994), representing the praxis 'voice' genre, state that the most important aim of investigating psychotherapy is the empirical study of the process of psychotherapy, i.e., examining the actual meeting (or interaction) between the psychotherapist and client and the potential changes that follow it. Similarly Greenberg (1991, 1999), also of the 'praxis' stance, posits that it is imperative to understand how psychotherapy works and what the process of change consists of, as well as what elements of the psychotherapy process trigger this change. Thus psychotherapy practitioners comment with increasing frequency on the need to further investigate the process of psychotherapy, an aim which can be pursued through a thorough examination of patterns of language use in therapy.

Since change as a result of psychotherapy – i.e., the client's qualitative change in his/her life – comes about through interaction not just through language, researchers must more fully explore how a successful outcome, viz.: a client's self-transformation (cf. Gerhardt and Stinson 1995: 635), is brought about linguistically. How is psychotherapy linguistically realized? How is it contextually and interactionally achieved? These are important questions to address not only considering the growing number of people who seek psychotherapy on various grounds but also the increasingly diverse social contexts in which therapeutic skills and talk are purposely applied.

The aim of the current project, representing discourse-oriented studies but also drawing on praxis perspectives (cf. Ainsworth-Vaughn 2001), is to investigate what makes talk between the psychotherapist and client therapeutic, i.e., what language features, communicative and interactional strategies – or, more generally, what verbal and non-verbal practices – transpiring in the psychotherapy session gradually lead to the client's self-transformation. How are the goals of psychotherapy – the 'talking cure'– discursively and linguistically achieved?

To accomplish these aims, a 65-hour corpus of authentic psychotherapeutic interactions has been qualitatively analyzed with the methods of broadly conceived discourse analysis. The data collected for the study features one male psychotherapist engaged in a one-to-one dialogue with twenty-five clients.

As a researcher I was permitted to observe and record the sessions. The project was very much data-driven (cf. Dörnyei 2007: 37–38; Johnstone 2000: 29; Braun and Clarke 2006); the fieldwork began without specific strategies having been identified as targets or particular categories defined. Rather, as prominent regularities emerged from the data, my sense of what makes talk therapeutic and what communicative and interactional strategies occur in this process, developed with the time spent at the sessions and the review of the collected data. Thus the more interactions I observed and recorded, the better my understanding of the therapeutic functioning of communication. When the project started I had no experience with psychotherapy, neither in the professional sense nor as a client. I believe that this 'blank' approach to the data enabled me as a discourse analyst to determine the most salient aspects of the data under scrutiny without the analytic preconceptions.[8]

In my description of the research site (see Chapter 1) I refer to a 'workshop' setting, as this was the (official) name under which the therapy sessions were conducted. These workshops were organized for those professionals who deliver various forms of psychological help themselves (e.g., psychologists, psychotherapists, social workers). Although such a context for therapy may appear to be an atypical format, the idea behind the sessions was, first and foremost, to create space for these professionals to deal with their own personal issues. This is to say that the issues that the therapist and clients worked on during sessions, and which are presented and discussed in this study, constituted the participants' real source of personal trouble, pain and dilemma at the time of the research. In other words, the collected corpus of psychotherapeutic interactions and the extracts presented in the study show real therapy material. At the same time, however, since other participants observed the individual sessions, these professionals were provided with a unique opportunity to witness and, in effect, learn the techniques used by the psychotherapist who worked with them. In other words, the meetings did not follow a typical workshop format where the educational goal is of primary importance, rather this was a side effect, absorbed through the opportunity to observe a seasoned psychotherapist engaged in intense, focused, one-on-one work with genuine clients with actual issues. Although, this is not a usual situation in therapy when one's (actual) psychotherapeutic work is being watched by others, such a format allowed the master therapist to combine the *personal* (for the benefit of the individual client in session) and the *educational* (for those observing the session) aspects of his work in the context under scrutiny.

The choice of this particular psychotherapeutic setting offered a number of benefits in accordance with the aims of the project. First and foremost it secured an access to rich authentic therapy material. Secondly, it enabled the observation and recording of various problems and issues subject to therapeutic intervention brought by twenty-five individual clients. Thirdly, in line with the interprofessional aspect of the project, the selected setting provided me with an opportunity and space to discuss the professional aspects of doing psychotherapy with the professional practitioners present at the workshops. In other words, I was able to gain first-hand professional insight on the psychotherapeutic work I was observing in an attempt to make the findings practice-driven (cf. Sarangi 2002). Finally, it could be argued that the very presence of the group of fellow clients as observers and workshop beneficiaries may have served to diminish the intrusion of having a researcher present.

As a researcher, I believe it is essential for discourse analysts to enter even the most restricted research sites (cf. Sarangi and Roberts 1999; Mullany 2007) in order to witness the actual interactions and collect the ethnographic details indispensable for the accurate data interpretation. My presence at the sessions secured a thick description (cf. Geertz 1973) of the site, allowed me to engage in the interprofessional dialogue with the therapist to understand his professional agenda and determine the extent of his conscious intent behind certain discernible patterns of method and technique. These aspects of my involvement in the project proved vital in the process of data transcription and analysis.

The study takes the view of social interaction being anchored within discourse norms which are then interactionally realized with certain verbal and non-verbal practices in the actual communicative contexts. Both verbal and non-verbal practices reflect general discourse norms upon which the activity of psychotherapy is based. Thus the book proposes three discourse norms which are indispensable for a social activity to be labeled psychotherapy and then demonstrates how these norms are operationalized, i.e., linguistically and interactionally realized in actual psychotherapy sessions. Two of these norms (*self-disclosure* and *communication of emotion*) have been arrived at by consulting the professional literature (psychological and psychotherapeutic) which extensively discusses these principles, yet leaves out the discussion on their situated and interactional realization. One of them (*the transparency of meaning*) has been arrived at by the qualitative scrutiny of the collected corpus of psychotherapy sessions as well as by juxtaposing a psychotherapeutic interaction with an ordinary conversation in terms of structure and goals. The phenomena of emotional support as well as the psychotherapist's emotional presence are also discussed as interactionally accomplished in the here-and-now of the therapeutic interaction. These two aspects of therapy talk are claimed to be indispensable for building a therapeutic relationship between the psychotherapist and the client.

To draw on Ochs's (1992) model of social meanings and indexicality, the current discussion will show how a social activity of psychotherapy is constituted by three fundamental stances which are indexed by specific verbal and non-verbal practices. The proposed discourse norms are assumed to be generally applicable to a psychotherapeutic activity as the collected and analyzed data represent the Relationship-Focused Integrative Psychotherapy approach, which incorporates the most important and commonly used psychotherapeutic theories.[9] Those theoretical perspectives can be found in almost every psychotherapy approach currently practiced. Thus the eclecticism of the Relationship-Focused Integrative Psychotherapy makes it an almost ideal therapeutic protocol to scrutinize for the defining characteristics of psychotherapy and its discursive workings. Since the aim of the study is to point out the interactional constituents of psychotherapy, the extracts selected for the discussion present successful interactions (from a professional point of view) between the psychotherapist and clients. This is to say that these interactions accomplished a certain, intended, professional task from the psychotherapist's (professional) point of view.

The linguistic and interactional realization of these norms may differ however, as no single feature of language or interactional strategy directly and exclusively indexes the therapeutic function of talk (cf. Ochs 1992). The therapeutic function of any verbal or non-verbal practice, as the analysis evinces, emerges in the local, interactional context which is, in turn, embedded in the speech situation of the psychotherapy session encompassing the psychotherapist's and client's interactional agendas. Thus of crucial importance for the current analysis is the significance of a certain form or strategy in the specific context of the interaction. Consequently, it will be demonstrated how certain therapeutic functions are achieved interactionally by applying microanalysis to a corpus of therapeutic talk.

Interestingly, and perhaps contrary to popular opinion, psychotherapeutic talk draws on the mundane. Quite unsensational and recognizable practices – whose *locally* emergent significance facilitates self-disclosive talk – help a client unveil and explore personal experience and focus on its emotional aspects, all in the safety of the therapeutic alliance. The therapeutic value of certain verbal and non-verbal practices is accomplished both by the client and the psychotherapist, commonly a facilitator of the dialogue. The psychotherapist remains in the interactional charge of the emerging talk and his communicative input is largely determined by the client's contributions. This is what makes psychotherapy a process which is constructed through the interaction of therapist and client.

The study should be of interest to linguists by demonstrating how their various tools and methods make it possible to unpack what is going on interactionally in psychotherapy. After all, language and communication are not only the means of expression in this context but through the use of verbal and non-verbal means, the client's experience becomes realizable and consequently understandable (cf. Sarangi 2001). In other words, language and communication function as professional tools in the hands of a psychotherapist enabling the client to make sense of traumas past and present for the ultimate purpose of living a better life. This ultimate goal however can only be accomplished if the psychotherapist and client engage in an *interaction*. Discourse analysts can offer systematic inspection of what happens in such an interaction, i.e., how psychotherapy is done. It is hoped that at the same time this discourse-oriented study of psychotherapeutic interaction, relying on the professional insights of psychotherapy can also offer practically relevant findings to the work of psychotherapists and counselors. These insights are indispensable in providing ethnographic background essential in understanding psychotherapeutic practices. The methods of discourse analysis and conversation analysis applied in the study "can make evident practices of which therapists are not explicitly aware" (Leudar, Antaki, and Barnes 2006: 28).

The present chapter has set the stage for the study presented in the book. It introduced two types of studies on medical encounters and considered a psychotherapy session to be a unique social and interactional research context both for professionals and discourse analysts. The discourse of psychotherapy was then positioned in the realm of discourses of health with an emphasis on the healing power of the therapeutic alliance developed between the therapist and client followed by the presentation of the aims of the current project.

Chapter 1 (*Situating the study*) comprises three main sections. Firstly, it introduces the aims and functions of psychotherapy presenting the recent changes in the field focusing on one of the most modern psychotherapeutic protocols, viz.: Relationship-Focused Integrative Psychotherapy. The interactions between the psychotherapist and clients collected and analyzed for the project represent this modern eclectic approach. The discussion then moves on to present another change concerning the discourse of psychotherapy, viz.: its increased infiltration of the new social contexts. Thus, why and how the therapeutic modes of talk are becoming increasingly common and intentionally re-contextualized is discussed, as well as the settings in which these modes have begun to emerge. Finally, issues related to data collection at the psychotherapy session as a restricted research site are discussed. Overall, the last section of Chapter 1 gives insight into conducting research at the site where language and communication function as professional tools. More importantly, it discusses the dynamics of collaboration between discourse analysts and professionals and thus it can be found particularly useful to researchers planning to undertake research at an (inter)professional site. It also underlines that only close and informed collaboration between discourse analysts and professionals can generate practically relevant findings. It begins with an overview of the language and communication-oriented studies into psychotherapy, concentrating on their 'know that' vs. 'know how' research perspectives. This is followed by a presentation of the merits of ethnographic research at the professional site. Next, the concept of the 'interprofessional discourse site' is attended to and its relevance to the context of the psychotherapy session is discussed. The diverging positions of discourse analysts and conversation analysts on the issue of 'interprofessionality' are presented. The status and identity of the researcher as a (non)-participant observer are also addressed, as well as various 'paradoxes' deriving from the researcher's involvement in the community under study. The discussion then focuses on the research ethics relevant to the interprofessional research project, drawing extensively on the observations and experiences collected by the author as a non-participant observer of the Relationship-Focused Integrative Psychotherapy sessions. The chapter concludes with a presentation of the current project. It describes the specifics of the research site, the type and amount of data collected, followed by a justification of the methodological apparatus and methods to be applied in the analysis of psychotherapeutic interaction.

The primary focus of Chapter 2 falls on the meaning of words and phrases proffered by the client, which is strongly preferred in the context of psychotherapeutic interaction. *The transparency of meaning*, referred to as explicit confrontation of the meaning of the client's verbal and non-verbal input by the therapist, is introduced as a salient discourse norm of psychotherapy. The discussion concentrates on how the client is urged to explore and account for an expression immediately after proffering it, i.e., in the interactional 'here-and-now'. The chapter starts with positioning a psychotherapeutic interaction both as an activity type and a discourse type. Then, the discussion concentrates on juxtaposing an ordinary conversation and a psychotherapeutic interaction, with an emphasis on how the meaning of the words and phrases is arrived at in these two contexts. The remaining part of the chapter is devoted to an analysis of three strategies used by the psychotherapist in order to bring out the personal significance of the client's verbal and non-verbal acts.

Chapter 3 discusses *Self-disclosure* as one of the most salient discourse norms of psychotherapy. The chapter commences with a presentation of forms and functions of self-disclosure. The function of self-disclosure in psychotherapy is discussed as conceptualized in the praxis literature of psychology and psychotherapy. Next, the discussion moves on to data analysis, demonstrating how self-disclosure in the context of psychotherapy (client to therapist) is a product of a joint interactional effort between the client and the therapist, as well as how the therapist tends to rely on the client's communicative and interactional strategies (verbal, kinesic, prosodic), yet redefines their functions in the local context in order to facilitate and frequently resume a client's self-disclosure. Here, several such strategies utilized by the psychotherapist are described.

Chapter 4 presents *Communication of emotion* as a further defining discourse norm of psychotherapy. Emotions in psychotherapy manifest themselves in a multitude of ways; thus the strategies used by the therapist to prod the clients to emotional experience and the clients' communication and construction of emotions are discussed. The chapter commences with the concept of emotion as envisioned by social scientists, and psychotherapists' perspective on the role of emotions in the process of psychotherapy. The bulk of the chapter is devoted to how emotions and emotional work feature in various forms in psychotherapeutic interaction. The empirical part of the chapter shows how clients are encouraged to enhance their emotional awareness as well as experience regulation and transformation of their emotions. The therapist, a significant agent facilitating the client's processing of emotions, undertakes a variety of emotion-regulating/ supporting interventions. This entails significant interactional effort from both the client and therapist. Finally, aspects of non-verbal communication are discussed as crucial practices in communicating emotions in psychotherapy as well as in demonstrating the therapist's presence for his clients.

Chapter 5 (*Emotional support*) discusses the therapist's strategies of emotional support and presence used in the interactions with the clients. The chapter begins with presenting emotional support as an integral part of the supportive communication. Then four strategies of emotional support are detailed followed by the description of how the therapist manifests his emotional presence for the clients in the interactional here-and-now.

Chapter 6 (*Conclusion: Reflecting on talk as therapy*) returns to the issue of the therapeutic function of linguistic forms and communicative strategies. By drawing on the findings from the empirical analyses, it demonstrates the necessity of taking different types of context into account in attributing a therapeutic function to a linguistic form. It also underlines the power of the dialogical encounter (between therapist and client) in promoting a qualitative change in the client's life and reiterates the main methodological issues concerning conducting fieldwork at the interprofessional discourse site.

Talk as Therapy is about disclosing one's (usually) dysphoric experiences, clarifying and exploring them in the interactional here-and-now as well as focusing on their emotional aspects in the safety of the relationship with the therapist. Therapeutic discourse with its potential to instill a change in an individual may be one of the highest cultural and intellectual achievements of human beings.

Chapter 1. Situating the study

> *Discourse research can offer a range of linguistic and rhetorical categories to capture the 'know how' of a professional group, while also being able to distance oneself from passing judgment about individual practice.* (Sarangi 2002: 127)

1.1 Relationship-Focused Integrative Psychotherapy

Despite numerous approaches to psychotherapy, its aim can be quite uniformly defined as "getting people to see things from new angles" (Gale 1991: IX). There are approximately 400 forms of psychotherapy to date (Bongar and Beutler 1995) and therapeutic eclecticism has become more common than adherence to just one school (Moursund and Erskine 2004; cf. also the so-called eclectic phrase, Gaik 1992: 272). Indeed many practitioners are now choosing to build their own, unique ways of doing therapy, taking what seems to them the best and most effective techniques from a variety of approaches. Moursund and Erskine (2004: 1) state that "any approach to psychotherapy inevitably overlaps to some extent with other approaches that are being used and have been used in the past".

Psychotherapeutic schools/approaches differ in specific methods applied in the work with clients and also the types of clients' problems. Speculation to the supremacy of a single method has been unfounded (Czabała 2006). According to Stiles et al. (1990), different psychotherapy approaches share the following: 1. focusing on the client's painful experiences; 2. finding a reference point for the pain/suffering to be understood; 3. a change is understood as the psychological change.

Psychotherapy can be approached as the main or ancillary method of treating certain psychological disturbances (Czabała 2006). It encompasses a variety of treatment techniques in which a professionally trained person establishes a therapeutic relationship with an individual suffering from emotional problems for the purpose of alleviating or modifying troublesome thoughts, memories, emotional reactions, or patterns of behavior (Pawelczyk and Erskine 2008). Through psychotherapy, clients shift their self-perception and new relational possibilities become available, making behavioral change possible. They discover facets of themselves, uncovering previously unconscious, suppressed or unexplored experiences. Successful therapy involves the therapist's phenomenological inquiry that facilitates the client's bringing back into consciousness that which has been unconscious – the unexpressed thought, the never verbalized affect, the interrupted fantasy, the intentionally denied experience – in order to reformulate psychological experience. While people may not need psychotherapists to enable them to talk about their feelings or to have authentic communication, still, the professional skills of a psychotherapist certainly facilitate and enhance the process of emotional expression. For some individuals the psychotherapist is the first person ever encountered who signals full interest in the client's phenomenological experience.

In the last 30 years, a major paradigm shift has occurred in the field of psychotherapy, wherein the focus of therapy is on a contactful relationship between client and therapist. The blank-screen model of a psychotherapeutic encounter has been replaced with a more relational approach across numerous psychotherapeutic schools (cf. Pawelczyk and Erskine 2008), whether they are contemporary Psychoanalysis, psychoanalytic Self-psychology, Integrative Psychotherapy, Transactional Analysis or Gestalt Therapy. Even many Cognitive-Behavioral psychologists currently recognize the importance of an effective interpersonal relationship as a basis for the client's making behavioral change.

The more relational model is based on the more contextually-sensitive, interactive forms of therapeutic dynamics (Gerhardt and Stinson 1995; cf. also Schafer 1992). The new model incorporates the indisputable fact of the dialogical nature of humans (cf. Staemmler 2004; Hermans and Dimaggio 2004; Angus and McLeod 2004), as commented on by one of the most renowned psychotherapists:

> ...a therapist helps a patient not by sifting through the past but by being lovingly present with that person; by being trustworthy, interested, and believing that their *joint activity*[10] will ultimately be redemptive and healing.
>
> (Yalom 1989: 227)

Thus it is in dialogue and through dialogue that one is able to arrive at clarifying one's views and attitudes.

The hallmark of the relational approaches is the crucial importance of the therapeutic relationship[11] or therapeutic alliance (Moursund and Erskine 2004) that must characterize the psychotherapist – client equation in order for the client to benefit from the psychotherapeutic work. According to the premise the need for a relationship constitutes a primary motivating experience of human behavior, and contact is the means by which the need is met. Contact occurs internally and externally; it involves a full awareness of sensations, feelings, needs, sensory motor activity, thoughts and memories that occur within the individual and a shift to full awareness of external events as registered by each of the sensory organs (Moursund and Erskine 2004).

Indeed, a review of the developmental psychology and psychotherapy literature reveals that the single most consistent concept is that of relationship – both in the early stages of life as well as throughout adulthood (Erskine 1989; Gehrie 1999; Lambert and Barley 2001; Horvath 2001). A contactful (interpersonal) relationship constitutes the source which gives meaning and validation to the self. Thus, as already presented, the role of psychotherapist is no longer limited to passing infrequent reflecting comments but instead he/she becomes a fully present (involved, attuned, inquiring) partner in the interaction: "today, the idea that a clinician's talk is instrumental in facilitating client change is as little contested as the idea that clients' talk can be a helpful indicator of their psychological well-being" (Russell 1987: 1).

The psychotherapy methods are based on the belief that psychological healing occurs primarily through the interpersonal contact of the therapeutic relationship. With such psychological healing it becomes possible for the person to face each moment with spontaneity and flexibility in solving life's problems and in relating to people. Anderson (1997: 234) states that therapy becomes, for the clients, a transformation event as the natural consequences of dialogic conversation in a collaborative relationship. In this communicative event the psychotherapist fosters an atmosphere of trust through his/her interest, respect, understanding, and empathy while encouraging open and direct communication by refraining from criticism and censure. As Moursund and Erskine (2004: 13) comment "our primary challenge as therapists is to create, maintain, and utilize a therapeutic relationship for the benefit of our clients". The therapeutic situation – in contrast to many non-therapy contexts – enables clients to learn about their feelings and (even) risk sharing them in the company of a therapist who "help[s] that exploration by maintaining a relatively constant posture of accepting, empathic interest and not adding the confusion of their own inevitably fluctuating feelings" (Kahn 1991: 153).

As Kahn (1991: 4) states "one of the reasons the therapist-client relationship has such therapeutic potential is that it is one relationship in the client's life that is actually happening during the therapy hour", and since in psychotherapy people are attempting to make meaning out of their experience, they can do it effectively within the context of a relationship and in a dialogue.

The interactions between the psychotherapist and clients collected for the project represent the Relationship-Focused Integrative Psychotherapy (Erskine and Moursund 1988; Erskine and Trautmann 1996; Moursund and Erskine 2004). Similarly to other relational approaches, Relationship-Focused Integrative Psychotherapy fully recognizes the importance of therapeutic relationship for creating a psychological environment which supports and encourages the client's change.

Relationship-Focused Integrative Psychotherapy is one of the most modern psychotherapeutic schools. The modifier 'integrative' refers to two aspects: firstly to the full synthesis of affective, behavioral, cognitive, and physiological theory and methods of psychotherapy and secondly, to the goal of psychotherapy, i.e. the integration or assimilation within the client of the fragmented or fixated aspects of personality "helping the client to assimilate and harmonize the contents of his or her ego states, relax the defense mechanisms, relinquish the script, and reengage the world with full contact" (Erskine and Moursund 1988: 40). Gold (1996) aptly summarizes the common characteristics of integrative psychotherapeutic approaches as follows:

> Theoretical integration involves the synthesis of novel models of personality functioning, psychopathology, and psychological change from the concepts of two or more traditional systems. Integrative theories ... generally attempt to explain psychological phenomena in interactional terms, by looking for the ways in which environmental, motivational, cognitive and affective factors influence and are influenced by each other. Causation is usually assumed to be multidirectional and to include conscious and covert factors, and most theoretical integrations include a focus on the ways that individuals re-create past patterns and experiences in the present.
>
> (Gold 1996: 13)

Relationship-Focused Integrative Psychotherapy is premised primarily on four theoretical perspectives: transactional analysis, Gestalt therapy, client-centered therapy, and behaviorism. It also relies considerably on psychoanalytic self-psychology, object relations theory and neo-Reichian body therapy (Moursund and Erskine 2004). It reflects the current eclecticism in psychotherapy, yet concurrently "provides internally compatible understandings of personality functioning, change, and technique" (Frank 1991: 540). The major premise of Integrative Psychotherapy is that the need for relationship constitutes a primary and motivating experience of human behavior, and contact is the means by which this need is met.

Two important principles guide Integrative Psychotherapy. The first one relates to the commitment to positive life change by affecting the client's life script ("a fixated series of defenses that prevent the feelings and unmet needs of childhood from coming into awareness" [Erskine and Moursund 1988: 30]). The second has to do with respecting the integrity of the client. This is to say that through respect and kindness, as well as maintenance of contact, personal presence is established which allows for an interpersonal relationship that provides affirmation of the client's integrity (Erskine and Moursund 1988). A contact-oriented, relationship-focused psychotherapy is based on the methods of inquiry, attunement and involvement. Most importantly, Integrative Psychotherapy practitioners believe that "change comes and remains solid as clients make their own meaning out of their own internal and external experiences" (Clark 1996: 313–314).

What is of great significance for the current study, Integrative Psychotherapy approach "attends seriously to what has been observed by all the major schools" (Wachtel 1990: 235) and thus constitutes ideal research ground to investigate the discursive workings of psychotherapy as a speech event. Indeed, the task of formulating discourse norms of psychotherapy as a speech event may appear quite daunting in view of the number of currently practiced psychotherapies. Relationship-Focused Integrative Psychotherapy with its reliance on the crucial and most respected psychotherapeutic protocols makes this task feasible. It is assumed, then, that the practices analyzed here can be generalizable to the larger community of psychotherapy professionals.

What is also noteworthy, the psychotherapeutic values and norms of interaction have entered a number of non-therapy social contexts. Thus the importance of psychotherapy in contemporary life is reflected in two aspects/ways. On the one hand, there is an increasing number of people who seek psychotherapeutic help and on the other, we can observe the recontextualization of therapeutic discourse in private and institutional settings.

What follows is the presentation of how (and why) the psychotherapeutic values and norms of interaction function in non-therapy contexts. Next the discussion will focus on selected aspects of conducting research at the restricted research site. Firstly, an overview of the 'language-oriented' studies into psychotherapy will be presented and the issue of how to study the professional sites will be addressed, followed by a focus on the interprofessional aspect of the setting under analysis. Issues of researchers' status and identity will also be addressed, as well as certain ethical aspects of the interprofessional research project (cf. Sarangi 2002). The discussion will extensively draw on observations and experiences collected by the author as a

non-participant observer of the Relationship-Focused Integrative Psychotherapy sessions. The chapter will close with presentation of the data collected for the project as well as methods and methodology used for the
analysis.

1.2 Psychotherapeutic discourse outside therapy room

> *...the therapeutic turn has produced a culture of
> the self, which draws extensively upon psychologi-
> cal knowledges and (quasi)-therapeutic techniques
> to know thyself and make thyself.* (McLeod and
> Wright 2003: 4)

Farber (2006: 7) states that nowadays, individuals "seem to be craving
more personal information about one another".[12] The *interest* in another
person's life and his/her experiences closely reflects one of the tenets of
psychotherapy, according to which one person (a therapist) is genuinely
interested in getting to know another person (a client). Orlinsky (1989)
talks about a contemporary individual as particularly vulnerable to the experience of conflict and loss and, as a result, in need of greater psychological help, while Giddens (1991) relates to 'personal meaningless' and
'existential isolation' as fundamental problems in late modernity. Fairclough (1992: 228) asserts that in the face of the increasing intrusion of the
economy and state on their lives, people try to manage their disorientation
and potential loss or crisis of identity by seeking various forms of therapy
and counseling. These perspectives clearly point to the current importance
of psychotherapy and psychotherapeutic discourse in people's lives.

It should then be of no surprise that selective discourse norms and
strategies of psychotherapeutic interaction, as well as discourse types and
properties of therapy talk, have entered new contexts and settings in two
most significant ways. Firstly, the terms 'therapy' and 'therapeutic' as well
as the vocabulary related to psychotherapeutic practice tend to be used
across many contexts as all-encompassing terms to invoke certain (positive), curative and beneficial aspects of events or situations in general. As
indicated on numerous pages of this book, people display and tend to claim
a high awareness of what therapy is about and on what methods it predominantly relies. Regardless of to what extent this folk perception and awareness is accurate, popular references to psychotherapy and its methods in

non-psychotherapeutic contexts are very common. For instance, President George W. Bush told an interviewer in 2004 that he wouldn't 'go on the couch' to rethink his decisions about the war in Iraq (Newsweek March 27, 2006). This succinct comment did not require any further elaboration and justification for the audience.

Secondly, and more importantly, there are areas of human activity which purposefully incorporate properties of therapy talk to gain well-defined/clear advantages. These new settings constitute particularly intriguing contexts, as they did not use to be based on or apply any therapeutic skills or features in their activities, yet now they put a major emphasis on them. As Cameron (2000a: 158) states, therapy is "an activity in which many of the themes of modern Western commonsense discourse come together". This new need, or rather an imperative, for everything being 'therapeutic' as well as a re-appraisal and recontextualization of therapeutic norms cannot be properly expounded without firstly consulting Giddens's (1991) concept of *reflexivity* as definitional of modernity in general.

In his view, the self in modernity becomes a reflexive project:[13] "– in our present day world – the self, like the broader institutional contexts in which it exists, has to be reflexively made" (Giddens 1991: 3). Reflexivity emerges as indispensable in the ontology and future of a person's life choices (Lupton 1998). The current social and cultural contexts demand that individuals constantly make and remake themselves (their 'selves') in order to find a place for their personal histories in a larger social history which, in turn, is characterized by rapid and continual changes: "the narra-tive of self-identity has to be shaped, altered and reflectively sustained in relation to rapidly changing circumstances of social life, on local and global scale" (Giddens 1991: 215). A person's identity can only be maintained by integrating events that occur in the external world and, more importantly, sorting them out into the ongoing story about the self (Giddens 1991: 54). Thus the salient aspect of one's identity is keeping a particular narrative going. This, in turn, implies enhanced awareness of the external and then internal experience of the world. Lupton (1998: 92) adds that emotional management constitutes an integral aspect of reflexive work upon the self, as "individuals in contemporary western societies are encouraged continu-ally to examine, and to work upon, their emotional selve'". As the re-searcher explains, the emotional 'work' refers here to improving the character of the emotional self, attempting to change it.

Therapy has the potential to teach and instill in an individual an ability to fully experience every moment of life and "integrate the inherited past and present into a coherent ongoing narrative which leads to a 'better future'" (Cameron 2000a: 4). This new *reflexive* conceptualization of identity can be first achieved and then maintained through therapy or self-therapy. *Reflexivity,* as one of the core characteristics of psychotherapy, enables an individual to continuously experience an enhanced awareness of one's thoughts and feelings. In this way it makes it possible to make sense of the rapid changes of the contemporary (global) world. Consequently in Giddens's view, therapy in contemporary social conditions should not be understood and evaluated only as "a means of coping with novel anxieties" (1991: 34) but rather, first and foremost as a 'methodology of life-planning' (1991: 180). The function of therapy in the modern world can also be understood in terms of an 'expert system',[14] i.e. "modes of technical knowledge which have validity independent of the practitioners and clients who make use of them" (Giddens 1991: 18). As Giddens argues, counselor and psychotherapist constitute core aspects of the expert system of modernity. What this implies then, is that (selective) therapeutic norms and values are no longer characteristic solely of the unique interaction (and relationship) between the client and the therapist, but they have entered new contexts. This idea very much echoes Fairclough's (1989, 1992) concept of 'technologization of discourse':

> We can usefully refer to 'discourse technologies' and to a 'technologization of discourse'... Examples of discourse technologies are interviewing, teaching, counseling and advertising...[I]n modern society they have taken on, and are taking on, the character of transcontextual techniques, which are seen as resources or toolkits that can be used to pursue a wide variety of strategies in many diverse contexts. Discourse technologies...are coming to have their own specialist technologists: researchers who look into their efficiency, designers who work out refinements in the light of research and changing institutional requirements, and trainers who pass on the techniques.
>
> (Fairclough 1992: 215)

Thus following Fairclough's line of reasoning, therapy has expanded its original purpose (a treatment of mental health) and has come to be regarded as applicable in many other contexts. Fairclough (1992: 223) asserts that what all discourse technologies share is "the property of being applied forms of social scientific knowledge". Numerous 'helping' organizations (cf. Fairclough 1992: 222) constitute examples of such applied forms of social scientific knowledge and are referred to as 'therapeutic technologies' (1992: 223). When psychotherapy and counseling assume that social ills can be removed on the basis of the hidden potential of individuals, they can be considered ideological practices. Fairclough also refers to Michel Foucault who regards 'confession', which incorporates aspects of psychotherapy and counseling, as the basis of social control. To recap, Fairclough positions therapy and counseling as key discourse types which have 'colonized' many institutional orders of discourse.

Still, Czabała (2006: 12) argues that psychotherapy is a method of treating mental disorders, but nevertheless offers numerous examples of how psychotherapy norms and values have expanded beyond the actual psychotherapy room. Orlinsky (1989), for instance, conceives of contemporary psychotherapy as a type of culture whose distinguishing features are counseling and providing people with a sense of relief.[15] Furedi (2004: 22) asserts that a culture becomes therapeutic when this form of thinking expands from informing the relationship between the individual and therapist to shaping public perceptions about a variety of issues. Following Furedi (2004), Becker (2005), Lasch (1979) and Rieff (1966), McLeod and Wright (2009: 123) refer to therapeutic culture as "a diverse range of social practices and cultural discourses unified by the imperatives of talk and self-disclosure, the privileging of the psychological and emotional realms, and a heightened concern with the self and interior life". In this view psychotherapy ceases to be a clinical technique only and it starts influencing everyday interactions and practices.

Cameron (2000a: 158) states that therapy lends itself to technologization, since its discourse norms are based on beliefs and values which also permeate other contexts, thus they can be easily adapted for different purposes in new settings. Therapy outside the psychotherapy room entails very eclectic and selective paradigms. Their eclecticism manifests itself in assembling concepts representing quite opposing psychotherapeutic approaches under one paradigm, while selectivity concerns adopting only those concepts which are relevant for a particular task.

What, then, are the novel contexts (activity types) which prominently feature therapeutic discourse norms and strategies? Hochschild (1983) states that the management of emotions has become increasingly commercialized, as evidenced by the number of 'emotion workers' whose number has been rising since the early decades of the twentieth century. Hoschschild relies on the term 'emotion worker' to refer to employees who are remunerated to adjust their feelings to the needs of the customer and the requirements of the work situation. In this way, as Hochschild asserts, feelings have become harnessed to economic imperatives.

Psychotherapy in its original setting and purpose entails the therapist's working with the customer's positive and negative emotions in a constructive way in order to understand them anew or make sense of them. 'Emotionality' becomes then one of the hallmarks of psychotherapy which gets trickled down first and foremost to other (non-psychotherapy) contexts, and in these settings 'therapeutic' is mainly indexed by emotion management. According to Cameron (2000a, 2000b), aspects of therapy talk have recently entered the global service sector, where they have become an invaluable resource for companies to draw on in their interactions with customers. The sharpened focus of the companies on the therapeutic styling of their employees' talk with the customers seems to be a consequence of the philosophy of 'customer care' which prioritizes quality service and customer satisfaction (cf. Taylor and Tyler 2000). In the current highly competitive global service sector, the customers should feel that they are not just served but, equally importantly, individually and intimately approached and 'cared for'. The direct consequence of a 'customer care' philosophy for the employees is that they are put in charge of managing other people's, i.e. their customers', feelings and emotional states, which they project in business transactions. In this way, they are required to perform 'emotional labor' (Hochschild 1983), which as Taylor and Tyler (2000: 77) state, refers to "feeling management during social interaction within the labour process, as shaped by the requirements of capital accumulation". Taylor and Tyler (2000) found that the delivery of quality service in the airline industry draws upon employees' capacities for feeling management. The work of telephone sales agents of airline services and flight attendants involves *caring* physically and emotionally for others. Emotional labor becomes a prominent aspect of employment within this economic sector. According to Cameron (2000a: 339), customer care training materials and management books about customer care relations rely predominantly on the register of therapy and counseling. The author also provides examples of advice given to service workers:

> If a customer comes across as being kind and caring then respond in the same way, ensuring that your voice is soft, rounded and undulates smoothly to reflect your own feelings of compassion.
>
> (Freemantle 1998: 109)

Consequently, a service worker in the globalized market economy needs to take on the role of a quasi-therapist in the interactions with customers. This is to say that he/she not only has to offer a solution to the product-related problem but also deal with the customer's projected emotions (cf. Taylor and Tyler 2000; Kiełkiewicz-Janowiak and Pawelczyk 2004).

A global institution that extensively draws on aspects of therapeutic discourse is the call center (henceforth CC). As the research carried out by Cameron (2000a, 2000b) and Kiełkiewicz-Janowiak and Pawelczyk (2004) evinces, CC operators are specifically trained to emotionally care for the customer.[16] Some of the aspects of doing emotional labor in the CC context include: projecting empathy to the customers, the technique of mirroring, i.e. demonstrating awareness of the interlocutor's mood and reflecting it back to him/her, or facilitating extended talk to build rapport (cf. Kiełkiewicz-Janowiak and Pawelczyk 2004). CC operators are also prescribed to ask questions that show concern for the customer and produce a style of service which is highly affective. Cameron (2000b: 335) explains that CC operators are trained to model their intonation in the direction of such qualities as warmth, sincerity, excitement, friendliness, helpfulness, confidence.

Cameron (2000a) discusses how therapy has become the underlying theme in current communication training texts. Thus there exists strong pop-psychology literature on advising ordinary people how to function as friends, spouses, lovers, etc. This advice, as Cameron asserts, originates in the practice of the 'talking cure'. This is to say that to be a successful communicator, one needs to (selectively and eclectively) rely on the discourse types and communicative strategies germane to psychotherapy. Cameron (2000a: 154), for instance, found recommendations from the theory and practice of 'assertiveness' and terminology of 'transactional analysis' in a sample of materials created for workplace training or for general public consumption under the heading of 'self-improvement'. Similarly Lupton (1998) comments on how the original language and concepts of psychoanalysis had, by the mid-twentieth century, entered everyday contexts. For example, concepts such as 'repression' and 'frustration' as well as the key concept of the unconscious are frequently used by lay public. Another example would be the therapeutic approach of confessing emotions that "has also successfully moved into current popular discourse on the emotion" (1998: 94–95). The psychotherapeutic concept of being open about one's innermost feelings has been perceived as one of the ways of handling the modern complexity of society and social relationships. As a result, a proliferation of 'discourse around intimacy' (Luhmann 1986) can be observed. Within this discourse, close relationships in particular emerge as a safeguard of achieving and maintaining intimacy by sharing emotions with others.

White (1992) discusses 'technologized' aspects of psychotherapy that can be found in certain television programs (mainly talk shows). The author elaborates on the point that psychotherapy as a specialized discipline within medicine "has also been rewritten in a wide range of professional and popular psychologies" (1992: 12). What unites the different non-psychotherapy contexts in which psychotherapeutic discursive norms are applied is the *process* of therapeutic engagement. In the contexts discussed by White (1992), the strategies of recognition, acknowledgement and confession of problems are highlighted and prevail over the final cure. Therapeutic discourse as featured in television talk shows refers to the processes of negotiating and working through one's social subjectivity (1992: 12). Thus within the pop psychology genre, as evidenced in numerous television talk shows, certain selective aspects of the psychotherapeutic process are individually valued, for instance merely self-disclosure and not necessarily actual improvement of one's psychological well-being.

It needs to be emphasized that all of the 'outside psychotherapy room' contexts entail less than 'pure' forms of psychotherapy, since the function of the adopted therapeutic norms and strategies diverges from the original purposes of the psychotherapist-client interaction. These new contexts incorporate some forms of 'hybrid' or 'technologized' aspects of the strategies that a therapist uses for the benefit of the client in the psychotherapy room.

Norcross and Freedheim (1992), referring to the future of psychotherapy practice, state that its future form will increasingly often incorporate more direct forms aimed at solving the client's current problems. The authors also point to future psychotherapy as a method of learning better communication skills. As Cameron (2000a) showed, this function has already found its place in numerous contemporary contexts.

Having presented an increasing number of contexts which import the definitional properties of psychotherapy and appropriate them for the new settings, I will now discuss issues related to conducting research at restricted research sites of which the psychotherapy session constitutes the prime example.

1.3 The psychotherapy session as a research site

1.3.1 Introductory remarks

The professional practices of legal, medical, educational and business settings have been extensively investigated (predominantly) by sociolinguistic and discourse-analytic studies[17] (e.g., Drew and Heritage 1992; Sarangi and

Roberts 1999; Mullany 2007; Gunnarsson 2009). The professional context of psychotherapy sessions is not an exception, yet at the same time it constitutes a unique research context, as representatives of numerous branches of scientific research might have their own particular motivations in unveiling what is (*really*) happening during a psychotherapy hour. Psychologists, psychotherapists, linguists, and communication studies experts, just to name a few, recognize the talk transpiring between the psychotherapist and client as crucial to addressing the issues and/or questions pertaining to their own disciplines (cf. Russell 1987). In this way, their research findings contribute to the so-called 'know that', i.e., the knowledge theory of their own disciplines (Sarangi 2002). In this sense, the researchers emerge as knowledge workers. The investigation of the psychotherapy session conducted by Labov and Fanshel (1977), for example, produced a mere corpus of generic rules of discourse coherence as a theoretical contribution to discourse comprehension from which the very practical aspect of the psychotherapeutic undertaking is conspicuously absent. In other words, their study did not contribute to the so-called 'know how' of psychotherapy, i.e., it failed to explicate what discursive strategies and conversational practices constitute psychotherapeutic practice. In this sense, Labov and Fanshel (1977) did not come out as (discourse) practitioners (cf. Sarangi 2002). The tension between the 'know that' and the 'know how' research (cf. Ryle 1949) raises one of the questions addressed in this chapter, i.e., what kind of contribution sociolinguists and/or discourse analysts should make to the fields of professional practice, and in the case of the current project, to the field of psychotherapy.

1.3.2 Early and current studies

Nowadays, the context of psychotherapy constitutes one of the main research topics for conversation analysis (CA).[18] This is not to say that before the CA involvement in identifying the conversational practices of psychotherapy, the psychotherapeutic context was out of the research focus. In the early 1950's Bateson (cf. Reusch and Bateson 1951) and Fromm-Reichmann (1950) were concerned with, among other aspects of psychotherapeutic endeavor, the communicative aspects in psychiatry and psychotherapy. Fromm-Reichmann (1959) drew attention to the demanding interactional position that a therapist occupies in the therapeutic equation, and the magnitude of the therapist's accurate decoding of a client's communication:

The psychotherapist is expected to be stable and secure enough to be constantly aware of and in control of that which he conveys to his patients in words and mindful of that which he may convey in empathy; that his need for operations aimed at his own security and satisfaction should not interfere with his ability to listen consistently to patients, with full alertness to their communications per se and, if possible, to the unworded implications of their verbalized communications; that he should never feel called upon to be anything more or less than the participant-observer of the emotional experiences which are conveyed to him by his patients....On the surface, these rules seem obvious and easy to follow; yet they are not... In actuality, none of us will be able to live up to all of them.

(Fromm-Reichmann 1959: 86)

Pittenger and associates (1960) conducted an analysis of 5 minutes of an audio-taped and filmed psychotherapeutic interview. In their analysis, they concentrated on context-dependent meanings of prosodic cues, voice quality and body motions. They also provided nine general principles of interpersonal communication.[19] One important observation in terms of 'know how' of psychotherapy, made by Pittenger and colleagues (1960), is that if a therapist misses some crucial sign from a patient, the very fact that it is crucial means that it will resurface at some later stage of the psychotherapeutic work with the client, perhaps in a more intelligible manner. Still, the conclusions that the authors offered have relevance to the general theory and method of research on spoken interaction, rather than psychotherapy (Peräkylä et al. 2008).

The 1970s featured an important contribution of Turner (1972) whose study of group therapy generated certain characteristics of therapeutic talk, e.g. *reflection* (cf. Sarangi et al. 2004). Scheflen's 1973[20] study focused on the organization of kinesic behavior during psychotherapy, and made a major contribution to the social scientific study of gesture (Peräkylä et al. 2008). And the already referred to Labov and Fanshel (1977), in what seemed to be a groundbreaking publication, discussed the epistemic organization of the psychotherapeutic interaction, and were also concerned with prosody and lexis, as well as gestures, at the expense of identifying actual action and practices germane to psychotherapeutic interaction. Finally, in 1994 Kathleen Ferrara's *Therapeutic Ways with Words* attempted to address the question of therapeutic use of language. Additionally, similarly to Labov and Fanshel (1977), Ferrara aimed at describing general principles of discourse by looking at a specific type of situated speech interaction, i.e., psychotherapy. In terms of the theory vs. practice dialectic, these early studies were more concerned with making a contribution to their own disciplines, i.e. the knowledge theory of their fields. The 'know how' aspect (with some exceptions, notably Ferrara [1994]) was extensively left out of the early investigations.

Conversation analysis[21] – relying on recorded interactions of naturally occurring speech – offers a fine-grained empirical analysis to describe how aspects of (our) social lives are done. This qualitative approach to talk-in-interaction aims at identifying how people, through talk, accomplish actions and make sense of the world around them (Madill, Widdicombe, and Barkham 2001). As Madill and associates (2001: 415) state, the three distinguishing features of conversation analysis, i.e., its activity focus, turn-by-turn analysis and emphasis on participants' orientation to the business at hand make it "ideally suited to examining empirically the nature of the psychotherapeutic process". Contrary to other qualitative approaches applied to psychotherapy context,[22] conversation analysis does not draw on the therapist's insights, dictates or recommendations that can be found in psychotherapeutic literature; rather it bases its research on the growing literature on how conversation works.[23] In this sense, CA is very much a data-driven perspective from outside the institution of psychotherapy, and its conclusions are based on the details of what actually occurred in the interaction:

> Unlike traditional process research, CA is not searching for underlying entities or attitudes which generate talk and behavior, but rather, it is a detailed examination of how the talk itself is a performative action that helps to both interpret and produce behaviors.
>
> (Gale 1991: 3)

Conversation analysts regard *sequentiality* as well as participants' *oriented-to* understandings as fundamental in explicating what is unfolding in the interaction between the psychotherapist and client. In this view, psychotherapy makes systematic use of the basic property of interaction with the aim of creating favorable change by inviting the therapist's particular understanding of what the client offers and by the therapist responding to a client's understanding in a particular way (Peräkylä and Vehviläinen 2007). The conversational analytic scrutiny into the level of interactional detail enabled the researchers to identify and explicate such conversational practices characterizing the psychotherapeutic process, as: formulation (e.g. Peräkylä and Vehviläinen 2003; Antaki, Barnes, and Leudar 2005a; Hutchby 2005; cf. also Bercelli, Rossano, and Viaro 2008), extension (e.g. Vehviläinen 2003), and statement design (cf. Peräkylä and Vehviläinen 2007).

Yet, at the same time conversation analysts themselves acknowledge a number of methodological problems, weaknesses and challenges that pre-

vent scholars working within this paradigm from arriving at a better understanding of this unique social context[24] (cf. Peräkylä and Vehviläinen
2007). In fact, in Peräkylä and Vehviläinen's (2007) view, conversation
analytic exploration of the interactional details simultaneously constitutes
one of its own major drawbacks, as this approach fails to recognize the
'global picture' of this unique social context, i.e., how therapy is actually
done. The mere investigation of the interactional sequences does not significantly contribute to an understanding of how the talk transpiring between the therapist and client improves the client's psychological well-
being and his/her relationships with other people. Related to this problem is
the issue of how to demonstrate psychological change that the client is undergoing by relying on the insights of conversation analysis. Additionally,
the interactional position of the client remains largely under-investigated in
the conversational analytic framework. For instance, the client's interactional agenda is not taken up by conversation analysts. Also different ways
of eliciting client's talk seem to be a less covered territory. Furthermore,
Peräkylä and Vehviläinen (2007) underline the necessity of demonstrating
how psychotherapy can be distinguished from other speech situations. Finally, conversation analysts – having identified interactional sequences and
conversational practices of the psychotherapeutic process – should investigate whether these sequences and practices can be found in seemingly dis-
similar psychotherapeutic approaches and protocols. In the words of
Peräkylä and Vehviläinen (2003: 728), "CA research on institutional interaction has not actively discussed issues such as 'competent practitioner' or
'good practice' or compared competing approaches within the same practice". Peräkylä and Vehviläinen (2003: 747) advocate a dialogue between
researchers (conversation analysts) and professional practitioners (psychotherapists) in order to gain mutually beneficial findings (see the discussion
below). This in turn, as Peräkylä and Vehviläinen (2003: 747) explicate,
entails incorporating text-analytical and ethnographic components along
with 'straight' conversation analysis.

I entirely recognize the conversation analysts' concerns regarding certain
(referred to above) shortcomings of their method. This, however, raises the
question of how to study, i.e. what methods should be applied in investigating
a psychotherapy session (or any other professional – client interaction), to
understand not merely how language mediates psychotherapeutic activities,
but also how the communicative and interactional strategies used in the sessions promote a qualitative change in the client's life, as this can be assumed
to be the main goal of different psychotherapeutic schools and protocols.

1.3.3 Researching the professional setting

With its sensitivity to context, qualitative research[25] is able to generate a micro-perspective of the psychotherapy session. The qualitative type of research refers both to the type of data used and to its further analysis and interpretation. Ethnography as a qualitative method of discovery appears to be the ideal way in which (socio)linguists can collect their data in professional settings. This approach constitutes the hallmark of qualitative research (cf. Dörnyei 2007: 129) and aims at providing a thick description[26] (Geertz 1973) of the investigated setting. For this purpose, ethnography relies on an eclectic range of data collection techniques, such as participant and non-participant observation, interviewing, and the ethnographer's own diary with field notes and journal entries; these can also be complemented with film and audio recordings as well as authentic documents (Dörnyei 2007: 130). This is referred to by Sarangi and Roberts (1999: 27) as triangulation of data sources, subsuming: 1) traditional participant observation; 2) audio and video recording; and 3) the collecting of documentary evidence. In this sense, triangulation of methods can generate a 'thick description' of the investigated setting "in order to produce a convincing interpretation of the data under scrutiny" (Mullany 2007: 54).

Psychotherapy session can be regarded as a restricted research site (cf. Sarangi and Roberts 1999) to which an access is not easily gained. Still, it is imperative for a (socio)linguist interested in describing professional discourses (e.g., the context of a psychotherapy session) to *enter* even a very restricted research site himself/herself. This presence, manifested by his/her position of the participant or non-participant observer, will provide the researcher with specific 'insider' knowledge indispensable for exploring and explaining the practices of the investigated setting. Postulated here then, is that in order to accurately describe the communicative practices which a professional site is comprised of, the (socio)linguist's scope must not be limited merely to transcribing and interpreting data (especially that collected by others). The professional practices are deeply (contextually) embedded in the setting in which they occur; if devoid of context, these practices are at risk of losing their specific communicative and interactional meaning(s):

> Language and other social practices are interdependent. Knowing something about the ethnographic setting, the perception of and characteristics attributed to others, and broader and local social organizational conditions becomes imperative for an understanding of linguistic and non-linguistic aspects of communicative events.
>
> (Cicourel 1992: 294)

Similarly Roberts and Sarangi (2003: 342) advocate the presence of the researcher at the research site as indispensable for collecting the ethnographic information concerning, for instance, how decisions are made, how queries are responded etc.: "research-based insights into the medical world are no substitute for the necessary ethnographic knowledge which comes from hanging around with doctors in a range of real life settings".

Highlighting the importance of ethnographic fieldwork, Cicourel (1992) points to the ways in which it can help locate a stretch of talk within a larger institutional context. The status of (non-)participant observer enables the researcher to arrive at a holistic view of the setting whose data he/she interprets. Observing (and/or participating in) a professional site, recording the interactions, transcribing them and then interpreting the collected data make it possible for the researcher to offer a description of the setting that "leaves nothing unaccounted for and that reveals the interrelatedness of all the component parts" (Hornberger 1994: 688). Additionally, the (socio)linguist analyzing the discourse(s) of professional settings makes claims about the context whose norms and principles define and/or determine the actual communicative and interactional strategies and practices. Consequently, the researcher's presence in the natural setting grants him/her access to capture the professional intricacies from another perspective, thus demonstrating the merits of a discourse analytic framework for analyzing professional practices. Finally, if the researcher wants to make the findings available and, more importantly, applicable to the actual work of the professional, his/her direct experience of being in the specific context enhances the credibility of the claims and findings made. This presence should also ideally facilitate cooperation between the discourse analysts and professionals. As Sarangi (2002) asserts, a joint research effort of the discourse researchers with the discourse workers (i.e., professionals) will not only secure interpretative ecology but, more importantly, it will provide for the potential recognition and acceptance of the findings.

As far as data analysis and interpretation is concerned, the motivation behind relying on specific (qualitative) analytic tools should be dictated by the goals as well as specific stages of the research. For instance, regarding the interactional context of the psychotherapy session, the conversation analytic tools already referred to can be applied to demonstrate the fine-grained organization of the event, yet prove insufficient in identifying the discourse norms upon which the communicative situation of psychotherapy is based or its interactional dynamics. This position echoes Silverman's (2005) and Dörnyei's (2007) call for adopting a *pragmatic approach*, i.e., selecting the research methodology and methods according to the research problem. In the words of Tashakkori and Teddlie (1998: 167): "The best method is the one that answers the research question(s) most efficiently".

My own presence as a researcher at the psychotherapy sessions enabled me not only to witness and audio-record interactions between the psychotherapist and clients but also to discuss with the therapist a number of professional issues that transpired in his interactions and appeared of significant importance to my study. My questions and queries were always responded to and not only did I gain the practitioner's perspective on these issues but I was also recommended specific 'praxis' literature to consult. Quite often these discussions proved how two professionals (a discourse analyst and a psychotherapist in this case) rely on the same terms in their descriptions of interactional practices but their understanding of them is quite divergent. Since I was permitted to audio-record but not to videotape the sessions, I decided to take thick field notes from the very first day of the sessions. The complete thick notes include not only the comments I obtained from the psychotherapist and the clients but also detailed descriptions of occurrences of participants' nonverbal behavior.[27] Thus the data at my disposal include audio-recorded sessions, field notes of the sessions themselves as well as the comments obtained from the participants and the professional texts (i.e., 'praxis' literature) that I was recommended to read. The combination of these sources of data can be seen as a form of triangulation (cf. Sarangi and Roberts 1999; cf. page 27 above). The reliance on these different sources in the process of data analysis can generate an adequate and thus convincing interpretation of the therapeutic use of language and communication.

The on-site presence of the sociolinguist and/or discourse analyst for the purpose of researching the discourse practices should potentially facilitate a dialogue between them and discourse workers (e.g., doctors, nurses or therapists, cf. Sarangi 2002). After all, doctors, nurses and therapists, as the focus of many discourse-based studies, use language themselves "to elicit and narrate symptoms, offer diagnosis, arrive at treatment decisions, etc." (Sarangi 2002: 96). This common interest and reliance on language and discourse both by discourse workers and discourse researchers is what makes, from a discourse/communicative perspective, any professional discourse site interprofessional by definition (Sarangi 2002).

1.3.4 The interprofessional discourse site

'Interprofessionality' of discourse sites recognizes an interdisciplinary research effort[28] that should be undertaken in order to describe how discourse norms, as well as communicative and interactional strategies, in fact, constitute these sites. Among the key manifestations of interdisciplinary trends in research is the so-called 'linguistic turn'[29] (Grant, Keenoy, and Oswick 1998) which encourages the blending of various disciplines and branches of linguistics (cf. also Mullany 2007; Jones and Stubbe 2004) and echoes a keen interest in language and the importance of (effective) communication from professional practitioners (Mullany 2007; cf. also Gunnarsson, Linell, and Nordberg 1997; Cameron 2000a; Jones and Stubbe 2004). A reciprocal curiosity emerges: on the one hand from professional practitioners (or discourse workers; cf. Sarangi 2002) in why and how (socio)linguists and discourse analysts investigate the professional contexts, and on the other hand from the discourse researchers in how professional practitioners rely on language and discourse to perform their jobs. The context of the psychotherapy session – where help is to a large extent provided through language and discourse work – clearly constitutes an interprofessional discourse site. This, in Sarangi's (2002) view, poses a question of what is so distinctive about the way discourse researchers investigate the practices of other professionals, for example, the practices of psychotherapists. More generally, the question relates to identifying what the aims of investigating professional communities by discourse researchers should be. Thus, should discourse researchers' main aim be to contribute to the general theoretical knowledge of their own scientific fields, or should their findings rather be applied to resolving some specific professional dilemmas (cf. Sarangi 2002)?

According to Sarangi (2002), the discourse researcher should assume the identity of a *discourse practitioner* in the interprofessional community he/she is investigating. This implies that, most importantly, his/her work should be characterized by collaborative interdisciplinarity. Consequently, in order to understand what is taking place at a specific moment in a given situation of therapist – client exchange, a discourse practitioner needs (extensive) assistance from the professional. This is to say that, in the words of Sarangi (2002: 103) "if our work were to be practically relevant, we need to align our interpretation with the professional practitioner's 'knowing in action', which is not always linguistically manifest".

An excellent example of such interdisciplinary collaboration is the work of sociolinguistics researchers and workplace practitioners that ensued from the 'Language in the Workplace Project' (LWP) (Jones and Stubbe 2004), in the process of which the sociolinguists moved across a continuum from a 'research on workplace' perspective to a 'research with practitioners' practice. Jones and Stubbe (2004: 189) also underline that the 'Language in the Workplace Project' team was "committed to research that would inform ...

practice and would not simply be addressed to fellow linguists and discourse analysts but would achieve 'real world outcomes'". In other words, the researchers abandoned the traditional model of applied research which leaves open the question of how the findings could be translated into practice. Collaborative modes of inquiry, which include collaborative interpretative practices,[30] can generate a much more coherent understanding of what is transpiring in interprofessional discourse sites. Such a collaborative mode of inquiry additionally presupposes that a discourse practitioner looking into the practices of psychotherapy, for instance, will not merely offer linguistic and/or pragmatic theories of interaction (this would be counterproductive to being a discourse practitioner) but instead will present some insights into the 'know how' of psychotherapeutic practice:

> Sociolinguistics – and discourse-based researchers have to show they can make a distinctive contribution to a given field of professional practice, while underscoring the fact that language is one of the major social variables that can account for differences at the level of performance.
>
> (Sarangi 2002: 101)

It follows that while maintaining language focus, discourse-based studies must be oriented for potential professional consideration, regardless whether their findings will ultimately be adopted in professional practice or solve a specific problem (Sarangi 2002). In fact, such an adoption does not always take place and discourse analysts are not always able to solve the professionals' problems (cf. Roberts and Sarangi 2003). Still they can offer 'meaningful problematisation' of an issue (Luhmann 1990; cf. also Roberts and Sarangi 2003) to the professionals by raising their awareness and possibly their understanding of the investigated object. Discourse specialists, as Roberts and Sarangi (2003: 351) underline, should "find a persuasive way of looking at a problem in a new light and providing specific on-going advice". This position significantly departs from Peräkylä's (1995; cf. also Peräkylä and Vehviläinen 2003) view that interaction research should not seek to resolve the problems and dilemmas faced by professionals. Though researchers differ in their positions on the application of findings, the recommendations of discourse-based studies can only be accepted and/or taken into consideration by professional practitioners if the offered claims are significantly robust (cf. Sarangi 2002).

Summing up this part of the discussion, discourse researchers entering interprofessional discourse sites remain knowledge workers (by offering verification or expansion of linguistic or pragmatic theories) yet their primary task in such settings is to offer insights into the 'know how' of the investigated contexts, ideally by collaborating with the professionals (i.e. discourse workers). The 'collaborative' aspect underlines the necessity of consulting the discourse worker (e.g., a psychotherapist) in order to get some insider's perspective essential for interpreting the professional practices. The insider's perspective relates to the concept of professional vision (Goodwin 1994: 606), which "consists of socially organized ways of seeing and understanding events that are answerable to the distinctive interests of a particular social group". This points to a professional practitioners' ability, unavailable to an outsider, to see the relevance of certain practices.[31] In Sarangi's (2002) view, working with professional practitioners will ensure interpretative ecology and facilitate, at the same time, the potential recognition and acceptance of findings. Jones and Candlin (2007) discuss the potential problems and issues that need to be addressed and dealt with in the context when a discourse practitioner and professional practitioner get involved in the (highly recommended) collaborative interdisciplinarity. One of the most important tasks for interprofessional collaboration or 'contact zone' (cf. Jones and Candlin 2007) is to agree on the meaning and importance of the categories. This is especially salient in a situation where the same term can have divergent values for the researchers (cf. the comments above). In fact, the categorization of practices, i.e. interdiscursive 'coordination' (cf. Jones and Candlin 2007) emerges as the foundation of such collaboration and is, as the author assert, doable:

> Two groups can agree on rules of exchange even if they ascribe utterly different significance to the objects being exchanged; they may even disagree on the meaning of the exchange process itself. Nonetheless, the trading partners can hammer out a local coordination, despite vast global differences.
>
> (Galison 1997: 783)

For instance, the interprofessional collaboration can take the form of working on focal and analytical themes (Jones and Candlin 2007; cf. also Roberts and Sarangi 2005). Focal themes of professional participants refer to categories and concepts representing (their) knowledge, expertise, interpersonal skills, etc. They emerge from professionals' reflexivity and typically need to be translated into the analytic terms of discourse practitioners. Thus such focal themes as empathy or good listening skills need to be discussed by discourse practitioners as specific contextual features or interactional strategies.

Scholars working within the paradigm of conversation analysis (cf. Peräkylä and Vehviläinen 2003) also recognize the necessity for a dialogue between discourse researchers (in their case, conversation analysts) and discourse workers.[32] Yet, it seems that their idea of 'collaborative interdisciplinarity' takes a considerably different form as it focuses on the relationship between conversation analysis and *interactional theories* used by professionals, referred to by Peräkylä and Vehviläinen (2003) as 'stocks of interactional knowledge' (SIKs). Stocks of interactional knowledge[33] as defined by Peräkylä and Vehviläinen (2003: 729) are normative models and theories or quasi-theories about interaction which constitute part of the knowledge base of many professionals. Since these theories and models are held by professionals to be valid, conversation analysis can address them by explicating the potential differences and similarities between the CA findings and the written, codified versions of the professionals (SIKs). In fact, the results of CA findings can have various relations to professionals SIKs:

1. CA falsifies and corrects assumptions that are part of an SIK.
2. CA provides a more detailed picture of practices that are described in an SIK.
3. CA adds a new dimension to the understanding of practices described by an SIK.
4. CA expands the description of practices provided by an SIK, and suggests some of the missing links between the SIK and the interactional practices.

(Peräkylä and Vehviläinen 2003: 731–732)

It seems that the most important task of conversation analysts is to address the fourth relation, i.e. to demonstrate what principles and/or aims, unmentioned by SIKs, are oriented to by professional practitioners (Peräkylä and Vehviläinen 2003: 744). At the same time, it is claimed that the systematic articulation of the relationship between the CA findings and SIKs will bring more interest to CA work from professionals, thus it will "enhance the 'usability' of conversation analytical research" (Peräkylä and Vehviläinen 2003: 729). This, in turn, may be vital for the wider social relevance of conversation analysis. As far as "distinctive contribution to a given field of professional practice" (Sarangi 2002: 101) is concerned, conversation analysis has the tools to point out that the actual practice performed by the professional practitioner in his/her interaction with the client is not (fully) referred to in the professional interactional theories (SIKs). In other words, conversation analysts have demonstrated that they possess the necessary methodological tools to prove a gap between theory and practice.

Psychotherapists constitute a highly intriguing community of practice (Lave and Wenger 1991; cf. also Eckert and McConnel-Ginet 1992), as verbal and non-verbal practices not only enable them to distinguish themselves from other communities of practice, but more importantly, these practices function as their professional tools. This fact makes a psychotherapy session a very sought-after discourse site for a number of other professionals, including sociolinguists and discourse analysts. Any researcher entering a professional discourse site needs to keep in mind that it is, by definition, an interprofessional discourse site (cf. Sarangi 2002). Thus the findings emerging in the course of the research should not only be addressed to fellow discourse analysts, for example, but should always be practically relevant (cf. Roberts and Sarangi 1999). This is to say that they should ideally reflect not merely the 'know that' but more importantly, the 'know how' perspectives. The latter aspect of practical relevance appears to be a certain way to encourage professionals to avail themselves of the sociolinguistic and/or discourse analytic findings from their own professional settings: "the onus is on discourse practitioners to present themselves as a 'community of interprofessional practice' in order to make their research both credible and socially relevant across professional boundaries" (Sarangi 2002: 129).

Linked to the matters of data collection and analysis that reveal the communicative and interactional strategies pertaining to a certain professional setting, is also the issue of the researcher's status and identity in the community he/she is investigating.

1.3.5 Researcher and the community

As discussed above, it is highly recommendable for the sociolinguists or discourse analysts interested in researching the language and/or discursive practices of a certain professional context to enter even the most restricted research site in order to collect natural interaction data. Conducting his/her own fieldwork at the discourse site, the researcher is also able to observe what discourse practices make up the professional practitioner's professional vision (cf. Goodwin 1994). Yet, without a doubt, the status and identity of the discourse researcher in the investigated community have serious consequences as to what type of data, in effect, he/she will be able to collect and, in the longer perspective, whether the actual research findings will find any resonance with the professional practitioners.

Studies into interprofessional sites entail, to a different extent, aspects of observation. However, as Dörnyei (2007: 179) presents, observation tends to be dichotomized into 'participant' versus 'non-participant observation'. This binary opposition assumes that a participant-observer becomes a fully involved member of the community, participating in the activities, while a non-participant observer tends not to be engaged (and if so, then only minimally) in the setting he/she is investigating (cf. also Tusting and Maybin 2007). Dörnyei (2007), referring to Morse and Richards (2002), clearly articulates that such a dichotomy does not reflect the numerous ways in which the researcher is watching and listening. Morse and Richards (2002) claim that "no observer is entirely a participant, and it is impossible to observe in almost every nonexperimental situation without some participation" (Dörnyei 2007: 179). This echoes Sarangi's (2002) suggestion of a continuum of the researcher's participation categories: at one end there is the researcher as a 'participant observer'; at the other, he/she emerges as a 'participant as interactant'.[34] The position of the discourse researcher conducting fieldwork at a psychotherapy session also questions a clear-cut opposition between participant observer and non participant observer (see the discussion below).

Sarangi (2002) states that the researcher-role identities in interprofessional discourse settings are multi-faceted. It seems, however, that the researcher's identity in the community he/she is investigating is contingent on how the researcher negotiates it with the subjects as well as how the subjects will perceive him/her. There are numerous possibilities available, such as researcher as insider or outsider, agent of change, and animator or overhearer (cf. Sarangi and Hall 1997). These labels used to refer to the researcher's identities, mark his/her different levels of participation and involvement with the research subjects (Sarangi 2002). Jorgensen (1989: 53–55) states that the role the participant observer adopts in the community under research affects what can be observed, as well as how and when. Johnstone (2000) claims that a participant observer needs to aptly combine the statuses of both an insider and an outsider. Not affiliating with the subjects and possessing no role except this of the researcher does not qualify, in Johnstone's view, as participant observation. On the other hand, Johnstone (2000) cautions against overzealous involvement aimed at underlining the insider status of the researcher (cf. also Duranti 1997). This 'going native' or 'becoming the phenomenon' (2000: 89) in turn may lead to losing the critical and analytical distance necessary for the relevant findings. It seems then that researchers should exercise their professional expertise in terms of his/her relationships to the participants under study. This is also to say that these relationships will not likely to be stable, fixed identities, rather the researchers will have to reshape them in context-sensitive ways (cf. Cicourel 1992).

Another important issue for a researcher to consider when engaging in a research project on an interprofessional discourse site is how to ensure the high quality of collected data and, related to this, the quality of findings which should ideally be found practically relevant by the investigated community. This is where the concept of *paradox* comes in, addressing the issue of authentic data and practically relevant findings in the context of discourse studies in the professional settings. The well-known concept of *the observer's paradox* conceptualizes the researcher as having a unified identity (Labov 1972). This notion, well-recognized in sociolinguistic studies (cf. also Hutchby 2007: 41–42), does not account for the fact that a discourse researcher, as already discussed, may be accessing interprofessional sites in various capacities (Sarangi 2002). Furthermore, Sarangi (2002) claims that the concept of the observer's paradox has been overstated at the expense of other paradoxes which characterize discourse studies in professional settings. For instance, the concept of the *participant's paradox* (Sarangi 2002) relates to a situation when participants are, in fact, observing the observer. This can take a number of positions and even claims from the participants to the researcher. Thus participants may be oblivious to the presence of the researcher-observer and the recording equipment at different stages of the interaction, or quite to the contrary, very aware of the researcher's presence. The concept of the *analyst's paradox* (Sarangi 2002) addresses the issue of the quality of data as, in order to ensure their ecological validity, the researcher needs the professional practitioner's insights on the data. The paradox lies in the fact that the professionals' insights are collected to inform analytic practice. Thus the participant (i.e., the professional) takes on the role of analyst himself/herself.[35] As Sarangi (2002) maintains, ecological validity (cf. Cicourel 1992) requires the alignment of the participant's (i.e., the professional's) perspective with the analyst's perspective:

> As discourse researchers, we remain, for most part, peripheral but legitimate participants, eager to rely on our subjects' insights so that we align (rather than transform) analyst and participant perspectives.
>
> (Sarangi 2002: 122)

Such perspective alignment, in which discourse researchers verify their interpretations against the participants' theories of practice, brings a double benefit: participants can become reflexive about their practice while discourse researchers can challenge their own theories which may not always be data-driven (Sarangi 2002).

The data for the current project were collected at two residential psycho-therapy workshops (a detailed description of the research site can be found in the section: *On data collection and transcription, participants and context* below) where participants (mostly with some background in psychology and/or psychotherapy) had individual therapy sessions with a therapist, yet in the presence of other participants. As a researcher I was also present at all the sessions. Thus, taking into account the fact that I did not have my individual therapeutic sessions with the psychotherapist, my status could be referred to as a non-participant observer. Yet, I claim that my position did, in fact, in-volve some aspects of participant-observation. As a researcher, I witnessed all the individual sessions, making sure that the interactions between the psycho-therapist and participants who consented to take part in the research would be recorded. It is a well-recognized psychotherapy argument that listening to another person's revelations makes the listener internally experience and re-late to what he or she is hearing. Consequently, the researcher at the psycho-therapy session cannot really escape emotional involvement and/or detach-ment from others' stories and experiences. Thus, on the one hand, the researcher is undergoing his/her own private psychotherapy, though without any direct dialogue with the psychotherapist. On the other hand, witnessing the heart-wrenching stories of the psychotherapy clients makes the researcher (voluntarily) relate to the participants in a humane way. I also believe, how-ever, that the impact of the observer's paradox on the performance of the cli-ents was minimal due to two main reasons. Firstly, the participants were informed well in advance of my presence as a researcher as well as my (gen-eral) research aims. Most of them were very accepting both of my research interest and research agenda, underlining their awareness of the importance of investigating this highly intimate context from a more linguistic perspective. On the first day of every workshop, I presented (again) the aims of my study and there was also time allocated for the participants' questions and com-ments. Secondly, as discussed in more detail below, the participants (includ-ing the researcher) lived together in the same house for the period of ten (workshop one) and three (workshop two) days. Being away from the duties of everyday life and spending all their time together, sharing meals, and being engaged in lengthy discussions at the end of each day, significantly contrib-uted to the almost unconditional acceptance of the researcher. Still, in my view the phrase 'in' and 'out' (referring to insider and outsider respectively) best describes my own position in the communities under scrutiny. On the one hand, in order to secure the participants' acceptance I did my best to be perceived as a member of the group even though I did not receive psycho-therapeutic treatment, which was the defining characteristic of the participants. At the same time, however, my main purpose of being there was to collect high-quality data of various sources even at the risk of sacrificing my insider status. It seems, then, that this balancing act between the positions of being an insider and an outsider, and thus in fact the *flexibility* of the researcher at the research site, indeed guarantees the collection of high quality data.

Sarangi (2002: 121) states that: "participants may remain conscious of the researcher's presence and even wish that the researcher were a legitimate participant, albeit with restricted interactional rights and obligations". What Sarangi (2002) claims then is that the researcher's presence, without any participation, may become uncomfortable for some participants. This seems to be quite a common situation faced by researchers at (group) therapy sessions. Actually, my presence as a researcher at the first site provoked a lengthy discussion among the participants whether or not I should also undergo psychotherapy. In other words, the participants (particularly those with psychology and/or psychotherapy backgrounds) expressed their concern about my psychological well-being as I was witnessing (thus relating to and internally experiencing) their intimate life stories, yet I did not share my stories with them.[36] This situation echoes Clarke's (2000) comment that participants may find the 'uninvolved' stance of the researcher as unnatural and disturbing. It is highly difficult, not to say unwelcome, for a researcher to stay uninvolved, thus not showing any signs of participation, even emotional ones, in this very intimate context. It can be claimed that the researcher's participation in certain research contexts may also be manifested emotionally, and this emotionality is expected of him/her by the participants. Therefore, to avoid the status of an outsider, I ran two briefing sessions for the participants at the first research site, where I was attempting to explain what patterns and strategies were beginning to emerge in my data.[37] This often triggered the psychotherapist's feedback on the presented material (cf. *professional practitioner's knowing in action* Sarangi 2002). It must be clarified however, that one of these sessions was specifically asked for by the participants. This incident very much resembled what Sarangi and Candlin (2003) refer to as 'hot feedback' where subjects of the discourse analytic study request analyst's comments on his/her finding prior to the completion of the project. This, as the authors assert, implies a "genuine interest on the part of the practitioners" (2003: 277). Additionally, being present at the research site and recording the sessions enabled me to address the participants (both clients and the psychotherapist) with questions and comments regarding their interactional choices and/or communicative patterns used during psychotherapeutic sessions.[38]

1.3.6 Research ethics

Any study that concerns people's lives in the social world needs to address the ethical issues linked to the process of researching it, and the context of psychotherapy session is no exception.

Dörnyei (2007) stresses that qualitative research tends to intrude into the private human sphere, consequently there is the increasing recognition of ethical issues in (applied) linguistic research. Interestingly however, it is the variationist (quantitative) sociolinguistic research that has generated robust insights regarding the ethical issues linked to data collection and researcher − researched field relations. Sociolinguists have clearly voiced their views on matters related to surreptitious recording as well as the researcher's responsibilities to the community under study.

Indisputably, one of the fundamental principles of ethical research is the principle of informed consent (Milroy and Gordon 2003: 79). This entails both the participants' agreement on participating in the research as well as their awareness of what such participation involves. Interestingly, Dörnyei (2007: 67) claims that the 'informed' aspect of the consent refers to "how little information is enough to share in order to remain ethical". In his view, the participants of the research study have the right to be informed about the following:

1. As much as possible about the aims of the investigation and the purpose for which the data will be used.
2. The tasks the participants will be expected to perform during the study.
3. The possible risks and the potential consequences of participating in the research.
4. The extent to which answers will be held confidential.
5. The basic right of the participants to withdraw from the study at any point.

(Dörnyei 2007: 69)

Point 4 could be slightly elaborated, as it should be clearly underscored that the participants will remain anonymous at the stage of data analysis and findings presentation (for instance, at various conferences and in different publications), i.e. any information that could in any way identify them will be altered. This is a particularly sensitive issue for the participants of psychotherapy research.

Informed consent tends to take the form of a written statement,[39] yet the participants may also be informed verbally about the recording and the aims of the research, and provide a verbal (dis)agreement which must be recorded. For instance, in the current study a group of the participants (workshop one) was provided with the research description, thus the participants, before their actual psychotherapy sessions commenced, were familiar with the research aims and with the fact that at the workshop there would be a researcher and recording equipment present. The time gap between being informed and the actual workshop enabled them to make a decision whether they would consent to their sessions being recorded, their material analyzed and finally published. On the first day of the workshop, the participants were again reminded of the aims of the project (they were also given a chance to address any questions to the researcher) and asked to state whether they granted their consent to be recorded or refused it.[40] Their statements of agreement or disagreement were recorded. Interestingly, the participants gave a strong support of their decisions of either participation or withdrawal.[41] All in all, out of seventeen clients of the first workshop, three chose to withdraw from the study. In the second workshop the clients also received a description of the project before the actual sessions, but this time they were asked to fill out an informed consent form with their signature indicating their consent. In this case, all of the clients (eleven people) chose to participate in the project.

Even though opinions between sociolinguists still remain divided on the issue of recording speakers covertly (cf. Milroy and Gordon 2003), Labov (1984) refers to practical disadvantages of candid recording, such as jeopardizing the researcher's relationship to the community and the poor quality of such recordings (Milroy and Gordon 2003). The borderline, however, between overt and covert recording can become very blurred, especially in the context of long-term participant observation (cf. Milroy and Milroy 1978). The reasonable way out seems to be recognizing the general principle which states that the researcher should "avoid any act that would be embarrassing to explain if it became a public issue" (Labov 1984: 52).

Dörnyei (2007) refers to the *researcher's integrity*, i.e., the moral character of the researcher as an area of research ethics that is fundamental in any investigation. The researcher's integrity subsumes certain responsibilities to the field. For instance, Dörnyei (2007) presents the obligations[42] that educational researchers should abide, and these can be more generally applied to discourse researchers. Most importantly, researchers must not "fabricate, falsify, or misrepresent authorship, evidence, data findings, or conclusions" (Dörnyei 2007: 67).

Cameron and associates' (1992) division into 'ethical research' and 'advocacy research' underscores the stance of many sociolinguists that 'doing no harm' to the subjects is not enough, and that sociolinguists' work should offer something back to their subjects. Thus the concern of 'ethical research' is to "minimize damage and offset inconvenience to the researched" (Cameron et al. 1992: 14) while the alternative 'advocacy research' is not merely conducted *on* but also *for* the subjects. Therefore, in the latter paradigm, the researcher emerges as indebted to the subjects she/he studies and is required to make the research findings available to them. The 'advocacy perspective' echoes Labov's *Principle of Error Correction*:

> A scientist who becomes aware of a widespread idea or social practice with important consequences that is invalidated by his own data is obligated to bring this error to the attention of the widest possible audience.
>
> (Labov 1982: 172)

As well as his *Principle of the Debt Incurred*:

> An investigator who has obtained linguistic data from members of a speech community has an obligation to use the knowledge based on that data for benefit of the community, when it has need of it.
>
> (Labov 1982: 173)

It seems, however, that regardless of the obtained results, researchers should always serve the communities they investigate. This attitude has been referred to by Wolfram (1993) as a *Principle of Linguistic Gratuity*:

> Investigators who have obtained linguistic data from members of a speech community should actively pursue positive ways in which they can return linguistic favors to the community.
>
> (Wolfram 1993: 227)

Still, Cameron and colleagues (1992) refer to 'empowerment' as the third type of relationship between researcher and subjects. In this view, the researcher is obliged to get the subjects involved in the study. This view is premised on the following assumptions:

> 1. Persons are not objects and should not be treated as objects.
> 2. Subjects have their own agendas and research should try to address them.
> 3. If knowledge is worth having, it is worth sharing.
>
> (Cameron et al. 1992: 23–24)

Thus the 'empowerment' position advocates that research subjects indeed do have a role to fulfill in explicating what they do, as well as in putting forward the research questions of particular (practical) interest to them. Yet, as Johnstone (2000: 50) explains, since sociolinguists do not substantially rely on people's self-reports regarding their own pronunciation, they will similarly assume that people "will also be poor reporters of their linguistic behavior on other levels". This position substantially diverges from Sarangi's (2002) view on 'interpretative ecology', i.e., combining the insights of the analyst(s) and participant(s) in the research. The latter suggestion, however, refers to an interprofessional discourse site and is mainly tackled by discourse and communication types of research.

In fact, Sarangi (2002) claims that at a professional discourse site the ethical issues should extend beyond data collection and researcher – researched relations.[43] He discusses them under four headings such as: *Where do we look, Do we identify a set of problems that might be of interest to our participants, To what extent do we involve participants in the interpretive process*, and finally, *Do we tell our participants everything we find* (cf. also Dörnyei 2007).[44] All of these questions, classified under the heading of 'discourse ethics', touch upon the issue of collaborative interpretation, thus the research cooperation of discourse worker and discourse practitioner. Sarangi (2002) suggests, for instance, that if the research problem is jointly negotiated then the research findings are more likely to be interpreted favorably. Another issue raised by Sarangi (2002) as reflecting the ethical dimension is the fact that a discourse researcher needs to verify his/her interpretations not so much against theories of language use but rather against the participants' theories of practice. Worth mentioning also is the point of providing feedback on contrastive performance (cf. also Bloor 1997). Presenting both good and bad instances of practice can be considered to be good pedagogy for enhancing awareness among practitioners (Sarangi 2002).

A discourse researcher entering a professional discourse site, the setting of a psychotherapy session for instance, should be familiar with its stocks of interactional knowledge (Peräkylä and Vehvilläinen 2003) as "the study of action is not possible without an adequate understanding of situated notions and concepts in a given social system" (Sarangi and Candlin 2001: 142). The proper understanding of the situated notions and concepts additionally requires from the discourse researcher his/her presence at the discourse site, i.e. fieldwork. This presence, as discussed above, is indispensable for a number of reasons.

Importantly, the discourse researcher's presence at the discourse site can facilitate a dialogue between him/her and the discourse worker, which can secure collaborative indisciplinarity of the research project. This project then becomes ecologically valid as it takes into account the perspective of a professional practitioner in order to comprehend what is going on in a certain situation of the professional practice. Taking into account the perspective of the professional practitioner underscores the fact that discursive studies into professional settings should not constrain themselves to offering insights applicable to their own (or related) field(s). Studies into professional settings are interprofessional by definition (cf. Sarangi 2002), thus they must be first and foremost practice-driven. Discourse analysts, with their methods and methodologies, are able to significantly contribute to the 'know how' of professions in which language and discourse function as professional tools. One such professional context is the setting of a psychotherapy session, where the primary task of a discourse researcher should be to demonstrate, on the basis of his/her own fieldwork at the psychotherapy site and collaboration with professionals, what discourse norms and principles are salient in the process of psychotherapy and to exemplify how they are manifested by certain interactional and communicative strategies. Practical relevance of the findings in this context relates to addressing the question of what discourse norms as well as features of language and communication make a conversation between two interlocutors (here the psychotherapist and clients) therapeutic.

1.4 On data collection and transcription, participants and context

As already presented, the data used for the analysis come from a 65-hour corpus of psychotherapy sessions recorded during fieldwork at 2 residential psychotherapy workshops in the summer and autumn of 2004. The first of them took place in the United States (10 days, with only native speakers of English, from the US, the UK, Canada, and Australia present) and the second one in Sweden (3 days, with participants of a variety of nationalities who used the English language during therapy). There were twenty-five clients at both workshops (five men and twenty women). Both events were held in residences which were rented for the purpose of psychotherapy sessions and only the session participants were present there. Thus participants of both workshops (including the researcher) stayed in the same house during the meetings, sharing meals and generally being in the presence of one another. Both residences were located away from a city thus providing the clients with numerous opportunities of spending time together and getting to know each other as well as with a chance to reflect in peaceful atmosphere on the issues brought up in their therapies.

The sessions were conducted by the same American male psychotherapist, well-experienced with over 30 years of practice. The therapist talked individually with the clients, but in the presence of other participants (other clients and the researcher). Thus the sessions in a way resembled 'therapy-in-the-group' as an individual participant's therapy session was observed by others, including the researcher. Indeed, it is only resemblance as all sessions were conducted on a one-to-one basis only (psychotherapist – client). As already stated most of the clients practice providing psychological help/support on a daily basis themselves. Yet their sessions with the psychotherapist were focused on their own unresolved *personal* issues, traumatic situations and events in their private lives. Their *professional* dilemmas were consulted with the psychotherapist at the end of each day on their demand.

The timetable of both events looked quite similar. The individual sessions started at 9 a.m. and stopped for the lunch break at 1 p.m., to resume at 3 p.m. The sessions finished around 7 p.m.

All clients, whose interactions were recorded, consented to take part in the study (see the discussion above). The sessions were recorded with a small, unobtrusive high-quality digital Dictaphone, then the material was downloaded into a computer file to be transcribed later. Even though the excerpts discussed in the present study are verbatim transcripts of the actual therapeutic sessions, participants' confidentiality has been fully protected at the stage of data transcription, as any personal information that could potentially reveal their identities has been omitted or changed (see transcription conventions).

The recorded material has been transcribed with a focus on both utterance and interactional content. In accordance with Schiffrin's postulation (1987: 68), none of the examples presented and discussed below is based on a single occurrence of the investigated strategy; rather, all constitute instances of typical patterns found across the whole corpus. At the same time, since the analysis has been confined to the context of psychotherapy, the functions of discussed communicative and interactional strategies should be interpreted in terms of sequential accountability (cf. Schiffrin 1987: 69). The applied transcription style is based on the CA representation of talk (cf. Jefferson 2004; Hutchby 2007). The CA system captures "in fine detail the characteristics of the sequencing of turns, including gaps, pauses and overlaps; and elements of speech delivery such as audible breath and laughter, stress, enunciation, intonation and pitch" (Hutchby 2007: 20). Thus it allows for the demonstration of the discursive complexity of managing the psychotherapeutic interaction by its participants as well as to evincing "the jointly constructed, socially engaged nature of what is going on" (Potter and Hepburn 2005: 289).

1.5 Methodology and methods

The methodological approach to the data analysis adopts the functional view of language (cf. Schiffrin 1998). This view regards language as a societal phenomenon and studies it in relation to its societal function(s). At the risk of some overgeneralization, functionalism is premised on two general assumptions. One conceives of language as possessing functions external to the linguistic system itself, and the second assumes that external functions influence the internal organization of the linguistic system (Schiffrin 1998: 22). Within the functional view, discourse is assumed to be interdependent with social life and its analysis intersects with meanings, activities, and systems outside of itself. Thus discourse is defined here as a socially and culturally organized way of speaking through which particular functions are realized (Schiffrin 1998: 32). Importantly, those functions are not constrained to tasks that can be accomplished by language alone, but they can include such tasks as maintaining interaction or building social relationships. As a consequence, functional analysis concentrates on how people use language to different ends as well as on the unintended social, cultural, and expressive meanings stemming from how their utterances are embedded in contexts.

The theoretical framework that is used for the analysis of the interactions between psychotherapists and clients is broadly conceived discourse analysis subsuming, for the purpose of the analysis, aspects of such approaches as conversation analysis, pragmatics, and interactional sociolinguistics, which possess methods for the linguistic analysis of discourse. Despite the fact that each of these approaches adopts a different view of discourse and utterance analysis,[45] the methods and conceptual apparatuses they offer can be applied to the same context of a psychotherapy session in order to investigate the therapeutic features of interaction arising between psychotherapist and client. It is claimed here that a combination of methods and approaches can better address the research question(s) at the interprofessional discourse site thus, in consequence, produce actual practically relevant research findings. In this sense it is the research question that dictates the choice and reliance on certain methodological approaches and research tools (cf. Braun and Clarke 2006: 80; Mullany 2007). For the purposes of the current analysis, the umbrella term of discourse analysis is referred to as the main analytical framework (cf. Cameron 2001: 7).[46] Discourse analysis analyzes aspects of the form and function of real samples of language use. According to Schiffrin (1998: 416), all approaches to discourse share a set of underlying principles. The most salient of them are discussed below as applied in some of the most important discourse analytic studies and as the underlying analytical framework for the current analysis.

Discourse is defined as language-in-use, and spoken discourse as talk as well as nonverbal communication (Roberts and Campbell 2006). Brown and Yule (1983) state that:

> The analysis of **discourse**, is necessarily, the analysis of language in use. As such, it cannot be restricted to the description of linguistic forms independent of the purposes or functions which these forms are designed to serve in human affairs.
>
> (Brown and Yule 1983: 1, emphasis in original)

A psychotherapy session, which is primarily a language-oriented activity, yet is accompanied by extensive reliance on non-verbal communication, perfectly lends itself to discourse analytical work. Discourse analysis recognizes the multifunctional and highly context-specific nature of language use and looks at the ways in which speakers design the content of their talk, their turns, and how interactions are sequenced and managed as well as speakers' choices in terms of vocabulary, grammar and rhetoric (Roberts and Campbell 2006). This approach to data analysis consists of identifying recurring features and structures in a corpus of data that point to the relationship between the structural organization of language and its functional interpretation in context[47] (Barton 2002, 2004). Johnstone (2000: 124) states that within the discourse analytical research "what we need is a way to make sure we are systematically paying attention to a variety of reasons why a stretch of discourse might have turned out the way it did". One of the tenets of discourse analysis is the assumption that any communicative event is co-constructed by the interacting parties (cf. Schiffrin, Tannen, and Hamilton 2001; Drew and Heritage 1992; Sarangi and Roberts 1999). Discourse analysis also pays attention to the ways in which language in interaction is often indirect, thus requiring certain inferences for the interpretation of the utterances. Discourse analysis is particularly sensitive to the unfolding argument of the whole encounter and the patterns of interaction that it reveals. Thus by applying discourse analytic tools, the talk under scrutiny can be slowed down to demonstrate the interpretive processes and overall pattern of an activity (Roberts and Sarangi 2005).

According to Sarangi and associates (2004), a central tenet of discourse analysis is the coding of transcripts along the thematic and interactional lines (cf. also Roberts and Sarangi 2002). While the thematic maps locate certain content areas (e.g. risk), the interactional maps identify contextual features, such as interruptions or overlaps. From a discourse analytic perspective, thematic maps are realized through various linguistic as well as interactional means. At the micro level, discourse is concerned with the largely hidden ways in which meaning and attitude are conveyed through intonation, rhythm and other linguistic features (Roberts and Campbell 2006).

The current analysis is based on the premise that discourse is an achievement of the parties involved in an interaction, rather than an effect of "a pact signed at the beginning, after which the discourse is produced entirely as a matter of individual effort" (Schegloff 1981: 73). Therefore, it must be treated as an interactional accomplishment of a moment-by-moment collaboration of all the parties involved, an ongoing achievement (Schegloff 1981). Face-to-face conversations (including the speech event of psychotherapy) are interactive and locally managed rather than preordained. Consequently, psychotherapy as a communicative event must be accomplished by the interacting parties, i.e. the psychotherapist and the client. Their interactional and linguistic strategies and choices construct psychotherapy (or psychotherapeutic discourse).

The present analysis will also draw on the tenets of the interactional model of communication (cf. Schiffrin 1998), premised on the assumption that what underlies communication is behavior and that all behavior in an interactional situation has message value (cf. Watzlawick, Beavin, and Jackson 1967). This is to say that "activity or inactivity, words or silence" (Watzlawick, Beavin, and Jackson 1967: 48–49) do carry interactional significance for an apt interpretation of what is transpiring between the interlocutors. Importantly, within this view, aspects of nonverbal communication, such as instances of silence for instance, can communicate messages even if they are not intended to do so (Schiffrin 1998: 399). This model tends to characterize studies which focus on the situated use of language. The notion of 'situated use' points to communication being less code-dependent and more context-dependent. The concept of 'context' also includes the information that interlocutors bring to the interaction, such as psychological states. The interactional model does not assign great importance to the interlocutors' intentions. Rather the message that is communicated is much more likely to emerge from "interactions among information intentionally emitted by an actor and unintentionally emitted by an actor" (Schiffrin 1998: 401). The interactional model of communication seems to be a particularly apt construct to be applied to the analysis of the psychotherapy session in view of the current shift in approaches to doing psychotherapy.

In order to explicate what makes the talk between the therapist and clients therapeutic, i.e., why and how certain communicative and interactional strategies take on therapeutic function, the concept of indexicality (Ochs 1992; cf. also Silverstein 1985) will be drawn on. The theory of indexicality entails the creation of semiotic links between linguistic forms and social meanings (Ochs 1992; Silverstein 1985). According to Bucholtz and Hall (2005) indexical processes occur at all levels of linguistic structure and use. Ochs (1992) states that indexicality is a property of speech through which cultural contexts, such as social activities (e.g., the psychotherapy session) are constituted by particular stances and acts. Even though Ochs (1992: 337) discusses indexicality as applying to the context of language and gender, the author underlines that "these comments on language and gender should be taken as exemplary of a more general relation between language and social meaning". To follow Ochs (1992), no features of language directly and exclusively index therapeutic talk. Clearly, a certain linguistic strategy can index more than one dimension of the sociocultural context. In order to pin down its therapeutic function, the pragmatic function of the strategy in question needs to be considered along with the local expectations vis-à-vis the distribution of these functions and their variable expression across social activities (Ochs 1992). This is to say that a certain strategy can perform a number of pragmatic functions. Yet its specific function (in discourse) is defined by the socio-cultural setting in which it transpires, e.g., its goals. This function however is not preordained, rather it is brought off in the local interactional context. It will be demonstrated how the discussed features and strategies take on a therapeutic function by considering both the socio-cultural as well as the local interactional contexts in which they transpire.

The current analysis will also draw on selected insights from psychotherapeutic theory or, more specifically, from the Relationship-Focused Integrative Psychotherapy (cf. Erskine and Moursund 1988; Erskine, Moursund, and Trautmann 1999; Moursund and Erskine 2004) for a better understanding and contextualization of the strategies used by the psychotherapist. Furthermore, the interprofessional focus requires the voice of the professional practitioners to be taken into account when examining how psychotherapy is contextually and interactionally accomplished.

In sum, this chapter has discussed a number of complex aspects that need to be seriously considered when researching an (inter)professional discourse site. As discussed, a psychotherapy session constitutes a restricted research site where issues such as the aims of the project and, linked to it, the issues of the researcher's identity, potential collaboration with professional practitioners and research ethics, have to be carefully considered. The current study retains to a great extent its interprofessional focus since my presence as a researcher at the psychotherapy sessions enabled me to gain the professional's perspectives on the data and discuss with the practitioner our research interests regarding the study, as well as to observe what constitutes the 'professional vision' at the site. Moreover, the discourse analysis of the collected data is informed by the stocks of interactional knowledge of the Relationship-Focused Integrative Psychotherapy. It is hoped that the multi-method approach both to data collection and data analysis as well as the interprofessional focus of the study will offer a comprehensive examination of a therapeutic interaction and ultimately produce the results that professional practitioners will find applicable to their daily work with clients.

The following chapters present the discursive workings of psychotherapy.

Chapter 2. The transparency of meaning: Personalizing the meaning in psychotherapy

> *"You've got some feelings about that?"*
> *"Sometimes. But sometimes I think restraints are good. Without them I might run wild".*
> *That was a curious moment. "What does 'running wild' mean? Do you mean extramarital affairs?"*
> *My question shocked Marvin. "I've never been unfaithful to Phyllis! Never will be!"*
> *"Well, what do you mean by 'running wild'?"*
> *Marvin looked stumped. I had a sense he was talking about things he had never discussed before. I was excited for him. It had been one hell of an hour's work. I wanted him to continue and I just waited.* (Yalom 1989: 247)

2.1 Introductory remarks

According to Sarangi (2000), the therapeutic setting, defined by the talk between the client and therapist which takes place in it, significantly differs not only from everyday conversations but also from mainstream medical encounters. O'Hanlon and Wilk (1987), on the other hand, proposed that ordinary language constitutes the medium for therapeutic communication, recognizing no distinction between the two beyond aim:

> 'A fly on the wall' who did not know we were doing psychotherapy would not necessarily suspect that that was what we were doing: he would see and hear only an ordinary conversation. What defines the conversation as psychotherapy is simply our goal in conducting the conversation.
>
> (O'Hanlon and Wilk 1987: 177)

The quotation aptly captures the seeming similarities, yet factual differences, between the two types of social interactions.

An ordinary conversation is construed as the prime medium of interaction in a world of social relationships, and thus can be regarded as an unmarked communication context (cf. Levinson 1979; Schegloff 2001; Sarangi 2004). It is precisely the type of interaction that a person is firstly exposed to and through which the socialization process proceeds (Drew and Heritage 1992: 19). The basic form of mundane, ordinary talk constitutes a kind of benchmark against which other more formal or 'institutional' types of interaction are recognized and experienced. Explicit within this perspective is the view that other 'institutional' forms of interaction will show systematic variations and restrictions on activities and their design relative to ordinary conversation (Sacks, Schegloff, and Jefferson 1974: 629; Atkinson and Drew 1979; Heritage 1984). Labov and Fanshel (1977), in their study of the discourse of psychotherapy, convincingly argued that therapy is a type of conversation and a communicative event in which the involved parties (the client and psychotherapist) work together under the conventional constraints and patterns of face-to-face interaction, i.e., an ordinary conversation. According to Lakoff (1982) psychotherapeutic discourse adheres largely to the rules of ordinary conversation, but with a few, highly significant exceptions. Certain things can be permissibly said and understood in one context but not the other. Therapist and client learn to adapt their knowledge of the techniques and purposes of ordinary conversation to the therapeutic interaction. Lakoff posited that if the ordinary conversation substantially differed from a psychotherapeutic interaction, a client would have to undergo some sort of training in order to properly function within the context.[48] While fluency in the discourse of psychotherapy is strongly based on skill in ordinary conversation, it can be observed that conversational skills need to be recontextualized when applied in this unique communicative context.

Psychotherapy however, to a greater extent than conversation, entails *explicit* interactional work on the meaning of words and phrases performed by the psychotherapist and client in terms of their potential referential and interactional import in the specific context of therapy. What I call the transparency of meaning, i.e., the result of an overtly confrontational approach to clarifying the sense and significance of a client's verbal and non-verbal input – in stark contrast to the negotiation that occurs in an ordinary conversation – constitutes one of the most important discourse norms in psychotherapy. A psychotherapist must be certain that his/her and the client's (referential and interactional) grasp of what the client communicatively offers 'here-and-now' are identical. Progressive work in the course of psychotherapeutic treatment tends to be contingent on sharing the meaning of occurring verbal and non-verbal acts between the psychotherapist and client. Despite that psychotherapy is widely believed to be based on ordinary conversation, how interactants come to understand the meaning significantly differs in these two communicative situations. Let us consider the following situation:

Husband:	I'm tired.
Wife:	How are you tired? Physically, mentally or just bored?
Husband:	I don't know. I guess physically, mainly.
Wife:	You mean that your muscles ache, or your bones?
Husband:	I guess so. Don't be so technical.
	(after some delay)
Husband:	All these old movies have the same kind of old iron bedstead in them.
Wife:	What do you mean? Do you mean all old movies, or some of them, or just the ones you have seen?
Husband:	What's the matter with you? You know what I mean.
Wife:	I wish you would be more specific.
Husband:	You know what I mean! Drop Dead!

(Adapted from Garfinkel 1967: 7)

The above quite recognizable extract may be illustrative of a failed attempt to conduct a regular conversation between two people. Though an outcome of an experiment,[49] it adequately demonstrates how the two parties fail to communicate effectively as one of the interactants (the wife) persistently challenges the other (the husband) by demanding clear specifications of the expressed states and opinions. Even a cursory look at the exchange suffices to realize that this is *not* how an ordinary (friendly) conversation between two people (let alone intimates) should proceed. It makes explicit, however, how much of what is conveyed and expressed in a conversation gets implicitly negotiated without challenging the conversational partner about every uttered thought and/or idea. An ordinary conversation is a context in which the meaning of proffered words and phrases is jointly arrived at in the *course* of an interaction. What is meant by 'meaning' here is not the general referential (propositional) aspect of the word or phrase. For example, in the exchange presented above, both interlocutors – as members of the same speech community – share an understanding of the referential (propositional) meaning of the adjective 'tired'. Yet, what the wife seems to be aiming at by challenging the husband about the meaning of 'tired' is the *personal* framing of the adjective. After all, the feeling of tiredness may involve a number of states and quite different experience(s). She demands that her partner provides her with the individual specification of the expressed states and concepts immediately after proffering them, and in this way refuses to collaboratively work towards arriving at personalizing this concept over the course of the conversation. Nor is the meaning of the expression understood here in terms of what is referred to as the concept of ambivalence in pragmatics (Thomas 1995). This is to say that the investigation of the range of illocutionary values of a speaker's statement is beyond the scope of the current discussion. The aspect of meaning that constitutes the core interest is how it relates to the client's personal (and often very intimate) experience. That is, the analysis will concentrate on how the client is urged on to explore and account for the used expression immediately upon proffering it, in the interactional 'here-and-now'.

This chapter explores the observable distinctions between the communicative situation of psychotherapy and an ordinary conversation to arrive at identifying the constituents of one of the most salient discourse norms of psychotherapy, i.e., how the meaning of the client's proffered expression(s) is arrived at. The discussion will firstly concentrate on juxtaposing an ordinary conversation with a therapeutic interaction with a special emphasis on meaning construction and negotiation in these two contexts. Then the most salient aspects of psychotherapeutic interaction will be presented, after which a psychotherapeutic interaction will be examined as an activity type and discourse type. Secondly, attention will be focused on how the meaning of the client's expression tends to be interactionally established in the psychotherapy session as well as how and why it diverges from an ordinary conversation.

2.2 Positioning therapeutic interaction: Therapy as activity type and discourse type

A number of researchers have attempted to pinpoint to what extent an interaction between a therapist and client in psychotherapy resembles an ordinary conversation, and at what points they diverge.

Ferrara (1994), for example, referring to an ordinary conversation as an unmarked form of discourse (cf. also Agar 1985; Hutchby 2007), contrasts it with psychotherapy on a model of seven dimensions. According to Ferrara, the rule of parity is suspended during psychotherapy. This is to say that interactants in psychotherapy enter into a relationship that is not equal, i.e., one is the helper and the other will be provided with help. Therapists direct the interaction, thus they decide about regulating and terminating the therapy. This is a clear departure from an ordinary conversation in which power and responsibility are shared by interlocutors. Next, reciprocality is presupposed in a conversation, yet extensively limited in psychotherapy. As Ferrara states, even in view of given variations across psychotherapy schools, it is generally predetermined in psychotherapy who will speak and in which manner, as well as to what extent. On the whole, the focus is concentrated on the client and, in accordance with an underlying precept of psychotherapy, the therapist must not make any personal emotional demands on the client. Another differentiating aspect has to do with the organization of the psychotherapeutic event. Ferrara labels this a routine occurrence in order to underline the fact that a client comes on a fixed schedule at a fixed time to the same room in order to undergo therapy. The standard session takes fifty minutes. Needless to say, conversations as spontaneous events can occur anytime and place. The criterion of bounded time constitutes another dimension. It signifies that the time frame for psychotherapy is both extended and restricted. It is noteworthy that beginning therapists are trained in what techniques they should use to terminate sessions (cf. Ferrara 1994: 40). The restricted topic further differentiates the two activities. It is assumed that "the topic of preference will revolve around the feelings, attitudes, and behavior of the client and will pertain to his or her mental and emotional health" (1994: 41). It is also the client's responsibility, with an extensive facilitation on the therapist's side, to offer the majority of talk. Although Ferrara states that it is uncommon for therapists to share personal information with the client, Farber (2006), referring to the research on therapist disclosure, underscores a division of opinions between psychotherapists on the issue. Therapists vary widely in their views on self-disclosure to clients and underline that the *moment-to-moment* decisions to disclose are not only based on their theoretical stances but are also influenced by a number of variables, e.g., the gender configuration of the therapeutic dyad or even the amount of time left in the session (Farber 2006: 149). It also needs to be underlined that client and therapist disclosure are not complementary interactional phenomena. Even though both therapist and client disclosure lead to a positive therapeutic outcome, clients are expected to reveal their problems and secrets but, as Farber asserts, "none of this is true for therapists" (2006: 149).[50]

Another difference between psychotherapy and ordinary conversation concerns the aspect of remuneration. Sarangi (2001) relates it to the consumerist model of health and social care. The psychotherapist is "paid to listen" (Sarangi 2001: 41–42). This professional listener, whose presence is professionally legitimated, is able to make sense of the client's experience and life story and compare it against other people's experiences. Unlike psychotherapy sessions, conversations tend to be voluntary and not remunerated.

The last distinguishing feature discussed by Ferrara (1994: 42) is the so-called regulatory responsibility "with which the therapist is empowered by mutual consent". This is to say that there is, in fact, no place for negotiating openings, closings or turn-takings, as the therapist remains in charge of the therapeutic part of a psychotherapy session.

Still, a basic principle of (good) psychotherapy is nonjudgmental acceptance of what the client discloses to the therapist (cf. also Rogers 1951). Ferrara (1994: 42) poses a very intriguing question, "we would like to know the moment at which conversation ceases to be conversation and becomes therapy, and conversely, how therapeutic discourse ceases to be therapeutic and returns to the world of ordinary conversation". In line with this question, the communicative event of psychotherapy cannot be conceptualized as 'either / or' communicative situation, but rather as one incorporating elements of an ordinary conversation and possibly elements of more asymmetrical discourses, depending on the stage of the actual interaction. Ferrara's query then implies that a communicative setting of psychotherapy does indeed incorporate certain aspects of conversation. For instance, Ferrara points to the openings and closing of psychotherapy sessions as significantly resembling their conversation counterparts. The author states that these edges of a psychotherapy session reflect equality between the involved parties, thus symmetry. This is unlike the rest of the event (i.e. actual therapeutic work), where asymmetry prevails. Ferrara also points to certain semiformulaic expressions that are used by therapists to terminate chatting and commence therapeutic work. Ferrara says that therapists would often make references to the time span between sessions to mark the beginning of actual therapeutic work, e.g. "How'd it go this week?", "What's going on?" (1994: 43). In my data the therapist often relied on the phrase 'Let's do some work' to signal the end of a conversational exchange or small talk and the start of psychotherapeutic work. Another common therapeutic gambit used by the therapist was 'How are you doing?'. Unlike a phatic communion phrase, it was proffered by the therapist not at the beginning of an encounter, but long after introductory remarks, and marked the beginning of therapeutic work as the clients commenced talking about their emotional states and moods. Sarangi (2000: 2) states that the talk format, e.g. 'how are you' derives its meaning from the activity type in which it is embedded and different responses to it (re)define the role-relations between participants as well as the boundaries of an activity type.

Lakoff (1982) argues that the differences that exist between an ordinary conversation and therapeutic discourse are more widespread than the *apparent* similarities. According to Lakoff, psychotherapeutic discourse uses the rules of ordinary conversations but with marked differences. In this sense, psychotherapists recontextualize the premises of a conversation to a new purpose, which is "effecting change" (1982: 136). Both a therapist and a client adapt their knowledge and experience of an ordinary conversation to a therapeutic encounter. Lakoff, similarly to Ferrara (1994), refers to the Principle of Reciprocity as the underlying rule of an ordinary conversation. Reciprocity in an ordinary conversation enables interlocutors to feel good about themselves and other participants of an interaction. Reciprocity also constitutes an important means of achieving rapport. Lakoff (1982: 139) also draws attention to the so-called microstructural reciprocity: "Whatever kinds of speech acts one participant may engage in, so may the other, and within those broad types, whatever one speaker may say or expect the other to say, the other is entitled to a symmetrical expectation". Yet, as she claims, although basically nonreciprocal in nature, psychotherapeutic discourse has a superficial veneer of reciprocity discourse.

Another difference lies in the fact that, in psychotherapeutic discourse, there is a greater emphasis on 'interpretation' which is carried out unilaterally. I will come back to this aspect further in the discussion. Lakoff (1982) concludes that the greatest support for the differences exists in negative evidence, i.e. the conversational aspects which are not found in psychotherapeutic discourse. Lakoff (1989) draws attention to differences in power between an ordinary conversation and therapeutic discourse. As she explains, unlike an ordinary conversation, there is no correlation between power, turn-allocation and topic-choice. In therapeutic discourse, the party who does most of the turn-taking, i.e. occupies the conversational floor (the client) "demonstrates less power in lacking the ability to refuse to take a turn when invited (whereas the therapist may remain silent at will) without interpretation; and lacking the ability to determine topic-choice" (1989: 105). An analogous comment has been made by Friedlander (1984), who says that in most relationships, the quantity of talk by each speaker is determined by his/her social worth (cf. also Goffman 1967: 36). Yet, as Friedlander (1984: 336) claims, this particular rule does not apply to psychotherapy, as in this (social) setting "the talk ration generally favors the client, the party with lower social status". According to Lakoff (1989), overt equal power distribution in conversation manifests itself in the ability to share equally in turn-taking. Covert power relations are evidenced when one interlocutor possesses the ability to interpret and thus control topic choice. Lakoff (1989) takes issue with the claim, advocated by a number of psychotherapists, that the potential power imbalance (cf. Spinelli 2006) inevitable at the start of therapy gradually disappears as the process continues/advances. In her view, the communicative event of psychotherapy never becomes truly equal as it is the client who is always interpreted and not the therapist. Yet, the inequalities are accepted by participants as the therapy is not perceived mainly for the purpose of interaction (Lakoff 1989: 106; cf. also Sarangi 2001). Even though psychotherapy does indeed have the interactive form of ordinary conversation, it aims at discovering (personal) truth. Finally, Lakoff (1989: 112) refers to the (potential) intimacy present in therapy as purely conventional, and not a sign of true intimacy: "the fact that it is used for unilateral disclosure via unilateral interpretability underscores this point: true intimacy would be fully shared".

Sarangi (2001), analyzing transcripts of an interaction between a client and therapist in a psychotherapeutic clinic, points to an ordinary conversation in which participants *share* communicative practices. If one discloses personal troubles, the other participant in an ordinary conversation is supposed to take the position of the recipient of troubles talk (Sarangi 2000: 13). Yet, this, as one of the clients explained, often involves prematurely providing some sort of advice or sympathy to another interlocutor and, in this way, thwarting therapeutic activity (Sarangi 2001). It implies that, unlike in an ordinary conversation, in therapy talk one interlocutor (therapist) should *actively* listen to what the client is disclosing as well as attempting to disclose, and support him/her in this challenging endeavor, focusing his/her attention on the client and his/her experience.

Furthermore, judged against an idealized context of everyday conversational interaction, therapeutic talk "becomes recognizable as 'distorted', as talk between strangers" (Sarangi 2001: 41). The 'distorted' aspect seems to lie in the fact that revealing highly intimate aspects of one's life should take place in the context of an intimate/well-established relationship and not in the company of a stranger. Yet, a client entering a therapeutic relationship agrees to that type of scenario. Sarangi (2001: 49) underlines that in the therapeutic setting, the client's agency is foregrounded: "the patient takes on an active role in the categorization of feelings and experiences". She/he is "the speaking subject" (2001: 42) while the therapist occupies the position of an involved listener. As Sarangi (2001: 42) expounds, this is a clear divergence from everyday talk in which participants do not "occupy differentiated receiver roles". What seems to be, however, the most salient discrepancy is that, in the therapeutic talk, explanatory understanding is given the utmost priority. This is to say that immense effort is made by the therapist to enable the client to understand the traumas and difficulties in his/her life. Such a priority does not characterize an ordinary conversation. Self-understanding, as Sarangi explains, is possible through self-reflection, which constitutes a characteristic feature of therapeutic talk. Self-reflection, as the core activity, positions participants (the client and therapist) in a very specific interactional framework which involves unequal power relations implicit in the context of psychotherapeutic interaction. The inequality relates to the fact that it is the client (not the therapist) who should self-reflect. Yet Sarangi (2001) also advises against juxtaposing a therapeutic interaction with an ordinary conversation without taking into account the goals and perspectives of participants. Indeed, judged against an ordinary 'normative' conversation, psychotherapeutic interaction appears very asymmetrical, as the therapist relies on his/her jargon, is in charge of the interaction and takes on the stance of an expert.

Needless to say, the features of a psychotherapeutic talk cannot be analyzed and evaluated without allowing for the context in which they transpire and the purposes they serve. The aim of even the most distant schools of psychotherapy remains uniform: to help the client lead a better, more fulfilling life. The client is at the center of attention in all communicative endeavors undertaken by the therapist. The client is the participant of therapy who should benefit the most from a psychotherapeutic interaction. Yet, as discussed above, in the psychotherapeutic interaction, the therapist appears to be more powerful as he/she possesses the (communicative and interactional) tools to help the client self-reflect, self-understand and consequently, in the long run, lead a better life. It needs to be underlined, however, that those tools are used to the benefit of the client. Thus it can be claimed that in the context of psychotherapeutic interaction, we are dealing with a very unique discursive phenomenon of reverse power relations. This aspect of 'doing therapy' can be succinctly presented with the words of a well-known psychotherapist:

> When one person, the therapist 'treats' another, the patient, it is understood from the beginning that the treatment pair, the two who have formed a therapeutic alliance, are not equals or full allies; one is distressed and often bewildered, while the other is expected to use professional skills to disentangle and examine objectively issues that lie behind that distress and bewilderment. Furthermore, the patient pays the one who treats. The very word treat implies non-equality. To 'treat' someone as an equal implies an inequality which the therapist must overcome or conceal by behaving as though the other were an equal.
>
> (Yalom 1989: 221)

The participant who appears more powerful in directing the course of the interaction utterly adjusts his/her communicative behavior to the benefit of the other, i.e. the client. In this sense, psychotherapeutic interaction extensively departs from an ordinary conversation in which every interacting party should benefit equally. Psychotherapeutic talk is generally non-reciprocal, i.e. it is premised on the assumption that the client and not the therapist verbalizes certain (traumatic) experiences and emotional states, which in turn constitute the major topic around which a therapeutic interaction revolves, aiming at enlarging understanding and insight.

According to Sarangi (2000), therapy constitutes both a type of activity and a form of discourse. In his conceptualization of an activity type, Sarangi (2000) draws on the same concept proposed by Levinson (1979), who considers it to be any culturally recognized activity characterized by a period of speech or its lack. An activity type is then defined as a "fuzzy category whose focal members are goal-defined, socially constituted, bounded events with constraints on participants, settings and so on, but above all on the kind of allowable contributions" (Levinson 1979: 368). It seems that the key aspect of the concept is constituted by the *allowable contributions*, which comprise not only what is said but also how, when and where something is said. Certain model examples of activity types are, according to Levinson (1979), teaching, a job interview, a football game, etc. As Sarangi, referring to Levinson, aptly illustrates in his discussion, types of activity perform a main role in language usage. This is to say that, on the one hand, a specific social context restricts what can be contributed to, but on the other, it helps to determine "what kinds of inferences will be made from what is said" (Levinson 1979: 393). Thus, an activity type appears to be a means of characterizing settings (e.g. a medical check-up, a service encounter). Sarangi (2000: 2) conceives of discourse type as a way of characterizing the forms of talk (e.g. medical history taking, interrogation, troubles telling). Yet, activity types are generally dynamic (communicative) events, thus they rarely depend upon a single discourse type, which in turn can perform different functions in different contexts. Sarangi relies on the term 'interactional hybridity' "in order to understand how certain discourse types are overlaid within and across activity types" (2000: 12). The author also inquires when certain discourse types become marginal in one activity type but occupy the central point in another.

The overlap between activity type and discourse type in the case of psychotherapy lies in the fact that aspects of therapy talk may transpire in a number of activity types and, in a similar vein, therapy draws on different discourse types.

Psychotherapy indeed constitutes one of the most commonly recognizable social activities (cf. Gaik 1992). The goal of this activity type remains well-defined, i.e. a professionally trained person establishes a therapeutic relationship with an individual suffering from emotional problems, for the purpose of alleviating or modifying troublesome thoughts, memories, emotional reactions or patterns of behavior. It is a socially constituted and bounded event. And what about Levinson's point concerning constraints on allowable contributions in the context of therapy as an activity type? As far as the therapist's contributions are concerned, I would like to concentrate on the 'what' and 'how' aspects, since allowable contributions also refer to how something is said (cf. Sarangi 2000).

Firstly, the content of the therapist's contributions should reflect, to a different extent at different stages of the therapeutic work, what the client is offering. This is to say that being *client-focused*, the therapist must not bring up topics or issues which do not constitute immediate reference to the client's situation in the therapeutic part of the interaction.[51] The therapeutic interaction is *about* the client and *for* the client's benefit. Secondly, the communicative and interactional strategies used by the therapist (*how* the content is packed) are also geared towards effecting client's change. Compared with an ordinary conversation these strategies may appear to be, for instance, too confrontational or challenging. Yet, their function must be evaluated in the context of the specific goals of the therapeutic activity. As far as the client's contributions are concerned, the therapist ought to accept what the client is offering unconditionally (cf. Rogers 1951 'rule of unconditional positive regard'). This unconditional acceptance also constitutes an exponent of the reverse power relations in this specific context: the therapist is in (interactional) charge of the direction of the interaction, yet must unconditionally accept what the client offers. This often involves further extensive work on reformulating the client's initial concerns (cf. Davis 1986; also Antaki, Barnes, and Leudar 2005a).

Therapy emerges as a unique context which functions as an activity type and a discourse type (cf. Sarangi 2000). This uniqueness derives from the fact that therapy is constituted, first and foremost, by talk entailing certain discourse types, thus it is frequently referred to as a 'talking cure'. Talk constitutes the foundation in many psychotherapy schools. Genuine involvement with another person (therapist) in sharing experiences provides clients with an opportunity to improve their lives in a most qualitative way. The question remains, then, what discourse types occupy the focal position in bringing about a (positive) change in one's life. Sarangi (2000) points to active listening as one of the definitional properties of therapy. Another important discursive strategy is self-disclosure and self-reflection, which enable the client to give voice to the hidden and often traumatic experiences in his/her life. Also, the transparency of meaning (pursued further on in this chapter) as well as a refocus from intellectual to emotional aspects of client's disclosive talk constitute the core discourse norms of the therapeutic interaction.

These definitional properties of psychotherapy as activity type permeate other contexts and settings (i.e. other activity types). Their positions there, however, range from focal to peripheral and, contrary to the context of psychotherapeutic interaction, not all of them have to transpire in a single activity type. Additionally, as advocated by Sarangi (2000) in accordance with 'interactional hybridity' their functions may differ from those performed in the context of an actual psychotherapy session. Thus, active listening, as represented by inquiry (a set of questions) may be applied not to attune to the client and form an alliance with him/her but, for instance in the context of questioning a witness in court, to build up an argument for the jury (cf. Levinson 1979).

There is, however, one aspect of the interaction between a therapist and client that tends not to be applied in any context other than a psychotherapy setting itself. The reason for this might be its almost non-existent status in an ordinary conversation (a basic model for human interaction) thus it has a lesser chance to be (easily) transferred into a new context. This aspect relates to meaning making in psychotherapeutic interaction.

2.3 Meaning making in ordinary conversation and psychotherapeutic interaction

Wardhaugh (1985) states that indirectness, rather than directness, constitutes the norm in speech. By 'speech' Wardhaugh means an ordinary conversation. Interlocutors seldom present their claims in fully explicit terms, but rather tend to rely on the intuitions of others as well as their common sense:

> You proceed through a conversation not as you would through an exercise in logic but rather in the manner in which you might try to find your way through a maze. You must be prepared to check, recheck, backtrack, hypothesize, and live with uncertainty for a while. If you are unwilling to live this way, misunderstanding would seem to be the inevitable consequence unless you choose to play the confrontational game.
>
> (Wardhaugh 1985: 36)

Excessively overt reliance in an ordinary conversation on unequivocal commands or confrontational questioning violates the basic assumptions people hold about the mutual trust and decency that a conversation should be based on.

The meaning of conversation, as Wardhaugh (1985) explains, is something that is negotiated during the course of the conversation rather than overtly expressed. The meaning of the current utterance in a conversation is contingent on what has happened before, what is currently happening, and what may or may not happen next. Thus it is not fixed but subject to constant review and reinterpretation. Similarly, Arndt and Janney (1987: 88) state that the major purpose of an everyday interaction (i.e. a conversation) constitutes an exchange of factual, personal and interpersonal information, and negotiation and mutual agreement on its meaning. The reason for this may be the fact that conversation is generally completely unrehearsed, and its content and structure is shaped in the course of the interaction. Wardhaugh draws attention to the fact that rehearsed, thus not spontaneous, parts (of a conversation) are highly marked and instantly become obvious (and suspicious) to those who hear them.

As far as *explicitness* of an ordinary conversation is concerned, according to Wardhaugh (1985), interlocutors tend to accept what they are told at face value. This is to say that they are prepared to accept a remarkable amount of unclarity and imprecision, and seek only occasional clarification of the proffered remarks or statements made to them. There is a tacit assumption that the potential unclarity will work itself out to the interlocutors' satisfaction. Consequently, witnessing certain exchanges which involve a significant amount of questioning and commenting implies facing interactions of a different kind, for example interrogations. If the interlocutors insisted on making everything their conversational partners say explicit, then conversation would become an extremely laborious enterprise.

As Wardhaugh (1985) states, unclarity and ambiguity must be tolerated in an ordinary conversation. One can not stop another interlocutor every time something is not clear, as such action can potentially obstruct what is happening; such behavior is not expected in a conversation. Furthermore, it breaks one of the most important qualities of a successful conversation, i.e. mutual trust between interlocutors, and can indicate a certain degree of disbelief or even rudeness. Constantly drawing the attention of others to the indirectness and unclarity of their statements may result in being labeled 'anti-social'. The general principle that interlocutors abide by when they enter a conversation is that a genuine account will emerge. Consequently, it can be assumed that people start a conversation not as skeptics and cynics but as potential believers. If an instant clarification is absolutely indispensable then it should proceed in such a way as to avoid any direct confrontation. Conversation is characterized by "occasional gaps, sudden leaps, a lack of explicitness, and a considerable and sometimes pervasive unclarity" (Wardhaugh 1985: 33). The author also underlines the fact that by participating in a conversation, one is partially held responsible for its coherence:

"you cannot rely on the speaker alone, but must 'help' him or her" (1985: 33). In this sense, a conversation emerges as a mutually constructed event.

Thus in listening to someone's account, another interlocutor needs to make the best of what he/she hears. Applying the quality of trust, interlocutors presume that the offered account makes sense and there is a certain sequence of the presented events, even though it may not be readily apparent from the description.

Lakoff (1982) states that unlike an ordinary conversation, in a psychotherapeutic interaction interpretation is carried on unilaterally, consciously, with greater regularity and frequency, and in much greater depth. Here interpretation is referred to as 'meaning making' of another interlocutor's statement. Both types of interaction (a conversation and psychotherapy interaction), however, share the same guiding principle for when and how to interpret, i.e. "interpret when the utterance makes no sense at face value" (1982: 141). Lakoff (1982) also presents three significant levels of meaningfulness, with respect to interpretability, in any kind of interaction:

1. The utterance is fully meaningful at face value; the addressee does not need to perform any work to understand it.
2. The utterance is not fully intelligible on its surface; the addressee must make certain assumptions (interpretations) whether consciously and overtly or not, to derive sense from it.
3. The utterance does not make sense and no amount of interpretation, using conventional, agreed upon (implicit) rules, will help.

(Lakoff 1982: 141)

The aspect of 'making no sense' in level (2) concerns principally pragmatic rather than semantic meaningfulness, while in level (3) it might be either. Lakoff (1982: 141–142) claims that level (3) occurs typically, though rarely in psychotic discourse, whereas level (2) becomes transparent "when someone says something that is internally coherent and rational, but whose purpose in the particular context of the discourse at hand is not immediately discernible; it is not clear how other participants benefit from the knowledge".

As Lakoff expounds, psychotherapeutic discourse and an ordinary conversation treat levels (1) and (3) similarly. The crucial difference between these two types of interaction, as far as meaningfulness and/or interpretability is concerned, lies in level (2). This is to say that one fundamental difference between (2) in an ordinary conversation and psychotherapeutic discourse is that in the latter, interpretation, i.e. 'meaning making' of what one interlocutor (the client) proffers is done openly and unilaterally (by the therapist). Lakoff asserts that in an ordinary conversation, that type of interpretation could indicate the end of any friendship if performed more than a few times (1982: 141). The author concludes that the differences between an ordinary conversation and psychotherapeutic discourse can be subsumed under two aspects.

Firstly, there is a lack of reciprocity in all types of therapeutic discourse. Secondly, there is a major reorientation of the client's expectations towards an interaction with a therapist. The client needs to relearn the metastrategies of conversation and consequently reexamine his/her forms of behavior in a conversation in which the client "has been engaging for years without giving it much thought, operating according to an implicit and therefore imperceptible pattern" (Lakoff 1982: 142).

The transparency of meaning constitutes a significant discourse norm of the therapist-client interaction. Its interactional realization consists in the fact that the therapist, at certain moments of the interaction, directly confronts the client about the meaning of his/her proffered statement.[52] To refer to Lakoff's (1982) line of reasoning, the client's utterance or statement is clear in terms of its semantic meaningfulness, i.e. it is internally coherent and rational. Yet, the specific context of psychotherapy demands that the statement (thus from the client) be consistent with the aims of this type of interaction. Clients are believed to present facts and experiences from their lives which they find emotionally difficult and constricting and which, in their view, carry potential importance for the therapeutic process. It is one of the tenets of psychotherapy that clients do not say things in vain, that is they offer the accounts of certain situations and events because they constitute troublesome contexts for them. These experiences packed in verbal and/or non-verbal form bear a certain significance for them. It is the therapist's task to uncover the personal, intimate anchoring, i.e. framing of the client's statement or behavior. This takes place in the middle of his/her revelations. The therapist is attempting to make meaning of the client's verbal and non-verbal behavior with his/her interactional and communicative strategies in the interactional *here and now*. This is a clear departure from what the clients have been socialized into and (unconsciously) involved in doing in an ordinary conversation. A therapist tends not to wait for the meaning of the client's statement to be worked out in the course of the interaction, but rather he/she directly confronts the client about the personal significance of the statement(s). Thus typically in psychotherapy, despite the lack of any interactional trouble in the course of an interaction, the therapist actively engages the client in providing a personal account of the proffered words and/or phrases in the interactional *here and now*.

2.4 Personalizing the meaning in psychotherapy

> *I saw my principal role as that of facilitating the*
> *means by which Mr. Jones could more carefully*
> *explore and clarify the meanings he had given to*
> *his symptoms.* (Spinelli 2006: 16)

In what follows, three strategies utilized by the therapist to bring out the personal framing of the client's proffered words or statements and aspects of non-verbal behavior will be identified and discussed. What unites all of them is the fact that they transpire, i.e. the therapist avails himself of them, in the middle of the clients' revelations. Thus as far as their organizational structure is concerned, the therapist interferes in the client's ongoing talk. The client is stopped by the therapist to comment, justify or reflect on the specific word, interactional strategy or even aspects of non-verbal behavior that he or she has just projected. The therapist's professional expertise (cf. Buttny and Cohen 1991) enables him to assess what facets of the client's narrative and experience are therapeutically relevant, and thus should be further worked on in therapy. What is also significant is that the clients may use in their disclosive talk certain terms, words or phrases and non-verbal behaviors which carry very personal meaning for them and the therapist may not be familiar with their immediate significance for the client's personal story. Consequently, the therapist needs to get into the personal meaning of the client's proffered words, phrases and non-verbal behavior. If the client and therapist fail to share an understanding of the key terms used by the client, the course of the psychotherapy treatment may easily be thwarted. As Thomas (1995) states, indirectness at some points in the interaction is risky and costly. This is especially important in view of the fact that current psychotherapy treatments tend to be generally much shorter, thus the criterion of time matters (cf. Ferrara 1994; Czabała 2006).

The strategies used by the therapist to access the client's personal meaning are of a very confrontational character (cf. Wardhaugh 1985: 36), yet in this way the participants in the psychotherapeutic interaction are able to evade possible misunderstandings and instantly share the client's personal meaning of the concepts he/she uses. Additionally, by being asked to reflect on a certain phrase immediately after proffering it, the client is learning how to be fully in touch with his/her emotional states. This is particularly important, as one of the goals of psychotherapy is to achieve awareness of one's emotions (cf. Labov and Fanshel 1977).

2.4.1 Probing questions

> *Your insistence, though, when you kept repeating*
> *the question, "Well, what does it mean – your writ-*
> *ing not going anywhere?" finally annoyed me. It*
> *was like a countdown in a fight. I knew I had to get*
> *up at that point, and say something or it was all*
> *over.* (Yalom and Elkin 1974: 5)

The most direct strategy used by the therapist in attempting to access the personal framing of the client's statement is the question 'what do you mean'. This type of question used by the psychotherapist in the interactions with clients has the function of probe. Probes (or probing questions) are follow-up questions that help an interlocutor clarify or expand his/her initial answer (Blache et al. 1996: 16).

Even though the most confrontational, it is the least interactionally complicated strategy to be used by the psychotherapist seeking elaboration on the salient content word used by the client. The therapist, however, does not rely on this question every time he is not positive about what the client is attempting to convey. Rather it seems to be the strategy to be applied when other (less direct) methods fail.

There are numerous places in the clients' narratives that might pose difficulties for the therapist trying to grasp their personal significance for the clients. Moreover, these 'veiled' words, phrases or even metaphors often disguise very intimate, private stories that the clients are able to convey at this point of their therapies only in an oblique manner. This is very much in line with Pomerantz's (1984) claim that delicate topics are often talked about with terms and glosses that relate to the problem without naming or identifying it. The therapist, however, needs to know what kind of significance these statements carry for the clients. It also happens that the therapist may have no doubts as to what the client specifically means by a certain phrase, yet he will still confront him/her about its significance. In this way, the client is being gradually instilled with the ability to be aware of the projected emotional states. Let us consider the following example:

Extract 1

1   T: Can I pursue with that '<u>trapped</u>' (.) it's no choice and it's impossible, <it <u>must</u>
2   permeate your life in some important areas.>
3   C: Yeah, it <u>was</u> (.) and it still is.=

4   T: =Can you name those areas?=
5   C: =Relationships.
6   T: You mean like friendships or   love life?
7   C: // No
8   no, love relationships.
9→   T: So I presume there is a sense of <u>hopelessness</u> that you can influence those
10   relationships in positive way.=
11   C: =°Yeah°, leading me to take pre-emptive action so >I don't come too close to it.<
12→ T: <Pre-emptive action not to come too close to it.> What does that <u>mean</u>? I know
13→   the di:ctionary meaning of those words but I wanna know what
14→   they <u>personally</u> mean to you:.
15   C: I think it has been a lo:ng going strategy for me to avoid getting into the trapped
16   feeling of having an impact (1.0) so I just end a relationship before I might
17   even get into that position or situation (.) I mean, that's
18   T: // So: if somebody
19   gets <u>romantically</u> interested in you or sexually interested in you
20   C: // I will
21   probably run away, °yeah.°

The above extract presents a part of the exchange which starts with the
therapist seeking permission from the client to focus on the theme of
'trapped' proffered by the client earlier in the interaction. The client is
also asked to name the aspects of her life that can be characterized as
'trapped'. Once relationships get pointed out by the client as troublesome
aspects of her life, the therapist offers disjunctive alternatives (cf.
Hutchby 2005) to spell out the types of relationships that pose difficulties
for the client. In fact, one of the interactional functions of such disjunctive questions is to encourage the client to pursue an active choice between the provided options (Hutchby 2005: 325). In line 9, the therapist
formulates the client's problem, which is rejoined by her with a latched
acknowledgment starting with 'yeah' and elaboration on the therapist's
formulation (line 11). This is, however, quite an oblique statement, devoid of any personal reference. In other words, this statement could be
used to refer to a large number of people's daily behaviors. Yet, needless
to say, the client's strategy of encoding the personal, often traumatic experience in general, abstract terms makes it easier for him/her to bring it
up in the session. The statement is very general thus there are multiple
ways of decoding its content and meaning. The meaning, however that
the therapist is mainly interested in is how the general, abstract content
relates to the client's personal experience. The characteristic of such all-

encompassing claims is their fleeting character. If left unexplained or un-elaborated on, they could potentially be denied by the participants at any point of the interaction (cf. also Arndt and Janney 1991). Thus in view of that, the therapist's task is to grasp their significance to the client's experience immediately after it is profferred by the client.

The therapist's statement in lines 12–14 aptly glosses the function of his 'what do you mean' used in the interactions with the clients. The therapist explains that he needs the client to translate the 'pre-emptive action' from the general term into person-specific acts. In this way, the therapist is able to anchor the client's individual experience from an all-encompassing claim. The immediate confrontational question triggers from the client a personal exemplification of her general claim. There is no doubt about the disclosure being highly emotionally-loaded (lines 15–17). The therapist however remains actively involved in the client's self-expression and understands its emotional load by co-constructing the client's expression (line 18). This is not a misattuned attempt, as the client provides a prompt rejoinder to the therapist's claim (lines 20–21). In Extract 1, by confronting the client with the probe 'what do you mean', the therapist enables her to tell her story by herself.

Upon hearing the therapist's 'what do you mean', the clients have at least two options for responding to it (cf. Pomerantz 1984). The client may directly address the prior talk (as discussed above), or he or she may look blank or questioning or make hesitating noises. The second option may indicate that the client fails to provide a coherent response and in this sense, his/her behavior is accountable, i.e. it is interpreted as manifesting some kind of a problem.

In Extract 2, the therapist is involved with the client in addressing her marital problems:

Extract 2

```
1   T:   I wonder if you sort of need to win your husband ba:ck (.) in a new
2        way (6.0) except that you can't be a co:smic mistake and do that at
3        the same time.=
4   C:   =No:, that's true, two different worlds.
5   T:   Yeah.
6   C:   Uh, they can't co-exist, (.) and there are only few °bridges.°
7→  T:   What do you mean?
8   C:   Not too many ↑connections when I'm fully in my real life then >I
9        don't feel like a cosmic mistake< and everything that surrounds
```

10   it, but when it comes into it then it can be a poison (2.0) nothing
11   is the <u>same</u> anymore, everything is >hollow, hollow< and this is
12   <u>nothing</u> compared to not existing (.) and even in the best
13   moments these thoughts come.
14 T: Tell me about your anger.

In lines 1–3 the therapist states a kind of proposal to which the client relates (line 4). Yet, the response provided by the client does not clearly resonate with the content of the therapist's statement. The response does not include any personal reference. The therapist, with the continuer 'yeah' (line 5), provides her with conversational space, thus encouraging the client to continue her self-reflection. The encouragement however results in a continuation of the metaphoric statement from line 4, preceded with a place-holder 'uh', and likewise misses any personal reference (line 6). At this point, the therapist attempts to refocus the client's disclosure from general to person – i.e., client-specific. The direct confrontational question from the therapist (line 7) solicits the expansion of the previous 'veiled'/general statements in terms of the client's real personal experience.

Schiffrin (1999) makes a distinction between a request for clarification of the statements and a request for elaboration. The differences between the two consist in the fact that the former indicates a reception problem which will be solved through upcoming clarification, while the latter "acknowledges receipt of information which has been sufficiently interpreted to allow the receiver to prompt its further development" (Schiffrin 1999: 280). Additionally, clarification requests aim at amending the old information while elaboration requests seek provision of new information. Schiffrin (1999) also explains that both clarification and elaboration requests demonstrate speakers' receipt of information (partial or complete) and simultaneously solicit further information. It seems that in the analyzed examples, the therapist's 'what do you mean' fulfills two functions at the same time. The client is asked to clarify his/her personal statement, but this clarification can only be achieved with his/her further elaboration on the initial statement. 'What do you mean' solicits from the client more details of his/her (traumatic) experience that help the therapist identify the troublesome aspects that lend themselves to psychotherapeutic work.

Extract 3 also illustrates how the direct, confrontational question is used by the therapist to tap into the client's personal experience when other interactional strategies failed to work:

Extract 3

1	T:	To hi:de what most of all? Of all your characteristics, what's the
2		most important thing to hide?
3	C:	Vulnerability.
4	T:	↑Vulnerability
5	C:	Yeah.
6	T:	Ok.
7	C:	Yeah.
8→	T:	No:w, what do you mean by vulnerability?
9	C:	I had to conceal e::verything that could be seen as deficient because
10		she would exaggerate it and when I was already on the floor >she
11		would step on me so<
12	T:	// Because if you showed a:ny vulnerability,
13		it was pro:ved to her that you weren't a good therapist (.) even
14		though you were only Y.
15	C:	I never cried, in my therapy I needed almost Z years when I first
16		time cried.=
17	T:	=Because if you cried, what would she do?
18	C:	>She would know that it was my weak point and next time she
19		would go directly there.<

Extract 3 presents a part of a talk about the relationship between the client and her mother; or rather its warped character. The exchange very much resembles a 'hyperquestioning' type of exchange (cf. Sarangi 2000). In lines 1–2 the client is asked about a quality she could not reveal in front of her mother. The client, in fact, provides the answer (line 3) which gets repeated by the therapist with rising intonation (line 4), indicating that the proffered answer requires elaboration from the client (cf. Bolinger 1982). The attempt to elicit more elaboration from the client fails, as she provides merely a token of acknowledgment 'yeah' (line 5), and another one in line 7 as a rejoinder to the therapist's 'ok' in line 6. Since other interactional strategies failed to solicit from the client the personal framing of *vulnerability*, the therapist resorts to the direct confrontation (line 8). This interactional move in fact refocuses the client's self-expression as she starts reflecting on what, exactly, was going on between her and her mother (lines 9–11).

It is also worth noting how the therapist's interactional strategies of seeming interruption (line 12) and latching (line 17) promote the client's reflection of her personal experience rather than a statement of some general claims as she did before. These strategies also function as the exponents of the therapist's empathy and attunement to the client's process of self-revelation. Even though the form of the therapist's contribution in lines 12–14 resembles an interruption, it aims at facilitating the client's difficult process of refocusing from general to personal. It also manifests the therapist's understanding of the client's emotional pain in revealing the most traumatic aspects of her existence. Thus from line 9 on, both participants collaboratively construct the account. This is nicely illustrated by the client's taking up a new personal aspect in line 15, following the therapist's intervention.

Extracts 2 and 3 discussed above have demonstrated how the therapist relies on 'what do you mean' to refocus the client's account from general to personal when other interactional strategies (e.g., continuers, repetition) fail.

In Extract 4, the therapist draws on 'what do you mean' twice:

Extract 4

```
1    C:   Let's see: how far we get (1.0) I think it's very very important to
2          address some issues that have been bothering me and uhm keep
3          me from contacting. I don't know (.) I'll start anyway. >The other
4          night we were talking over dinner why I didn't drink alcohol< and
5          I could drink alcohol but I get very much °afraid° to be out
6          of control. I like to be very much, have everything under control,
7          to be very much in charge so to let go, to relax, it's very very
8          difficult for me.=
9→   T:   =Now, what do you mean by out of control?
10   C:   That I can be ↑spontaneous, that I'm not holding back anything,
11         like flowing with everything that is going on and not criticizing me
12         inside.
13→  T:   Would you be funny? Angry? Would you be sexy? Would you be
14         crying? <What do you mean?> These are all the things people
15         might do: when they've been drinking.
```

Extract 4 depicts the beginning of a session in which the client, in her initial statement, declares what issue she would like to pursue in the current meeting. When the client mentions the problem of 'being too much in control' of her life, the therapist promptly rejoins the statement (an interactional strategy of latching) with a question to specify what 'being in control' of her life entails (line 9). What is significant in this extract is that the 'what do you mean' is prefaced with a discourse marker 'now' (Schiffrin 1987), which clearly marks a discontinuation of the client's disclosure and the beginning of the therapist's inquiry. The client starts elaborating on the theme of 'control' in lines 10–12. She offers examples of how 'control' defines certain aspects of her life. Yet this short specification is challenged by the therapist (lines 13–15) when he returns to the client's initial thought of avoiding alcohol as one of the aspects of 'being in control'. The therapist directly questions the client as to how she would behave under the influence of alcohol and closes this part of the statement with the confrontational 'what do you mean'. In the second part of the statement, the therapist asserts that the types of behavior he has mentioned constitute merely an exemplification of how one may act, and the client needs to specify how she would potentially act.

In Extract 5, the therapist makes a latched clarifying comment:

Extract 5

1	C:	And it doesn't get ta:lked about (.) you know, she <u>always</u> says:
2		'and if anything ever happens to me, will you whatever', but
3		it's always <u>if</u> ever anything happens to me.=
4→	T:	=Which means?=
5	C:	=If I die.
6	T:	<What's the importance of that talk?>
7	C:	Well (.) since I was a child I fee:l that I've been very much
8		in contact with <u>death</u>, uhm, the stories I've been told,
9		I've been preoccupied with deaths since I was a child, uhm,
10		the story my mother told me is that <u>poor</u> Mr. X had to die
11		in order to make room for me to come into the world,
12		(2.0) that story has <u>always</u> been with me.

Unlike in the examples discussed above, the therapist does not rely on the question 'what do you mean' in order to press the client to uncover the very personal and difficult aspects of their experience. The therapist's latched phrase in line 4 constitutes a syntactic continuation of the client's thought expressed in lines 1–3. This is to say that the therapist's remark could be made by the client to complete her thought. This, however, did not occur. The client, in lines 1–3, is attempting to verbally convey how the issue of 'death' gets talked about between her and her terminally-ill daughter. The statement is replete with a number of unspecified references: 'anything', 'whatever', 'ever', 'anything'. It is important to underscore that the therapist's inserted comment aims at eliciting from the client the overt labeling of what she and her daughter really talk about. There is no denying that for a loving parent, openly verbalizing the terminal condition of her daughter is excruciatingly difficult, yet it is therapeutically important. It seems that the therapist's collaboration in labeling 'death' makes it more bearable for the client to utter it. In line 6, the therapist embarks on some post-answer work about the significance of 'death talk'. This prepares the ground for the further discussion of the terminal condition the client's daughter faces as well as the client's handling of the emotionally difficult situation.

All of the therapist's 'what do you mean' discussed above can also be interpreted as instances of 'other-initiated repair' or 'next-turn repair initiation' (Schegloff 1981). This constructional format is positioned immediately after the trouble-source took place. Sacks and associates (1974) state that the ongoing talk can be interrupted to initiate 'repair' on the ambiguous segment any time participants think they are not able to sufficiently interpret a stretch of talk. 'Other-initiated repair' however, are marked forms of repair[53] (Schiffrin 1999). In the discussed extracts, the clients' statements are unproductive as far as the therapist being able to identify the personal significance of the word or phrase proffered by the client is concerned. Thus, for the client, the word or phrase that she/he offered is perfectly understandable in terms of its significance to his/her personal experience, but quite vague for the therapist, who challenges the client to elaborate on it. Berger (1979) states that one can afford to be fully explicit in presenting feelings and emotions only if there is not much at stake or if one is confident that his/her (conversational) partners will respond in a supportive, or at least unthreatening, way. Clients come to therapy to share their experiences with a person (the therapist) they do not initially know. The therapist needs to build a relationship based on trust in order for the client to be explicit in presenting his/her experience. Only then can the client let down their protective and limiting guard and get involved in the process of therapy. It seems that the trust that their innermost feelings and traumatic experiences will not be rejected or minimized enables the clients to respond to the therapist's confrontational 'what do you mean' with further and 'person-specific' elaboration of their personal/intimate dramas.

2.4.2 Overt continuers

Goodwin (1986) states that speakers, in organizing their ongoing talk, extensively depend on what their recipients are doing. Recipients avail themselves of a range of both vocal and non-vocal actions to display to speakers their alignment as hearers, as well as how they are analyzing and participating in the talk at the moment (Goodwin 1986: 206). 'Yeah', 'right', and 'uh-huh' feature prominently in talk recipients' turns.

As discussed above, words and vocalizations such as 'yeah', 'right', and 'uh-huh' fall into the category of backchannel cues or continuers. The major division lies in the fact that while backchannels do mainly supportive work in the interactional context(s) in which they occur, continuers reaffirm the interlocutor's right to an extended, i.e., multi-unit turn. Yet, in order to identify the function of a certain 'yeah' or 'right', the sequential context in which they transpire needs to be investigated. Goodwin (1986) closely investigated the placement and function of continuers in ongoing talk. Continuers, as Goodwin explicated, occur at the boundaries of turn-constructional units. With this specific sequential position of continuers, the recipients of talk are able to demonstrate that the unit of talk has been received and another one is now awaited (1986: 208). Continuers then treat a unit of talk as part of a larger series of units. Recipients of the talk, while relying on continuers, manifest their attendance to individual units as emerging elements of a larger structure that is not yet complete.

Similarly to Ferrara's (1994) findings, the corpus of psychotherapy sessions under current investigation also features a large number of backchannel cues and continuers. What is interesting is that continuers used by the therapist often take on a verbal form which clearly manifests that their function is to press the client to continue his/her disclosive talk. In this way, they explicitly grant the interlocutor (here the client) the right to an extended turn by indicating that what is being received is the talk in progress. Let us analyze the following extract:

Extract 6

1	C:	...Oh, <u>yes</u>, and then when you got home, >do you remember?< you
2		were the sta:rring role in <u>whatever</u> the school drama was and
3		although you coul:dn't play the <u>part</u>, you sat in the special place
4		(.) right against the stage. You liked that wheelchair a bit,
5		didn't you? Oh, X it feels like there is <u>so much</u> to say to you.=
6→	T:	=Yes, there <u>is</u>, so keep going.
7	C:	Oh, yes, I mean (.) I don't know whether you <u>remember</u> this
8		(.) do you remember the <u>night</u> after you've been racing without
9		having dinner in this caravan and said .hhh 'somebody is going to take
10		me out for dinner tonight' and I said, '<u>oh</u>, that's great! how are they
11		getting here?' and she said 'by boat' and this <u>boat</u> pulled up at the side
12		of the lake where our caravan was and uhm he got <u>champagne</u> and

13   they rode out >into the middle of the lake< and they sat out there for
14   hours and hours and hours and she said 'this is the <u>coldest</u> method of
15   being picked up for a date mom' ((LAUGHING))=
16→T: =Keep talking to X.
17   C: Well, a <u>bit</u> of me wants to stand behind the curtain and peep (.) another
18   bit of me wishes I'd be able to do something like that...

In Extract 6, the client is involved in a dialogue with her daughter. In this psychotherapeutic technique, the daughter is not present but she is directly addressed by her mother in the session. The therapist remains present in the session and his role is to facilitate the client's imaginary dialogue. The client in Extract 6 remembers a time when her currently terminally-ill daughter was healthy and fully enjoying her life. Lines 1–5 feature a very emotionally-charged mother's disclosure that ends with a comment of an abundance of memories that she could talk about. The therapist instantly urges the client to continue with the disclosive talk, as represented by a latching response (line 6). What is significant for the current discussion is that in this particular conversational slot, whose function is to reaffirm the speaker's right to an extended turn, the therapist does not produce a continuer in the form of 'yeah', 'right', etc. The proffered utterance functions as a continuer but takes a longer, verbal form. The therapist makes a link to the client's previous statement ('there is so much to say to you') with a rejoinder 'yes there is'. In this way he acknowledges that a unit of her talk has been received (cf. Goodwin 1986). The second part of the continuer 'so keep going' overtly encourages the client to continue with her story as another unit of her multi-unit turn is awaited (cf. Goodwin 1986).

The question arises why the therapist relies on the explicit 'keep going'. It seems that in the context of the ongoing (therapeutic) talk, the clear and overt statement unambiguously signals to the client to continue with the revelation. With the overt continuer, the client is not misled as to its function. The unmarked 'yeah' or 'right' could potentially signify to the client a function other than the right to a multi-unit turn. In fact, the client continues with her story (lines 7–15). In line 16, the therapist's statement again interactionally latches the client's statement with the overt continuer instead of typical conversational 'yeah', 'right', 'uh-huh'. The client picks up another thread of the personal story with the item 'well', which typically prefaces problematic utterances (Pomerantz 1984).

Extract 7, a continuation of Extract 6, demonstrates another example of the use of overt continuers by a psychotherapist in interaction with a client:

Extract 7

```
1   C:    Well, this is confu:sing; <this is such a confusing thing for me to
2         a:nswer> at the moment. When I see you happy, I'm completely
3         content, when I see you sa:d, >no matter how happy I feel<,
4         just the same; when you get ma:d I get mad, but it doesn't last
5         very long.=
6→T:      =Keep going.
7   C:    Because I have to keep reminding myself that you were in this
8         (.) and it's not mine ((CRYING)), it's the one thing I can't
9         fix, >you know< in some ways I'm thinking I've done you a
10        big disfavor because you happen to be absolutely the most
11        important thing in our lives as your parents (2.0) looking at
12        it now I can see that what we've tried to do is spot the dangers
13        before they arrive and do something about them, and you've got
14        to the stage now where there are so:: many dangers and so many obstacles,
15        you have to find out how to overcome obstacles, now at this point...
```

The client's emotionally moving direct address to her daughter in lines 1–5 is not considered by the therapist to be complete. Similarly to Extract 6, the client is pressed to continue with the revelation with the latched, overt continuer 'keep going' (line 6). The unambiguous message prompts the client to return to the incomplete story. It is noteworthy that the client restarts the story with the conjunction 'because' (line 7), which signifies the continuation of her talk. What seems to be very characteristic to the specific context of psychotherapy session, contrary to an ordinary conversation, is that it is the recipient of the talk (i.e., the psychotherapist) who *urges* the speaker (i.e., the client) to build a multi-unit turn. The clients bring to psychotherapy sessions a lot of painful experiences that are not always very easy to share, even with an understanding and emphatic recipient. The pain nevertheless needs to be verbalized, and thus constructed to be worked on in the session. The reliance on overt continuers enables the therapist to clearly signify to the client not only that the next unit of his/her talk is awaited, but also the (therapeutic) need to continue with uncovering other threads of the personal story.

Extract 8 presents another part of the same session:

Extract 8

```
1   C:    I really min:ded that you aborted your baby.=
2→T:      =Yeah, keep going.
```

3   C: >You rang me up just before the consultation< and you said
4   'Mom I'm pregnant', and I felt real thrilled, oh, I just felt so::
5   <u>thrilled</u> and then she said 'tomorrow I'm having an abortion'.

In line 1, the client is addressing her daughter with the resentment she holds about her abortion. In line 2 the therapist produces a latched response which not only indicates the reception of the client's statement but also anticipates further expansion. The overt continuer at the same time urges the client to expand on the unhappy event in her life.

Extract 9 features another part of the same interaction, in which the therapist manages to encourage the client to talk about the grievances she holds towards her sick daughter:

Extract 9

1   C: The <u>real</u> message is I want you to si:t in front of me and <u>listen</u>.
2→T: >Keep going,< tell her what o:ther things you don't like.
3   C: Sometimes I don't like the way you're going up with Dad, °seems to be at my
4   expense sometimes,° I fee:l hurt and he joins in with his jokes about me and
5   I say to you 'I feel <u>hurt</u> X' and you say >'Oh, that's just Dad, Mummy, you
6   should know him by now, you've been with him long enough.'< Why do
7   you <u>always</u> take his side?

Those are important aspects of the client's suffering which run very much against the dominant discourses of motherhood (cf. Coates 1997 and the discussion in the chapter on *communication of emotion*). In turn, the client manifests initial difficulties in addressing her sick daughter with the potential tribulations in their relationship. In line 1 the client begins a series of wishes and objections toward her daughter. The therapist, upon hearing the initial grievance, instantly pushes her to carry on with that thought (line 2). In the second part of the same statement, the therapist explicitly urges the client to elaborate on it. This is a very risky interactional move on the part of the therapist, as he, on the basis of the client's statement in line 1, in fact openly declares to the client that there are certain aspects of her sick daughter's behavior that she (the client) does not approve of. The therapist, however, succeeds in prodding the client to elaborate on the list of grievances. The client in fact adopts the therapist's 'don't like' phrase in commencing her list of complaints. The potential continuers are again replaced in the above extract with an explicit message which conveys not only the clear information for the client to continue, but also that she is expected to build a multi-unit turn, with every turn adducing more details about her personal suffering.

Continuers used by the therapist in sessions with clients often take on a verbal form. This overt form performs three functions in the specific context of a psychotherapy session. Similarly to a typical continuer, it signifies that the previous talk unit has been received and another is awaited. Additionally, its explicit verbal form presses the client to continue the story, thus constructing the client's talk as multi-unit turns. Within such a process, the emerging talk between the client and therapist constitutes the collaborative product of a process of interaction between speaker and recipient (cf. Goodwin 1986). Its transparency of meaning lies in the fact that the therapist's clear message, packed in the form of a continuer, cannot be misread/misinterpreted by the client. He/she is explicitly informed that another interlocutor (the therapist) is ready to hear another piece of the unveiling personal narrative. The transparency of the therapist's continuers secures for the client the right to the multi-unit turn and, at the same time, prompts him/her to continue releasing the emotionally difficult personal material. In other words, the therapist cannot let the client stop disclosing his/her experiences by inserting potentially ambiguous cues.

2.4.3 Non-verbal into verbal

Meaning is communicated not only through verbal means, but also through aspects of paralanguage (involving among others: voice quality, voice modifiers, independent sounds, silence and pauses) and non-verbal behavior (involving proxemics, body contact, kinesics, facial expressions and eye behavior, chronemics, tactile and olfactory channels). Key (1975) conceptualizes the Behavioral Event as a combination of 3 aspects: language; paralanguage, vocalizations and prosodic features; and kinesics, gestures and motions. In the current discussion, the term non-verbal also subsumes aspects of paralanguage. Nonverbal aspects of communication constitute, in fact, critical components of participants' messages, and the research documents that from 65 percent to 95 percent of all face-to-face communication is conveyed through nonverbal means (Madonik 2001).[54]

Verbal and non-verbal messages, however, are complexly intertwined. In studies on the relationship between verbal and non-verbal behavior, two major hypotheses have been put forward. According to the first, the independent systems hypothesis, gestures arise in response to speech failures. The second, integration theory, is based on the assumption that speech and gesture form an integrated system, thus they constitute two aspects of a single process. Within the second paradigm, gestures precede or coincide with speech.[55] Moerman (1990: 9) states that participants in an interaction use "all of the body's sensory modalities...The various sensory modalities... are used together and inter-organized" rather than relying on verbal and non-verbal aspects as separate systems. This very much reflects a current perspective that strongly advocates investigation of the interplay between verbal and non-verbal aspects. As early as 1969, Ekman and Friesen underlined that the non-verbal aspect "can repeat, augment, illustrate, accent, or contradict the words" (1969: 53). Similarly, Key (1982: 9) states that verbal message "is accompanied, modified, reinforced, enhanced, and nullified by nonverbal concomitants". These statements undoubtedly point to the unique relationship between the verbal and non-verbal aspects of communication.

Key (1982: 9) talks about "the indissoluble union of linguistic and extralinguistic messages" and singles out 5 types of paralinguistic and kinesic acts that are premised on their relationship to the accompanying verbal message (Key 1975). The Lexical types have a meaning in themselves, without the aid of speech. The Descriptive type is illustrative of the features of the item being described. The Reinforcing type emphasizes or highlights the verbal act. Key (1975: 30) gives the example of a clenching fist that accompanies an angry statement. As the author underscores, reinforcing gestures make the verbal act more forceful. The Embellishing type enhances the speech in the sense that without it, speech would be dull or unattractive. Within the Incidental type, the non-verbal behavior does not contribute in definable ways to the lexical event of the moment. It might also be conceived of as unintentional or involuntary communication.

A number of researchers (e.g., Kendon 1983, 1985) underline that the meaning of non-verbal aspects, gestures[56] for instance, can be specified only in the actual interactional context. Streeck and Knapp (1992: 12) explain that the meanings of gestures "depend upon the 'talk-thus-far' and are fully worked out only in the talk that succeeds them". Kendon (1980: 208) asserts that verbal and non-verbal aspects are manifestations of the same process utterance and thus one is not dependent upon the other.

Much of non-verbal communication entails the communication of emotion. Riggio (1992; cf. also Riggio 1986, 1989) discusses the concept of 'non-verbal communication skill' which refers to people's abilities to communicate through non-verbal channels. This concept implies a high degree of awareness not only to one's own, but also to another interlocutor's aspects of non-verbal communication. According to Riggio (1986, 1989), 'non-verbal communication skill' involves encoding and decoding nonverbal messages, as well as regulating and/or controlling nonverbal communication. Encoding non-verbal messages is often referred to as *expressiveness*.[57] Poyatos (1982) provides a list of 5 factors which need to be acknowledged as far as the process of non-verbal encoding is concerned:

1. The receiver is usually more aware of the emitter's non-verbal behavior than the emitter himself/herself. This is due to the often unconscious nature of non-verbal behavior.
2. The sign-meaning relationship, since signs can be arbitrary, imitative or intrinsic while "meaning itself can be shared or only idiosyncratic and understood by the sender, or it can be encoded but never decoded". (1982: 123)
3. The verbal messages are fully decoded in natural conversation only when words are perceived and decoded together with their corresponding non-verbal behavior.
4. The interrelationships of verbal and non-verbal systems must be considered.
5. The primary functions of each activity in relation to each other and the co-interlocutors must be taken into account.

(Poyatos 1982: 123–124)

As Riggio explains, much non-verbal expressiveness entails an ability to express felt emotional states. The ability to decode non-verbal cues is referred to as *sensitivity* to nonverbal behavior and is conceived of as a key component of empathy (Riggio, Tucker, and Coffaro 1989). It can be assumed that certain professions should involve greater adeptness at the 'non-verbal communication skill' for the benefit of the involved participants. One such professional area is the field of psychotherapy.

Aspects of non-verbal communication feature prominently in psychotherapeutic interactions.[58] Mahrer and Nadler (1986) point to particular aspects of non-verbal behavior as indicators of the so-called 'good moments'[59] in therapy, i.e., markers of a client's progress and high quality psychotherapy process. For instance, the client's active, energetic and vibrant voice may signify such a positive transitional point in therapy.

Psychotherapists, in their work with clients, stay very much alert not only to the actual aspects of non-verbal behavior displayed by the clients, they are also very attentive to situations when the client, while verbally conveying pain and/or sadness, does not signify such emotions in a non-verbal way (cf. Moursund and Erskine 2004). Key (1975) asserts that an extreme lack of movement on the part of the client constitutes a concern to the psychologist or psychotherapist. Certain gestures, for instance, make it easier for the clients to communicate to the therapist the trauma that they have experienced and bring with themselves to psychotherapy sessions. Researchers (e.g. Ekman and Friesen 1969; Zuckerman, DePaulo, and Rosenthal 1986) state that inconsistencies between a client's different channels of communication may be indicative of the client feeling ambivalent or attempting to hide certain information from the therapist. Therapists claim that the message conveyed in a nonverbal manner nearly always carries more significance than the words it accompanies (cf. Moursund and Erskine 2004).[60] In fact, Labov and Fanshel (1977) in their study on therapeutic discourse assert that in the case of some sort of incoherence between the text (i.e., the verbal message) and the accompanying paralinguistic cues, the latter define the underlying meaning of what the client is trying to communicate (cf. also Madonik 2001). Similarly, Philippot and associates (2003) state that nonverbal messages may be more indicative of the client's true affect and attitude. Consequently, they advocate that nonverbal behavior should constitute a major preoccupation in clinical settings. Consideration of nonverbal communication by the therapist permits the client to explore conflicting motivations. In the words of Beier and Young (1998: 252), "nonverbal behavior is the 'unconscious made visible'".

Aspects of non-verbal communication displayed by clients during their sessions become the focus of the therapist's work in two significant ways. Firstly, as already pointed out, therapists tend to look for lack of coherence between the client's non-verbal behavior and the accompanying verbal message.[61] In other words, they are very much alert to situations in which the client's verbal content is contradicted by his/her accompanying nonverbal behavior. This disharmony, as Key (1975: 33) states, evinces discrepancy between the words and real feelings of the interlocutor.[62] Ernesto Spinelli, one of the leading proponents and practitioners of existential therapy today, refers to such a strategy as very distracting, but still remains very aware of it and acknowledges "the apparent contradiction between ... stance and ... statement" (Spinelli 2006: 25). Witnessing such incoherence, the therapist makes the client accountable for it. As far as the second way of working with non-verbal messages is concerned, especially with the current focus on the transparency of meaning, the therapist explicitly asks the client for an interpretation of his/her non-verbal behavior that accompanies (or not) the proffered verbal message. This is a particularly salient strategy, as the proffered non-verbal behavior does not seemingly contradict the client's verbal message. This particular strategy, applied by the therapist, performs a number of important functions that aim at enhancing the therapeutic endeavor. First of all, drawing the client's attention to his/her non-verbal behavior has the potential of boosting the client's awareness of his/her emotional states (cf. Labov and Fanshel 1977). Clients often remain unaware of performing certain gestures, for example, during sessions. Yet these gestures often reinforce and/or modify the verbal messages they are communicating. The recognition and realization of displaying certain non-verbal behavior has the potential, in turn, to reassure the clients about their *real* emotional stances. A client's displayed non-verbal behavior can also manifest aspects of his/her suffering that have not yet been talked about by him/her during the sessions with the therapist, due to their emotional load. Thus they can be used as triggers to prod the client to talk about the as-yet unexpressed. Finally, the therapist's careful observation and reading of the client's communicative patterns signify his/her physical and emotional presence for the client. This, in turn, constitutes an indispensable factor in building a therapeutic alliance between the therapist and client.

In what follows, the therapist's work with the clients' projected aspects of kinesics and paralanguage will be discussed.

2.4.3.1 Aspects of kinesics

Let us consider the following example:

Extract 10

1	C:	I think the whole situation was a TORTURE, I couldn't trust my <u>mother</u>
2		who I stayed with the who:le day (.) she lied to me.
3	T:	<u>Tell</u> me about that. How did she lie?
4	C:	Sometimes she said if you do thi:s then you can go out
5	T:	// So she made conditional
6		promises.
7	C:	<u>Yeah,</u> and >when I did everything< I couldn't go out <u>anyway</u> because I
8		supposedly did things badly the day before.=
9	T:	=So she makes a contract with you and then breaks the contract because of an old
10		crime.
11	C:	Yeah.
12→	T:	Your head is <u>moving</u>, do it out <u>loud</u>.
13	C:	°I hate to be a victim.°
14	T:	I think that's true of <u>all</u> of us (.) I don't mean to discount what you said but that's
15		pretty normal.
16	C:	Yeah.

In Extract 10, the client expands on his difficult and in effect traumatic relationship with his mother when he was a child (lines 1–2, 4, 7–8). The therapist, with his interactional behavior, manifests his involvement in the conversation by providing a concluding comment (line 5), and latching rejoinders to the client's statement (line 9). In fact, both parties actively collaborate in building the interaction. In line 12, the therapist overtly comments on the client's gesture and in the second part of the statement the client is asked to account for the act. The client's explanation (line 13) constitutes an elaboration of his previous statements. He must have felt like a victim, being a (vulnerable) child, but that kind of treatment has always been rejected by him. The gesture performed by the client functions as a reflection and reinforcement of the accompanying verbal message. The therapist's overt comment helped the client to give voice to another aspect of his childhood experience (being a victim) that had grave consequences for his adulthood. The meaning of the client's gesture has become transparent, i.e., the client accounted for it in terms of his personal experience.

In another extract, a client begins to talk about her suicidal feelings:

Extract 11

```
1    C:    Well, I've sometimes felt ↑suicidal and it's not been about killing here and now.
2    T:    Have you talked to other people about your relationships? Keeping diary?
3          Talking to other people about it?
4          (3.0)
5→ T:    Are you shaking your head?  Wh:y are you shaking your head now?
6    C:    I try.
7    T:    I don't know what the phrase means 'I try', what do you mean when you tell me
8          'I try'?
9    C:    I don't even exactly know myself, I don't know what to say to anybody
10         anymore (.) I just don't know.
```

The second part of the client's disclosure in line 1 ('it's not been about killing here and now') reveals that the suicidal feeling has been accompanying the client in her daily endeavors. This is a very powerful statement fas far as its content is concerned, yet it does not get completed. Even though the client says that 'it's not been about killing here and now', she, in the same turn, does not continue what in fact 'it has been about'. It can be assumed then that in line 1 the client is attempting to introduce a new topical angle into the session (cf. the use of discourse marker 'well'). It might be that due to the emotional load of the disclosure, the client is bringing in the new story gradually, awaiting the therapist's reaction. In line 2 and 3 the therapist, with the strategy of hyperquestioning, attempts to encourage the client to talk about the ways she has dealt with the tragic situation. The series of therapist's questions is followed by a three-second silence. The client does not continue with expanding on the 'suicidal' theme. Even though not responding in a verbal way, the client still communicates in a non-verbal way. In line 5, the therapist openly comments on the client's shaking her head. This comment takes the form of a question aimed at eliciting from the client the function of this gesture at this particular point of the therapeutic session. In line 6 the client provides the meaning of the gesture, yet it is regarded by the therapist as not satisfactory as far as the therapeutic effect is concerned. Consequently, the therapist directly confronts the client (lines 7–8) with the question 'what do you mean'. This interactional move elicits from the client another example of her suicidal feeling, that is, a feeling of hopelessness (lines 9–10). The therapist's explicit comment on the client's non-verbal behavior enables her to talk about the difficult experience.

It is important to underline that the therapist resorts to a most confrontational routine to make the client uncover further aspects of her suffering when she, in the therapist's view, did not manage to account for the significance of her gesture earlier in the exchange. It might also be that the client is not aware of the particular gesture she has displayed and, consequently, is not able to precisely define its meaning. Yet, drawing the client's attention to her non-verbal acts enhances the awareness of emotional states. It is also noteworthy that the client's gesture could potentially function as an answer to the therapist's questions in lines 2–3. Thus it would indicate that she neither talked to other people about her problem nor kept a diary. If the therapist had not confronted the client about the meaning of the non-verbal act, she would not have revealed the traumatic aspect of the 'hopelessness' of her life.

Extract 12 features a comment offered to one of the participants of a therapy session:

Extract 12

1→T:		X, you were shaking your head in <u>recognition</u> of something. <Would you do it out
2		loud for all of us?>
3	C:	<u>All</u> of the stories are ve:ry familiar to me, <u>all</u> the humiliation at school and at
4		home (.) whatever. I remember from my earliest memories: you are <u>disgusting</u>,
5		you are <u>awful</u>, you are the worst thing. My ↑mom was envious of everything.

In lines 1–2 the therapist encourages the client to account verbally for the projected gesture. This interactional move by the therapist underlines his presence for the clients as well as his involvement in the session. The comment is addressed to one of the participants who was observing the work of the therapist with another client. The therapeutically relevant gesture is picked up on by the therapist. In lines 3–5 the client gives voice to what has been previously communicated non-verbally. The gesture, as the client explicates, signifies her identification with the stories and problems presented by other participants. In this way, the client's gesture becomes transparent.

Had it not been for the therapist's comment, the client would likely not have verbalized her identification with the issues discussed by other participants during the session. Thus the therapist's comment in lines 1–2 triggered a personal revelation from the client.

2.4.3.2 Paralinguistic cues

Clients' conversations with a therapist are emotionally charged communicative events. At many points in their revelations, clients utter exclamations and vocal outcries. These are often very short and spontaneous outbursts that tend to signify certain emotional states. This is no different from an ordinary conversation, which abounds in various types of exclamations and cries (cf. Goffman 1981). Response cries, i.e., exclamatory interjections provide a sense of "exuded expressions, not intentionally sent messages" (Goffman 1978: 800). Interestingly, response cries breach the rule of the self-control and self-possession that interlocutors are expected to maintain in the presence of others "providing witnesses with a momentary glimpse behind our mask" (Goffman 1981: 120).

However, what distinguishes a psychotherapeutic interaction from an ordinary conversation is that, in the former, these exclamations are often picked up on by the therapist, who momentarily stops the interaction and turns to the client to account for his/her reliance on the particular exclamation. The client is asked to elaborate on the personal meaning of the exclamation, i.e. to justify why it was used at this particular point of the client's disclosive talk. As already indicated, clients' exclamations may be "spontaneous, unplanned, instinctive externalization of internal affect that is not under conscious control and is not necessarily intended to communicate anything concretely to anyone" (Arndt and Janney 1991: 527). Additionally, their function may be purely cathartic, that is they are used to release emotional tension and help the speaker sustain psychic balance (Arndt and Janney 1991: 527). These functions tend to be rejected by the therapist, who presses the client to reflect on the exclamation immediately after he/she has uttered it. In this way, the client is not only able to give voice to his/her pain of finding himself/herself in certain life circumstances but also learns how to be aware of his/her emotional states.

In Extract 13, the client starts reflecting upon her difficult relationships with her father and stepfather:

Extract 13

1	C:	He was so:: busy with himse:lf, >I mean< the <u>only</u> function with this guy
2		was to sort of show myself, I mean the only <u>moment</u> I had the existence
3		when he could sort of say '<u>look</u> what I've made of this child', or <u>pff!</u>
4→	T:	Pff, very, very <u>powerful</u> phrase. Can you translate that in English? 'Look what
5		I've made of this child, pff!'
6	C:	What's in there is <u>now</u> in a way my ANGER at him and now I can see the fake,
7		(.) when I was a child I was afraid of this guy, I was <u>terrified</u> at him, but I guess
8		I was also angry at myself for being ↑afraid
9	T:	<u>Now,</u> I suspect that it is a displacement, <u>displacement</u>. <You rea:lly angry at
10		him for his self-centeredness, but you've already lost hope that you would
11		make an impact with your anger.>
12	C:	Yeah.

The initial brief statement (lines 1–3) closes with the exclamation 'pff'. It is noteworthy that the client's statement in lines 1–3 is not complete as the use of conjunction 'or' is indicative of another option that should be provided by the client. Instead, however, she utters 'pff'. It might be that her experience is very emotionally distressing, thus difficult to put into words and share at this stage of the psychotherapeutic process. The exclamation 'pff' nevertheless enables the client to give vent to whatever she has been through, yet without a fully verbal articulation of the experience. Thus by relying on 'pff' the client re-embodies, for the therapist, her experience. The client's 'pff' is repeated by the therapist (lines 4–5) twice, the second time with the accompanying client's statement from line 2. The client decodes her personal meaning of 'pff' in lines 6–8, explicating that the phrase stands for the accumulated anger at her father's behavior and his actions toward her. It may be assumed that by directly confronting the client about the proffered exclamation, its meaning becomes transparent, not only for the therapist but also for the client. The therapist's confrontation about the meaning of 'pff' lets her openly express her disappointing thoughts regarding her father.

Extract 14 constitutes a continuation of the same interaction with the client:

Extract 14

1	T:	You turned the <u>anger</u> on yourself. What's it like for <u>you</u> living with the
2		self-centered stepfather?=
3	C:	=Again, pff, it's just=
4→	T:	=Very important phrase, this pff.
5	C:	I don't <u>know</u>, it's like (.) what cho:ices did I have anyway? I mean=
6→	T:	=So <u>pff</u> is a choice less expression.
7	C:	YES, so yes it was <u>lousy</u> and <u>yes</u> >I would have preferred something different<
8		but ok this is what it was.
9	T:	And we know how <u>essential</u> it is for people to have <u>choice</u>, one's whole self
10		esteem is often wrapped up in having choice in a relationship.
11	C:	Yeah.
12→	T:	Pff means that you've been robbed of the choice.
13	C:	Yes, and even if I had a choice, then I would have a choice between one
14		depressed guy, and (.) I'd better not say what I <u>thought</u> anyway.
15	T:	<You've really been doing that for many years>, just go ahead and say what you
16		were about to say!=
17	C:	=What a depressed narcissistic asshole! I mean what <u>else</u> can I say?

The therapist continues with the theme of anger and addresses the client with a question about living with a self-centered stepfather (lines 1–2). In response to this request, the client returns to the exclamation 'pff' which constitutes (at least for her) an appropriate response to the therapist's question. The therapist recognizes the significance of the client's exclamation and builds the interaction around it. In line 5 the client begins to decode other meanings of 'pff' by indicating her lack of influence on the situation she has found herself in. In line 6, the therapist co-constructs the meaning of 'pff', to which the client readily provides an acknowledgment and further expansion of 'no choice' circumstances (lines 7–8). The comment offered by the therapist in lines 9–10 constitutes an excellent exemplification of the double alignment of the therapist (characteristic of the whole corpus), not only as an inquirer and expert but also as an involved, receptive and available person. In line 12 the therapist carries on uncovering the personal experience of the client behind the exclamation 'pff' which, as already clarified, relates to the lack of choice. The client again provides an acknowledgment token to it (line 13) and further elaborates on the theme, yet does not fully complete the statement. In lines 15–16 the therapist urges the client to openly express the opinion that she held back for many years.

It is worth noting how the therapist relies here on the proterm 'that' (line 15). Pomerantz (1984) states that speakers rely on proterms when delicate topics are discussed. By using the proterm 'that', the therapist does not identify what the client 'has been doing for a long time' but grants the conversational floor for her to give voice to the so-far unexpressed pain. It is also noteworthy that the therapist and client co-construct the meaning of the exclamation 'pff'. The therapist in lines 4, 6, and 12 states what aspects of the client's experience this expression may potentially entail. This function of suggestion is supported by the client's rejoining acknowledgment tokens (lines 7 and 13). Heritage (1984) states that the meaning of the words and, it may be adduced, exclamations is not preordained but "it remains to be actively and constructively made out" (1984: 310). Extract 14 nicely portrays how two interacting parties are constructing the meaning of the paralinguistic cue and building an interaction around it.

Extract 15 features another exclamation:

Extract 15

1	T:	See, I <u>wonder</u> if she has a good reason to act this way (.) you were not <u>pretty</u>
2		enough to [cure]
3	C:	[mhm]
4	T:	her depression, you were not <u>intelligent</u> enough to cure her depression, you
5		were not <u>creative</u> enough to cure her depression and she is angry with that.
6	C:	She is <u>suffering</u> because of her not good enough dau:ghter, oh!
7→	T:	Do this <u>oh</u> out loud, tell me what's behind that.
8	C:	Above >all the other things< you have this <u>daughter</u>=
9	T:	=WHO CAN NOT CURE HER DEPRESSION, and what profession did you
10		choose? I <u>wonder</u> if she has a good reason being a:ngry? She has a <u>baby</u> but
11		depression doesn't go away, ↑then >she is two years old< and you can <u>talk</u>
12		but you don't say the right words to cure her depression, and then you're
13		four, five years old and you can run around and <u>play</u> but the play does not cure
14		her depression, and then you go to school and you can <u>read</u> but you're not
15		reading the right psychotherapy books to learn how to cure her depression.
16	C:	And I would <u>never</u> be able, no matter how good
17	T:	// So what do <u>you</u> think of the
18		story I just made?
19	C:	It's true.

Extract 15 presents a part of an exchange that centers on the client's un-solved issues with her mother. In lines 1–2 the therapist is addressing the client's difficult relationship with her mother by enumerating all the aspects of her in life in which she potentially failed her mother's expectations. This formulation (*I wonder*) aims at showing the client the enormity of her mother's demands that no one would be able to fulfill. In line 3, in the middle of the therapist's turn, the client inserts a minimal response. Its function becomes clear in line 6 when she proffers a statement that echoes the content of the therapist's turn. In line 6 she joins the therapist in building the 'enormity of expectations' case when she implies her mother's potential psychological suffering brought about by the unkind daughter. This is, of course, a very tongue-in-cheek remark (echoing the therapist's statement in lines 1–2 and 4–5), as no matter what the client did, she was not able to satisfy her mother. The client closes this statement with the exclamation 'oh'. In his next turn, rejoining the client's 'oh' (line 7), the therapist asks her to 'unpack' the exclamation, i.e., to account for the use of it in terms of her personal experience. This is to say that, in the therapist's view, the client's exclamation, which for her may not be necessarily aimed to communicate any meaning to anyone (cf. Arndt and Janney 1991), can be purposefully pointed out to the client as a trigger to reveal more of the personal material. In line 8 the client attempts to account for the proffered exclamation and, continuing with the tongue-in-cheek frame, directly addresses her mother. Thus 'oh' becomes an ironic 'feeling sorry' for her mother who, despite her personal problems, had a daughter who was not able to alleviate her suffering. In lines 9–19 both participants collaborate in building the 'enormity of expectations' case.

Arndt and Janney (1991: 542) state that emotive messages which are not explicitly verbalized can be signaled vocally and kinesically, and that they are functionally equivalent to verbal expressions but not as binding. It seems that clients' reliance on aspects of kinesics, paralinguistic cues and additionally on verbal yet general, abstract notions helps them convey to the therapist personally important yet difficult to explicitly verbalize themes. At the same time, the non-verbal means of expression emerge as highly effective in the context of psychotherapy, enabling the client and psychotherapist access to therapeutically relevant material.

To sum up, the therapist's interactional focus on the client's exclamations has the potential to enable the client to voice his/her troublesome experience which has not been expressed before. This could be due to its traumatic load or because its content did not match the expectations of the societal dominant discourses. By concentrating and working on the exclamations she/he uses, the client is also learning to be aware of her/his emotional states. Finally, by attending to the details of the client's communicative behavior, the therapist underlines his presence and involvement in the client's personal work.

Extract 16 presents how an aspect of paralanguage becomes transparent in terms of its meaning and significance to the client's experience:

Extract 16

1	C:	And not only <u>that</u>, °he would slap me° and I would get in trouble with my mom
2		for opening my mouth.
3	T:	Yeah.=
4	C:	=For saying <u>anything</u>, why would I <u>say</u> that? Why would I do that? Why would
5		you do this? Why would you do that? Because you're no::t doing <u>anything</u> and
6		I want <u>you</u> to do something.
7	T:	<They probably didn't like the snotty, nasty way you talked to them.>
8	C:	I <u>know</u>.
9→	T:	What does that tone <u>mean</u> now 'I know'? Are you going to push me away?
10	C:	'Cause I always thought I was in trouble for how I said <u>things</u> or if I didn't say
11		anything, well (.) <u>Y</u>, she would stay quiet.=
12	T:	=That was true, you're always in trouble.
13	C:	Mhm.
14	T:	Period.
15	C:	Ok.
16	T:	You're always in <u>trouble</u> 'cause you had two troubled parents.=
17	C:	=Yeah.
18	T:	You had two troubled parents who were fighting with each other all the time.

In the above extract the client, partially regressing, reflects on her difficult and troublesome relationship with her parents. In this particular part of the session, the client starts expanding on the way she talked with her parents – in this way trying to manifest her lack of approval for some of her parents' actions. In reaction to the therapist's formulation in line 7 the client produces an acknowledgment 'I know' (line 8) with a marked pitch and as Key (1975: 47) underlines, much of the emotional effect in language is conveyed by pitch. In line 9 the therapist overtly comments on the client's marked pitch of the phrase 'I know', and in the same turn indicates its potential meaning. Thus the client is made accountable for *how* she presented the intended message.

Tannen (1986: 30) states, "how we say what we say communicates the social meaning". This particular, marked client's tone of voice in fact conveys an extra message in addition to signifying the cognitive state. This additional information conveyed by the pitch remains ambiguous, as it might signify potentially divergent messages to both participants. The therapist, in order to remain an attuned and involved participant, should share the same meanings (of concepts) with the client. Additionally, in the specific setting of psychotherapy, the 'how we say' may point to certain difficult personal material that the client is not able (at this point of her/his psychotherapy process) to convey in a verbal way. Thus aspects of paralanguage constitute an important resource for the clients to communicate their traumatic experiences without verbally stating them. In lines 10–11 the client makes the meaning of the marked pitch transparent by explaining that whatever she said and however she said it, it caused a rift in her daughter-parents relationship. In the same turn, she introduces her sister whose behavior differed markedly ('she would stay quiet'). The last portion of information gets ignored by the therapist, who instead focuses on the client (line 12). The message stated by the therapist in line 12 gets reinforced by repeating or slightly modifying it in lines 16 and 18.

The extracts presenting the client's interpretation of his/her non-verbal communicative acts feature a number of collaboratives (Sacks 1992 Vol. I: 57–60). This is to say that one participant's turns often constitute direct extensions of thoughts presented by another in the previous turns.

To conclude, the three strategies used by the therapist in his interactions with the clients – the probing question 'what do you mean', the reliance on overt continuers, and interpretation of non-verbal aspects of communication – aim at personalizing the clients' general and all-encompassing statements and promoting the clients' self-expression. The therapist's strategies make the personal meaning of clients' statements and experiences transparent, i.e., available not only to the client but also, thanks to the therapist's interactional effort, accessible to the therapist. The direct confrontation with the question 'what do you mean' enables the client to gradually let go of protective abstract notions in expanding on his/her personal experience, and instead directly address the experienced traumas. The therapist's overt continuers make it possible for the clients to continue elaborating on the intimate stories with the clear message from the therapist that they are granted the conversational floor to build a multi-unit turn. Finally, the interpretation of the non-verbal acts makes the clients aware of the emotional significance of the non-verbal messages they project. It also helps them to access intimate and/or traumatic aspects of their experience that would otherwise remain unexpressed, thus unavailable to therapeutic work.

In such a highly emotionally-charged setting as psychotherapy, clients' verbal and non-verbal expression may be potentially ambiguous – thus a client and therapist would have a divergent understanding of what the client in fact communicates. This would be a very risky and therapeutically ineffective situation. The transparency of meaning, i.e., uniform understanding of the client's proffered verbal and non-verbal acts enables both participants to work toward alleviating clients' suffering. Interestingly, participants in a conversation tend not to openly (i.e., verbally) decode certain aspects of their interlocutors' non-verbal behavior. This is to say that conversational intimacy tends to reject open, i.e. confrontational, decoding of another interlocutor's message in the middle of his/her revelations. The communicative situation of psychotherapy, on the other hand, by promoting the client's self-expression and the transparency of meaning of his/her communicative acts, highly encourages explicit sensitivity (decoding) of the therapist to what the client is attempting to communicate.

2.5 Concluding remarks

The interaction that transpires between a psychotherapist and his/her client constrains discourse behavior in a number of ways. These constraints emerge if a psychotherapeutic interaction is judged against the norms and expectations of an ordinary conversation. A psychotherapeutic interaction is based on an ordinary conversation, with few but profound differences. In a psychotherapeutic interaction, the discussed issues or topics revolve around the client and his/her life experiences. The client is the key participant of the communicative event, while the therapist controls the interactional order of the event. The therapist, unlike in many other social interactions, tends not to self-disclose, or does so only to the extent that is beneficial to the client, thus the Principle of Reciprocity (cf. Lakoff 1982) tends to be withdrawn. A psychotherapeutic interaction constitutes an intriguing example of reverse power relations, manifesting itself in the fact that the therapist, by being in charge of the interaction, unconditionally accepts the client's contributions. Additionally, the client is expected to hold most of the conversational floor, yet she/he lacks the ability to interpret, as this constitutes the therapist's unilateral right. Such a unilateral right to interpretation disqualifies any interaction to be labeled a conversation.

This chapter has focused on one important aspect of therapy talk which, nevertheless, does not figure prominently in non-therapeutic settings and, at the same time, is missing from an ordinary conversation. *The transparency of meaning*, i.e., therapist's and client's identical understanding of the client's proffered communicative acts in the effect of the therapist's ongoing interactional work, constitutes one of the key discourse norms in psychotherapy. Clients come to understand that their reliance on abstract and/or all-encompassing words and notions tends to be confronted by the therapist (cf. also Friedlander 1984: 336). The therapist indirectly imposes mindful use of language on the client. This is to say that, by pressing the client to account for and elaborate on the proffered word, exclamation or aspect of non-verbal behavior, the therapist creates an interactional context, as well as a safe interpersonal space, in which the client can unveil intimate, personal experiences. In this way, the meaning of the proffered communicative acts becomes transparent and accessible not only to the client but also to the therapist. Clients' focus on their own communicative acts instills in them an awareness of their own emotional states.

This chapter has presented how the important discourse norm of psychotherapy, i.e. the transparency of meaning, is accomplished at the level of language. It follows that, since the transparency of meaning is so significant for the client's progress in the therapeutic endeavor, the strategies used to evoke it can be referred to as therapeutic features of communication. Indeed, making the client accountable for his/her reliance on a certain communicative act has the potential to enhance certain norms that psychotherapy values. For instance, psychotherapy highly encourages self-reflection through the revelation of personal yet painful experiences. It also promotes explanatory understanding as the client, by accounting for his/her acts, is pressed to present (traumatic) facts that the therapist, in turn, helps him/her to comprehend. With this kind of assistance, clients realize the life circumstances they found themselves in and which, in fact, made them seek psychotherapeutic treatment.

The *transparent* personal communicative act enables the therapist to enter into the client's world and to better understand his/her current trouble. It needs to be underscored that the transparency of meaning can be ascribed a therapeutic function in the specific interactional, local context. Thus to conclude whether the norm of transparency of meaning and its strategies function as therapeutic in a certain context, the goal of the interaction needs to be taken into consideration. In the context of psychotherapy, the transparency of meaning is imperative in the long process that leads to the client's qualitative change of life. The strategies that lead to making the communicative acts transparent are used by the interlocutor whose role is that of repairing the life of the other person. In some other social context, it may happen that the same strategies are used by a more powerful interlocutor to the detriment of a weaker one, for example during interrogations. Thus, the strategies used to achieve the transparency of meaning are therapeutic as long as they promote a person's clarification of the communicative act in terms of his/her personal experience in the local interactional context in which they transpire, and the transparent meaning can be further used to the benefit of the interlocutor.

And finally, to relate to the form-function dialectic, a form can index a number of acts and stances (cf. Ochs 1992). The analyzed question 'what do you mean' can perform a number of functions, one of which can be promoting personal elaboration on the proffered act. This strategy can be labeled as therapeutic as long as it fulfills either a core or peripheral norm of psychotherapy. Hence 'why are you shaking your head now' remains therapeutic if it succeeds in encouraging another person to self-disclose, abandon the abstract/general terms in favor of personal narrative and, as will be discussed in another chapter, to re-focus the narrative from an intellectually-focused to an emotionally-focused account. Obviously, that can only be discovered by the analysis of naturally-occurring speech and the local interactional context in which it transpires. As a result, the claim that 'why are you shaking your head' constitutes a therapeutic form remains unsubstantiated unless proven in an actual interactional context.

Another defining discourse norm of psychotherapy is the principle of self-disclosure. Although this norm has been recognized and extensively discussed in the professional psychotherapeutic literature, its interactional realization has been significantly left out.

Chapter 3. Self-disclosure

Many times people are attempting to do something all alone and it can't be done all alone because it's got to be done in dialogue. Even when you think the same thoughts all by yourself, it's not the same as engaging in a dialogue. And there is something so healing about it. (Richard Erskine, workshop in 2004)[63]

3.1 Introductory remarks

Verbalization[64] – revealing, stating out loud and sharing some personally important (be they joyful or traumatic) experiences with others – is an everyday human undertaking. The label self-disclosure was introduced into the psychological and communication literature by the work of Sidney Jourard (1968, 1971; Jourard and Lasakow 1958). Although multiple definitions have been suggested in the literature, self-disclosure is in essence "the process of making the self known to other persons" (Jourard and Lasakow 1958: 91). Similarly, in 1999, Adler and Towne refer to self-disclosure as "the process of deliberately revealing information about oneself that is significant and that would not normally be known by others" (1999: 358). Jourard[65] (1959: 505) over fifty years ago proclaimed self-disclosure an indispensable means of achieving a 'healthy personality': "It is through self-disclosure that an individual reveals to himself and to the other party just exactly who, what and where he is". Jourard (1971) has substantially influenced the current research on self-disclosure, the interpersonal framing of which allows individuals to construct intimacy, closeness and love (cf. Petronio 2000: 3).

Self-disclosure as a mechanism that facilitates the development of mutual understanding and caring (Berg and Derlega 1987) is a significant aspect of interpersonal relationships. Even though self-disclosure can take the form of personal or interpersonal revelation, the present discussion will focus mostly on the interpersonal aspect of sharing (sensitive) personal information.

According to Cosby (1973), for an act of communication to qualify as an instance of self-disclosure it needs to meet three essential conditions: it must contain personal information about the sender; the sender must communicate this information verbally; and another interlocutor must be a target. Antaki and associates (2005b), however in their discussion on self-disclosure depart from the psychological conceptualization and focus on its 'situated interactional practice' character. They aptly argue that if revealing certain personal information is to constitute self-disclosure, it can only do so in the local circumstances of the production of the talk, thus a self-disclosure exists only in situ. Antaki and colleagues (2005b) propose three indexical features that tend to characterize a self-disclosure. First of all, for a statement to be described as a self-disclosure it needs to report personal information in terms of what Labov and Fanshel (1977) refer to as A-events.[66] Secondly, it needs to be significant in the local circumstances of the interaction. Often its significance will also manifest itself in what Pomerantz (1986) describes as 'extreme case formulations'[67,] i.e., the given information will be presented in highly colored terms thus its drama or newsworthiness will be enhanced. Last but not least, the potential self-disclosure should be understood as volunteered, thus as Antaki and associates explicate: "the speaker's production of something over and above what is mandated by the interactional business at hand" (2005b: 187). The examples discussed by the authors in the article, however mostly refer to self-disclosures as brought off in ordinary conversations and only a minority of them relate to self-disclosures in the context of psychotherapy. I will come back to Antaki and colleagues' (2005b) features of self-disclosure as to how they apply to acts of self-disclosure in the context of psychotherapy session in the section on self-disclosure in the process of psychotherapy.

Staemmler (2004: 49) observes, "one feels satisfied and is left with the impression that one has understood oneself fully" only after sharing one's preexisting meanings with another person. It follows that overtly stating out loud to others what one has been through helps one comprehend the experience. Moreover, he attributes verbalization to the human dialogical nature due to which an interpretation and understanding of one's experience is only satisfactory once it is co-created through an emphatic exchange. This is in line with Jourard (1971: 6), who similarly asserts: "no man can come to know himself except as an outcome of disclosing himself to another person" and Bakhtin (1984: 287): "...I become myself only by revealing myself to another, through another and with another's help". Furthermore, it is assumed that the meaning of what people convey verbally emerges from the dialogue in which they engage (Staemmler 2004: 39). Taylor (1992: 36) furthers this notion by asserting that self-understanding is very much dependent on sharing one's feelings verbally with others. Taylor's conceptualization also touches on the aspect of one's identity as existing only in reference to others with whom the experience is shared: "even as the most independent adult, there are moments when I cannot clarify what I feel until I talk about it with certain special partner(s), who know me, or have wisdom, or with whom I have an affinity…This is the sense in which one cannot be a self on one's own. I am a self only in relation to certain interlocutors" (Taylor 1992: 36). Staemmler (2004: 49) adduces: "my own preexisting meanings always feel more or less incomplete".

Naming an already experienced situation brings it into consciousness and facilitates its identification (Stubbs 1997: 371) and understanding. In this sense, language is not only the means of expression but through the use of words experience becomes realizable (Sarangi 2001). Needless to say, language and communicative strategies feature prominently in the process of verbalizing one's experience and thus in the process of repairing, stabilizing, or enhancing a sense of Self. Schiffrin (1996: 169) referring to Bruner (1987) states that narrative language offers a process of subjunctivization to an individual as it reveals presuppositions, allows multiple perspectives and permits subjectification. Petronio (2000: 3) says that through talk people "disclose primordial, primitive conditions of being-in-the-world". As Mercer (2000: 1) aptly states, we use language for thinking together as well as for collectively making sense of experience and solving problems. Yet, this function of language, as a tool for carrying out our joint intellectual and emotional activities, tends to be predominantly taken for granted. Self-disclosure, typically characterizing intimate discourse contexts, e.g., 'troubles talk among friends' (Jefferson 1988), 'conversation of intimate friendship' (Lakoff 1990), appears to play a crucial role in a person's self-understanding across various everyday contexts of communication.

In sum, verbalization of one's experience to a significant other who actively listens and provides an empathetic response clarifies and in turn validates one's emotions. Such a quasi-psychotherapeutic dialogue has the potential to bring emotions and repressed experiences into consciousness, thus allowing for the expression of the subjugated voice (cf. Frosh 1997: 75).

Psychotherapy offers clinical and conversational space for verbalization of emotions, intimate stories, and secrets, and such disclosure constitutes one of its salient characteristics. As Farber (2003) has observed, therapy is an exemplification of one of the few situations in life "when talking about oneself in not only considered appropriate but necessary". It is a place whose nearly total confidentiality facilitates people's self-disclosures. Disclosures in psychotherapy can be analyzed from multiple perspectives, for instance: therapist – patient (cf. Leudar, Antaki, and Barnes 2006), patient – therapist, trainee – supervisor, supervisor – trainee. The present discussion will focus specifically on one type of disclosure in psychotherapy, i.e., client – therapist. In the remaining part of the Chapter the role of self-disclosure in the process of psychotherapy will be scrutinized followed by an analysis of the strategies used by the psychotherapist to facilitate the clients' self-disclosures.

3.2 Self-disclosure in the process of psychotherapy

> *What helps clients most is not the imposition of a*
> *theory to explain their experiences, but the facilita-*
> *tion of self-discovery.* (Clark 1996: 312)

Disclosure of painful material has been the cornerstone of psychotherapy since its inception (Farber 2006: 17). Although therapeutic approaches indeed differ in the extent to which they emphasize disclosure, they all implicitly consider a client's disclosure the heart of psychotherapy. As Stiles (1995) states it is this heart from which all therapist interventions originate. Farber (2006), in the most recent publication on self-disclosure from the psycho-therapeutic perspective, aptly summarizes the current views on the usefulness of self-disclosure by making a distinction between two types of self-disclosure. On the one hand, there is the so-called ruminative self-disclosure, i.e., going over old material in the same old ways, on the other, there is the self-disclosure that gradually enables one to understand or frame issues in new ways (2006: 76). As Farber says the latter type constitutes the client's goal as it leads to making new sense of old problems: "to be effective, disclo-sures must ultimately lead to new cognitive or emotional patterns of process-ing information" (2006: 207).

Research on self-disclosure in psychotherapy is a post-1990s phenome-non (Farber 2006: 9).[68] Currently the focus of majority of psychotherapeu-tic schools is on a contactful relationship between client and therapist. This is in line with the claim that the self is truly immersed in a world of rela-tionships (cf. Verhofstadt-Denéve et al. 2004) as well as with the concept in communication studies according to which the most authentic self can be achieved and celebrated in intimate relationships, thus in private communi-cation. One's true self can be validated in intimate relationships as opposed to the superficiality of self in public (Rawlins 1998: 370). As Rawlins states, Sennet in 1974 claimed that "social relations of all kinds are real, believable and authentic the closer they approach the inner psychological concerns of each person" (1974: 259).

Hermans (2004) underscores the importance of the narrative construction of self in the context of psychotherapy by dialogical positioning of I – me in three ways. Firstly, the client's self-verbalization is mirrored with the psychotherapist's reflections. Consequently, from a fresh perspective the client is able to extract new meaning from the verbalized material. As Hermans claims, the active listening of the psychotherapist enables the client to re-engage with the distressing experience. Secondly, narrating thus verbalizing one's experience to oneself and the psychotherapist creates 'dialogical space'. The dialogue makes it possible for the client to incorporate existing story parts (experiences) as well as add its new elements that have emerged during the current interaction. Finally, the 'dialogical space' can only be established by a mutual involvement of the two interlocutors. That is, the client invests his/her 'enormous autobiographical memory database' (Angus and McLeod 2004: 79), i.e., his/her inner experiences, while the psychotherapist lends 'professional vision' or professional expertise (cf. Goodwin 1994; Hutchby 2004) in the form of theories and methods which enable to assess and possibly change the client's existing narrative. Being involved in their own narrative-telling enables the clients to be aware of feelings and emotions that have not been previously verbally recognized (Greenberg and Angus 2004).

In fact, in the process of psychotherapy clients are actively encouraged to express emotions and experiences (i.e., self-disclose) that cannot be easily articulated in other communicative contexts. As Farber and Hall (2002: 359) claim, "therapeutic success derives in large part from the patient's willingness to become aware of much that had been previously unavailable or inaccessible".

Emotional expression, the formation of identity and expressing the previously unexpressed are all the result of an intimate dialogue in psychotherapy. In the psychotherapeutic setting *self-disclosure* constitutes the most essential – even defining – speech act without which psychotherapy loses its primary function, i.e., bringing about a self-reflective stance to reveal problematic emotional material in order to understand it anew (Gerhardt and Stinson 1995) and possibly change behavior. As Russel (1987: 2) states, Breuer and Freud were the first therapists to notice the weight of verbalization of emotional states:[69]

> We found, to our great surprise at first, that each individual hysterical symptom immediately and permanently disappeared when we had succeeded in bringing clearly to light memory of the event by which it was provoked and in arousing its accompanying affect, and when the patient had described that event in the greatest possible detail and had put the affect into words... The psychical process which originally took place must be repeated as vividly as possible; it must be brought back to its status nascendi and then given verbal utterance.
>
> (Breuer and Freud 1957:6)

Thus Breuer and Freud's curative triad had to entail recollection, feeling, and verbalization. Since then it has been emphasized that in the context of psychotherapy, disclosure constitutes an intrapsychic process by which unconscious impulses and confused feelings acquire a verbal form and thus become conscious. Freud was clear about the fact that some emotions and their meanings become clear only by expressing them, or in talking about them to another person, or in reflecting upon them (Oatley and Jenkins 1996: 10).

In 1942, Carl Rogers recognized that one of the most significant features of any type of therapy is 'the release of feeling', i.e., the verbalization of "thoughts and attitudes, those feelings and emotionally charged impulses, which center around the problems and conflicts of the individual" (1942: 131). Although 'the release of feeling' can take on a non-verbal form, in this discussion, as already indicated, verbalization refers only to the experience that has been conveyed verbally. In order to help clients express the yet unexpressed, Rogers advocated building the counseling relationship between the therapist and the client of the quality that is markedly different from any other social bonds the client has experienced so far. This type of a relationship offers a type of 'therapeutic space' where people feel emotionally safe and are not inhibited in expressing all feelings and attitudes which complicate their lives. Rogers (1942: 167) also claimed that only the feelings and attitudes which have been verbalized by the client can be recognized by the therapist, who should not "bring to light those attitudes which the client is not yet ready to reveal". In other words, the psychotherapist should not express relevant emotional states for the client. Rogers claimed a very agentive role for a psychotherapist in the process of the 'release of feeling' as one of the major aims of the therapist is to help the client express freely the emotionalized attitudes which are basic to his/her conflicts (1942: 172). Today, there exists a general theoretical consensus about the psychotherapist's active role in promoting client's verbalization (cf. Russell 1987). Greenberg and Paivio (1997) talk about the need to evoke traumatic experiences in order to reprocess and restructure them.

A client's disclosure of his/her feelings or personal matters in the context of psychotherapeutic interaction constitutes an act of self-disclosure as it meets the three conditions outlined by Cosby (1973): it conveys highly intimate, personally framed information about the sender (the client); it (often) takes on the verbal form; and the target is another interlocutor (psychotherapist). However, the second and third conditions need some elaboration. Psychotherapy entails to a great extent certain aspects of non-verbal communication. For example, psychotherapists often look for a lack of coherence between the verbal and non-verbal messages communicated by the client. Such incoherence frequently points to some therapeutically relevant material that should be first verbalized by the client and then worked on by both parties. Arndt and Janney (1987: 66; cf. also Caffi and Janney 1994) explicate that since speakers in an ordinary interaction expect 'schema-consistent behavior', they pay more attention and are communicatively more alert to those communicative choices where the verbal mode is either not sufficiently confirmed by nonverbal modes, or where it is clearly contradicted by prosodic or kinesic choices. In cases of such contrastive patterning (e.g., a client stating *I am very happy with the life I lead* while pounding his/her hand against the table at the same time), there is a tendency to trust the nonverbal information more than the verbal information, as such indexical information is considered more 'caused' or unintentionally communicated than 'causal' or intentionally communicated. Besnier (1990) asserts that researchers from various traditions of inquiry have suggested that whenever there is a lack of congruence between different keys, such keys as intonation and facial expressions (aspects of prosody and non-verbal signs, or the more nonreferential indexical signs) override other signs.[70]

Yet as Arndt and Janney (1987: 139) claim there seems to be an unwritten rule in interaction that partners only interpret those communicative choices, which are supposedly intentionally communicated, i.e., those choices that reflect speakers' attitudes towards their partners and their (communicative) relationship. Since this unintentionally communicated 'caused information' features a fleeting quality, it can be assumed that speakers are often not very much aware of proffering such information and interlocutors usually deliberately overlook such information. Instead, their next utterances are built on information they take as intentionally communicated.[71] Nevertheless, the other information ('caused') is not ignored or considered irrelevant but contributes to the receiver's overall judgment of the communicative interaction with the partner.

In view of that there is a difference between an ordinary conversation where such incongruence tends to be neglected and the communicative situation of psychotherapy where this unintentionally communicated ('caused', Goffman's 'given off') information is treated as more significant and closer approaching the client's *real* attitude or emotional state. For example, in the collected data, the psychotherapist often loudly commented on the evident discrepancy between the client's verbal input ('casual', 'given' information) and the accompanying non-verbal contribution:

Extract 1

```
1   C:   If I relax and I'm I'm myself (.) then it'd be somehow (2.0) something a::wful,
2        >even though< I kno::w intellectually that (.) when I'm myself >people tend
3        to like me< even more 'cause I'm with sane ↑people (1.0) but that was never
4        my experience, >you know<, (2.0) I always had crazy people arou::nd and
5        it's kindda hard to trust that they are non crazy people (.) (.hhh) who would
6        respond in a non-crazy way.=
7→ T:    =So when X comes and gives you a kiss?
8   C:   Then (.) I >could< just think, oh, that was nice.
9→ T:    That's still only half way there and I'm watching your shoulder shake her off.
```

In the extract above the therapist poses a hypothetical situation for the client in which he is offered some unsolicited affection from another client whom he knows (line 7). Even though the client seems to be willing to accept the warmth from a female colleague (line 8), the therapist overtly comments on the accompanying non-verbal leakage from the client (cf. Ekman and Friesen 1967) that undermines the stated/verbalized acceptance (line 9). Thus the movement of the shoulder (non-verbal information, aspect of kinesics) stands in stark contrast with the declared acceptance of the fondness (verbal information). The incongruity points to serious therapeutic relevance of the discussed issue. As the extract evinces, the therapeutic setting permits the client to explore the conflicting motivations and he/she will experience and ideally understand the consequences of the hidden nonverbal communication and the motivation it represents. The professional stocks of interactional knowledge (Peräkylä and Vehviläinen 2003) of Integrative Psychotherapy (Moursund and Erskine 2004) refer to the therapist's recognition of a client's incongruence between verbal and non-verbal input as confrontation, and subsume it in the category of therapist's interpretations: "the client's facial expression may not match his voice tone, for instance and neither of them may fit with the content of what he is saying" (2004: 166). The aim of such confrontation is to broaden and deepen the client's awareness and enhance his/her well-being.

In the current discussion on self-disclosure however, only aspects of verbal communication will be considered. As far as the target of the disclosure is concerned, the psychotherapist's *active* involvement in facilitating a client's self-disclosure needs to be underlined. Thus, unlike in the context of homosexual coming-out or self-disclosures in private settings, the target of the verbalization (the psychotherapist) intentionally adopts communicative strategies that aim at promoting the client's emotional expressivity (see the analysis below). Although the recipient of the disclosive talk is the therapist, in view of the goals of psychotherapy, it can be claimed that it is also the client himself/herself whom the disclosure targets.

Now, looking at the criteria proposed by Antaki and colleagues (2005b) from a more interactionally-oriented and discourse-based perspective, to qualify as a self-disclosure a statement should constitute a report of personal experience and be significant in the context of ongoing interaction, as well as volunteered. How do statements of personal experience produced by clients in the psychotherapy session meet these criteria?

There is no doubt that self-disclosure is endemic to psychotherapy. There also exists quite widespread and common understanding of what the speech event of psychotherapy entails, i.e., why people come to psychotherapy (Gaik 1992).[72] Clients disclose their most intimate matters ensured by the knowledge that whatever gets revealed will be held in the strictest confidence by the therapist. There is plenty of room for self-expression of A-events (Labov and Fanshel 1977) as clients are actively encouraged by the therapist to give voice to their personal experience. Thus, the first criterion is met. The second criterion, however, poses a bit more difficulty in the specific context of psychotherapy. While in everyday life, to count as a self-disclosure, a personal statement often needs to be framed as newsworthy or dramatic and thus frequently takes the form of extreme case formulations (Pomerantz 1980), the context of psychotherapy does not seem to require this manner. The client is encouraged to verbalize what he/she personally finds to be troublesome or traumatic. The rule of 'unconditional positive regard' (Rogers 1951) directs the therapist to accept whatever the client offers and then work towards singling out the therapeutically relevant matters (cf. the discussion on formulations below). In other words, unlike in an ordinary interaction, the client does not need to use highly colored description of his/her statements in order to bring them off as acts of self-disclosure. As Farber and Hall (2002: 366) explain, "psychotherapy is a setting where an individual's focus on his or her problems and perceived flaws is expected and socially sanctioned and thus, can be thoroughly explored". The third criterion for a self disclosure, i.e., the volunteered aspect, also requires some more detailed handling. In the context of psychotherapy, the client, on the one hand is free to articulate his/her thoughts and feelings, yet on the other hand, the therapist is in a position to orient the client inward. This is to say that the task of the therapist is to help the client bring out troublesome personal material, which may have been previously inaccessible. This, in fact, entails the therapist and client often working in tandem for the client's self-disclosure. Consequently, applying Antaki et al.'s (2005b) features of a self-disclosure to the context of psychotherapy, it can be concluded that while the first feature is absolutely fundamental (a report of a personal experience), the second can be excluded (significant, newsworthy or dramatic information), while the third one (volunteered information) often constitutes an interactional achievement of both the client and therapist. The last feature constitutes the salient aspect of self-disclosure in the psychotherapeutic setting, i.e., a client's self-disclosure often constitutes an interactional achievement of psychotherapist and client.

Across the numerous approaches to psychotherapy, clients are encouraged to verbalize their experiences by adopting a self-reflective stance. In other words, a client is invited to scrutinize his or her thoughts, feelings, fantasies, motivations and behaviors (cf. Bruner 1990; Erskine, Moursund, and Trautmann 1999). This scrutiny is actively facilitated by a psychotherapist who continuously encourages the client to "symbolize, transform, and displace a stretch of experience from [...] past into linguistically represented episodes, events, processes, and states" (Schiffrin 1996: 168).

In the process of the client's verbalizing internal phenomena – facilitated by the therapist – the internal is manifested externally and becomes more real, part of the dialogue of the therapeutic relationship (Frosh 1997; Staemmler 2004). As already underlined, this process can only take place in a dialogical and contactful interaction.

There is a consensus among psychotherapy practitioners and researchers about verbalizing the client's 'landscape of consciousness' (Bruner 1990), i.e., his/her emotions, expectations and intentions that have not yet been symbolized in language as an essential starting point for the identification of the client's distress. Accessing and articulating, i.e., giving voice to the subjective world of the client by the therapist's active verbal involvement in turn leads to the client's reflecting on processing of emotions, motives, etc., and consequently towards self-transformation.

In 1999, Angus and colleagues proposed the so-called Narrative Process model which subsumes three modes of narrative processing (Angus, Levitt, and Hardtke 1999). Each of the modes has a therapeutic goal. In each of these stages the client's narrative processing takes place in a comforting therapeutic alliance; the narrative expression and the disclosure of salient personal memories is construed as foundational to the inception of personal change. The first one, external narrative processing, enables the client to freely express his or her story "in terms of what has been forgotten or never fully acknowledged, and hence, understood" (Angus and McLeod 2004: 81). Secondly, in internal narrative processing, the client relives a certain event or experience in order to access its emotional importance. The third mode, reflexive narrative processing, helps the client to comprehend the verbalized material anew and thus gain a fresh understanding of his/her experience (Angus and McLeod 2004: 81–82).

Linde (1993: 121) also claims that, in everyday contexts, the ability to render an accurate assessment of one's own life requires a person to adopt the roles of both a watcher and a narrator who are not identical. This separation enables an individual to promote and maintain the 'reflexivity of the self' by narrating certain life events and simultaneously assessing his/her behavior in terms of personal and social values. The division into the narrator and the watcher can be linked to Bruner's (1990) distinction between the epistemic self (representing one's beliefs, feelings, and wants) and the agentive self (which refers to actual social behavior and action). Thus the individual is aware of his/her epistemic self and, by assuming the role of a narrator, is able to assess his/her agentive aspects. One of the therapeutic aims is to encourage clients' self-verbalization of their experiences in the company of an empathetic listener (a psychotherapist) and to promote the subsequent skill to narrate one's life outside the psychotherapy contexts in terms of one's values (epistemic self) as judged against one's actions (the agentive self). In fact, the speech event of psychotherapy can be understood as "a significant cultural arena in which a sense of personal coherence can be constructed and maintained" (Angus and McLeod 2004: 77). Psychotherapists are also aware of the power of psychotherapy to enhance a person's 'narrative coherence' and, particularly, the crucial role of disclosure in promoting this function (cf. Mitchell 2002).

Verbalization of phenomenological experience redefines the relationship between the interacting parties, thus rendering the interaction intimate – an element of relational psychotherapy. Successful therapy involves the therapist's phenomenological inquiry that facilitates the client's bringing back into consciousness that which has been unconscious: the unexpressed thought, the never verbalized affect, the interrupted fantasy, or the intentionally denied experience. Although McLeod and Balamoutsou (2001) claim that the psychotherapist acts as a sensitive audience to the emergence of the disparate storylines within the client's narratives, his/her role is much more agentive than the position of a passive – yet understanding recipient. A psychotherapist's verbal encouragement of a client to disclose his/her troublesome landscape of consciousness has the potential to facilitate and change the organization of the client's self.

Psychology-based inquiries into self-disclosure tend to be content-oriented, i.e., they mostly focus on what clients typically talk about during their sessions with psychotherapists as well as what topics they typically evade (cf. Kelly 1998; Farber and Hall 2002).[73] Farber (2006) underlines the important role of the psychotherapist in facilitating the client's self-disclosure and reports a significant observation that follows from one of his recent studies, namely that clients would like their therapists to be more actively engaged in promoting self-disclosure (Farber et al. 2004). There is also a reference made to the fact that a client's disclosure is facilitated by a therapist's 'gentle' responses and that other means of promoting this process are also possible. Yet, there is no actual discussion on what communicative strategies the therapist may avail himself/herself on to promote the client's self-disclosure. It is, however, equally important to investigate how self-disclosure is facilitated by the therapist since, as proved by Antaki and colleagues (2005b), it is an act of interactional achievement. Even though, as Farber (2006) concludes, there is no explicit answer to the question whether expressing emotions and thoughts (i.e., disclosure) leads to better outcomes, it is imperative to investigate the facilitation of self-disclosure in the context of psychotherapy as in this way the strategies by which therapy is accomplished can be identified.

In sum, the aim of self-disclosure in therapy, as Labov and Fanshel (1977: 32) assert, is motivating a patient into introspection and the discovery of evermore profound aspects of Self. Psychotherapy is a "…struggle to resymbolize, to put into words that which has not been or cannot be spoken" (Frosh 1997: 76). Consequently, a therapist's communicative strategies play a crucial role in helping clients discover and explore the uniqueness of who they are both internally and in relationship with others.

3.3 Psychotherapeutic self-disclosure as interactional achievement

> *I asked myself to be there both with and for Mr.*
> *Jones, in that I sought to be both willing and able*
> *to embrace his way of 'being-in-the world' not*
> *merely to reflect it back to him but in order to dis-*
> *close accurately its implicit assumptions so that*
> *these could be more adequately examined.*
> (Spinelli 2006: 17)

In what follows, communicative and interactional strategies on which the therapist draws in the process of facilitating the clients' self-disclosures will be identified.[74]

Self-disclosure in the context of psychotherapy (client to therapist) is often a product of joint interactional effort between the client and the therapist. It might seem a safe assumption that, since self-disclosure is such an endemic and commonly recognizable practice in psychotherapy, clients offer their narratives generously and with little resistance. Yet, while the stories and experiences that clients bring into the psychotherapy room have taken place, they often have never been verbally expressed. This is often the case with the most traumatic experiences of any kind of abuse. Revealing those experiences, a trauma in itself, constitutes an indispensable step in the long process of change. Thus the therapist's role in assisting the client in this process of self-disclosure cannot be denied. In those difficult moments of verbalizing and sharing past experiences the therapist should facilitate the client's story in the yet still least obtrusive interactional way. This is to say that the therapist's verbal facilitation should be well-adjusted to the interactional here-and-now of the client's account.

The current discussion will not focus on what is done with the verbalized material, i.e., how it is worked on later in the session, but rather how the clients' self-disclosure is facilitated by the therapist. Particular attention will be devoted to the stages of psychotherapeutic interaction when the client, in the therapist's view, presents an incomplete account where for further therapeutic intervention a more detailed description is needed.

As has already been underlined, verbalization of the 'unexpressed', i.e., the release of some suppressed aspects of experience, along with pent up emotions, constitutes one of the most vital tasks a therapist faces in interactions with clients in many psychotherapeutic approaches, including the one under current analysis. Though merely preliminary stage, it is still an absolute necessity before a client can facilitate any significant personal change. Bruner (1990) refers to one's deeds, acts and experiences in general as aspects of agentive self, similarly Gerhardt and Stinson (1995) talk about aspects of experiential self. Those are the significant facets of self that need to be addressed by the client with the assistance of a therapist. Once self-disclosed, these facets become material entity (Frosh 1997) or manifest material (Staemmler 2004) amenable to therapeutic work. Erskine and colleagues' (1999) research confirmed that among the eight relational needs inherent in all human relationships are the needs for validation, self-definition and to make an impact on the other person. When these relational needs are responded to in psychotherapy, an individual can more readily express aspects of self that may have previously been unexpressed.

Analyzed material of psychotherapy sessions evinces that clients' self-disclosure in the psychotherapy session is facilitated, to a great extent, by the therapist. The therapist tends to rely on the client's communicative strategies (verbal, kinesic, prosodic) yet redefines their functions in the local context in order to facilitate and frequently resume a client's self-disclosure. The dependence on the client's communicative repertoire by the therapist is particularly salient in situations when the client seems to be quite advanced in expressing his/her experiences or emotions but quite abruptly stops it. Thus, it is fundamental for the therapist to remain within the client's frame of reference to ensure smooth continuation of the self-expression, thereby resuming an act of self-disclosure.

Therapist's communicative and interactional strategies for resuming a client's self-disclosure constitute an effect of the local interactional work conducted by the therapist and the client. Here the (interactionally sensitive) use of *you know*, the expression *I don't know,* repetition, information-eliciting tellings as well as reformulations will be discussed as strategies for promoting clients' self-disclosure The analysis of each strategy will commence with a brief theoretical background of the interactional strategy in question.

3.3.1 'You know' as a discourse marker

Although discourse markers (DMs) are used to indicate the relationship between discourse units thus creating coherence within a speaker's turn, the current discussion will focus on the function of the discourse marker *you know* as indexing the relationship between one speaker's utterance and another's response (cf. Schiffrin 1985). Despite different attempts to classify

DMs (cf. Redeker 1990; Jucker and Smith 1998), the most constitutive feature of DMs is that they are optional, in the sense that "the informational segmentation of the argument would remain intact without the markers" (Schiffrin 1987: 51). Schiffrin (1987: 31) defined DMs as nonobligatory utterance-initial items that function in relation to ongoing text and talk. In other words, the optional aspect of DMs manifests itself in the fact that they do not change the truth conditions of the propositions in the utterances they frame (Schourup 1999: 232). Even though DMs are not obligatory in the clauses, they perform much interactional work (cf. Fuller 2003); their functions can be multiple, rendering this conversational strategy highly context-sensitive.

One common discourse marker is *you know*. The literal thus referential meaning of this DM implies its function in information states. Yet, scholars tend to agree that *you know* creates focus on the information it frames and does not suggest that the hearer actually has knowledge about what is being said. As Fuller (2003) concludes, *you know* is frequently used in contexts where the hearer is clearly presented with new information (cf. also Fuller 1998; Brinton 1990).

Schiffrin (1987) offers a very elaborate discussion on the functions of *you know*. She advocates that *you know* does indeed mark information states but tends to be used in order to present new information which the speaker wishes the hearer to accept (cf. also Östman 1981). The use of *you know* aims at gaining hearer's involvement in an interaction as this DM "seems to be marking some kind of appeal from speaker to hearer for consensus" (Schiffrin 1987: 54). The author proposes that *you know* signifies speaker/hearer alignment in the conversation (1987: 54). Schiffrin also states that the intonational contours assigned to *you know* reflect pragmatic differences in the speaker's certainty about the hearer's knowledge. According to Schiffrin (1987: 291) *you know* with rising intonation is a sign of less certainty about shared knowledge between the speaker and the hearer compared to *you know* with falling intonation (cf. also Bolinger 1982).

Other researchers investigating this DM across numerous contexts, thus adopting the approach of distributional accountability (cf. Schiffrin 1987: 69), propose further functions of *you know*. He and Lindsey (1998) argue that the investigated DM increases the salience of the information it frames. Schourup (1985), on the other hand, claims that the fundamental meaning of *you know* is "to check the correspondence between intended speaker meaning and hearer information state" (Fuller 2003: 27). Holmes (1986: 18) concludes that no single function can be attributed to the use of *you know*: "there is no doubt about the fact that *you know* may be used primarily to appeal to the addressee for reassurance. It may equally be used, however, as an 'intimacy signal' and a positive politeness strategy, expressing solidarity by generously attributing relevant knowledge to the addressee". Although numerous studies have focused on the pragmatic functions of *you know*, the issue of how these functions feature across various social contexts has not been sufficiently addressed (cf. Fuller 2003: 25). Additionally, Schiffrin (2001: 66) stresses the fact that *y'know* poses a number of distributional and functional difficulties as, contrary to other DMs it is not always positioned as utterance-initial and it has variant degrees of semantic meaning. Schiffrin also admonishes that it should not be surprising that the status of a certain marker will differ depending on the type of data in which it occurs.

Freed and Greenwood (1996) found that although the occurrence of *you know* is endemic to the conversational context, the subjects of their study employed this discourse marker most often in the type of conversation referred to by the authors as 'considerate talk'. In this type of conversation the subjects were focused on the topic of friendship. Freed and Greenwood attributed the greatest use of *you know* by the subjects in this conversational context to their conscious engagement in talking to one another as well as the nature of the subject itself. It can be concluded then that a highly personal conversation (i.e., an intimate context) prompts greater use of *you know*. Consequently, it can be hypothesized that the conversational practices of psychotherapy should be abundant in *you know* tokens as clients share with the therapist the most intimate, personal aspects of their lives. Indeed, even a cursory perusal of client-psychotherapist exchanges validates this hypothesis. However, on closer discourse-based analysis there emerges a major qualitative difference between two types of *you know*.

Both types of *you know* tend to be used by the clients in reporting their personally important experiences, thus both of them can be generally referred to as an element of high-involvement style (cf. the discussion above). The key difference however, lies in the fact that the second type, germane to the current discussion, appears in moments of a client's self-disclosure when he/she suddenly stops the act of self-revelation. The client's interrupted selfdisclosure is interactionally repaired, i.e., resumed by the therapist via his reliance on the client's current verbal and interactional input *You know* in this particular context appears to be a way of dealing with extremely difficult experiences that are emotionally distressing to share or have never been openly expressed at all. Thus the second type of *you know* tends to precede emotionally difficult (for the client) yet potentially therapeutically relevant material. A therapist with expert knowledge (cf. Buttny and Cohen 1991) is able to recognize at what points of the interaction the client should be encouraged to continue his/her self-revelation. This encouragement requires from the therapist to perform some local interactional work. From this elicited verbalized material the therapist then singles out and (re)formulates issues that should be worked on.

3.3.2 'You know' facilitating intimacy

The examples discussed below exemplify the first type of *you know* found in my corpus.

Out of the above-discussed functions of *you know*, this DM may appear to be redundant as a strategy to present new information that the speaker (client) wishes the listener (therapist) to accept due to the rule of 'unconditional positive regard' (cf. Rogers 1951). Also, the use of *you know* to gain a listener's involvement should be excluded since a therapist is acutely aware of the importance of his constant involvement in what the client is saying (cf. the discussion above). *You know* as an intimacy-building strategy, tends to precede a potentially threatening or traumatic thought or idea that is about to be revealed by the client:

Extract 2

1	C:	On Friday evening >after< we did the presentations (.) several people came to
2		you for a HUG, and my first thought was, 'WOW, I'd like that too', I was
3		quite envious >actually.< And then I <u>noticed</u> that on Saturday >and
4		yesterday< I started protecting myself against that thought saying 'no:: ,
5		other <u>people</u> need it mo::re than you, you really need ↑that what for ?', and
6		(1.0) **you know**, that's the ARmor (1.0) also.
7		(.)
8	T:	'Other people need it more' is a <u>very</u> typical theme <that the oldest child in the
9		family> would <u>often</u> say to discount their own discomforts.

In Extract 2, new, emotionally and therapeutically significant material follows *you know* and the metaphor of *armor* provides an apt self-label to refer to the client's minimization of her self-esteem. What comes before *you know* is an example of some protective behavior of the client which later on, in line 6 gets labeled. *You know* precedes an element that the therapist topicalizes later on in that session. *You know* in the above example is juxtaposed with a pause (1.0) which signifies that the thought to be revealed by the client is of crucial significance in her experience. The metaphor of *armor* pertinently describes the clients' reservations as to whether she deserves any affection and is semantically tied to the material that precedes it. What is important in the use of the first type of *you know* is the interactional position of the therapist whose comments validate what follows the discourse marker, regardless of how shocking the revealed material might be (lines 8–9). The involved and client-attuned therapist instantly recognizes the importance of the metaphor and provides a comforting explanation, as demonstrated in the next example:

Extract 3

1	C:	>I don't know<, I d<u>on</u>'t think I would like <u>that</u>. I don't like <u>that</u>. People make
2		that sound like a wonderful ↑thing but I couldn't do that, (1.0) **you know**
3		(1.0) >like a one-night stand.< I need to <u>kno</u>w a little bit about somebody,
4		are they a good ↑person=
5	T:	=You sound romantic to me.

You know occurs in moments of self-revelation. Similarly to Extract 2, the long-awaited reference to what the client means by *that* (i.e., a one-night stand) is also accompanied by a pause adding to the significance of the verbalized thought. The client's apprehension in defining what is meant by *that* is further transferred onto the actual verbalized thought as it is spoken very quickly. The therapist again aptly identifies the emotional load of the information hedged by *you know* with a latched comment.

In both examples the clients disclose very private, potentially threatening yet intimacy-building material that is hedged with *you know* and relevant pauses. The client does this quite spontaneously without any local work performed by therapist. This DM in a way mitigates the impending release of often never-before-divulged personal views. *You know* as a 'mitigator' seems to be a necessary strategy for the client to protect his or her face in the context of revealing intimate material, often for the first time, and before a group, no less. As Tannen (1989) observes, telling the details creates intimacy and psychotherapists align with this view: "Details are wonderful. They are informative, they are calming, and they penetrate the anxiety of isolation: the patient feels that, once you have the details, you have entered into his life" (Yalom 1989: 188).

In another example *you know* builds intimacy by making an appeal to being understood and creating the salience of the information it frames:

Extract 4

1	C:	Well, (1.0) when we're in a <u>really</u> difficult phase and I >wanna< <u>say</u> to her 'Is
2		there anything else I can do? Can I <u>do</u> something to make it more <u>bearable?</u>',
3		she says: no::, just <u>stop</u>, just carry on being, **you know** (2.0).
4	T:	What happens inside of <u>you</u> when she says it?=
5	C:	=>I want to be worth it< my head knows <u>this</u>, my head knows I can't take
6		the pain, the humiliation, the depreciation that she is going through, which I
7		WANT TO, I WANT TO, **you know**, I (0.5) can't.

Although in the above example the investigated DM follows the revealed intimate material, *you know* points to the salience of what has been communicated by the client. Again, the therapist's responses to the emotional aspect of self-disclosure underline his presence and involvement in what is being verbalized. The client shares with the therapist the excruciating experience of witnessing, yet not being able to eliminate, her daughter's suffering. In lines 5–7 the client refers to the aspects of her daughter's illness that cause her (the client) psychological agony. This is done by presenting a three-part list ('the pain, the humiliation, the depreciation'). The three-part list signifies that the stated (individual instances) represent something more general (cf. Jefferson 1990; Potter 1996). Here the three-part list is symbolically attempting to convey the sense of misery and hopelessness the client experiences in dealing with her daughter's illness. The therapist's reactions to what either precedes or follows *you know* index this discourse marker as an intimacy-building strategy. In sum, the first type of *you know* mitigates the threat posed to the client in verbalizing highly intimate information and at the same time builds intimacy, which characterizes the discourse of psychotherapy.

3.3.3 'You know' and 'I don't know' in resuming self-disclosure

The second type of *you know* found in the corpus of psychotherapy sessions does not function merely as a discourse marker (i.e., as a propositionally optional element) calling for therapist's alignment, but its presence in the verbal performance of a client may be used by the therapist to help him/her express the previously 'unexpressed'. Clients tend to employ *you know* as a way of handling some emotional experience which has not been fully revealed (to the therapist). Thus clients partially disclose some aspects of it, leaving other parts unexpressed. Since the experiences clients reveal in psychotherapy are of distressing nature, their initial resistance[75] to self-expression may be due to its sheer emotional load. The interesting thing is that *you know* or *I don't know* follow 'self-disclosure in progress' and might appear to act as markers of resistance to more verbalization. Here, the therapist's verbal contribution and local interactional work is indispensable for *you know* to act as a verbalization trigger and at the same time to alter its potential resistance function. The analyzed material demonstrates two sequential patterns in which the client employs *you know* or *I don't know* and the therapist follows with verbalization-triggering contributions (*No, I don't know* + *what*; *What don't you know?*), which function as the second element of the adjacency pair:

Pattern 1:

C: ...,you know.
T: No, I don't know + (what)
C: [resumption of self-disclosure]

Pattern 2:

C: ..., I don't know.
T: What don't you know?
C: [resumption of self-disclosure]

The above observed patterns of the use of *you know* starkly contrast with the type one *you know* discussed earlier, as here this DM is cognitively *responded to* by the therapist and prompts the client to continue expressing highly private experiences thus resuming an act of self-disclosure. In the first type of *you know*, the therapist's response underscored his attunement and presence to what the client was saying.

The therapist's attunement to what the client is trying to communicate enables him to recognize that the client's use of *you know* conceals quite harrowing aspects of life scripts that need to be self-disclosed in order to become manifest material. This manifest material can then be further worked on by both therapist and client. Extract 5 exemplifies how *you know* hides some distressing experience. The client's *you know* is followed by the therapist's response *no, I don't know* + *what* which leads the client to further verbalization:

Extract 5

1	T:	And did you reveal any of your vulnerabilities?=
2	C:	=No.
3	T:	How did you make <u>sure</u> that in the army you <u>didn't</u> reveal any of
4		your vulnerabilities?
5	C:	You blend ↑in, become ↑invisible, you don't ↑speak, don't show any anxiety,
6		don't ever fear, swear, >don't drink<, (1.0) **you know,** (1.0).
7	T:	No, **I <u>don't</u> know,** train <u>me</u>.
8	C:	>Oh<, you have to be clear what kind of people you need to align yourself with
9		(1.0) and people you need to avoid so:: basically shut <u>up</u> and don't reveal
10		<u>any</u>thing or you're co::nstantly criticized.

In Extract 5, the therapist is involved with the client in the therapeutic inquiry about the client's problems in integrating with the group and finding a sense of belonging. At this point the inquiry revolves around the client's experience of being in the army, which, as expected, turned out to be quite an excruciating experience. In describing his method of survival in the army, the client provides a list of 'do's' and 'dont's'. The marked rising intonation on some of the enumerated elements denotes that these are merely some headings which could be further expanded on (cf. Bolinger 1982; cf. also Schegloff 1981: 79). The list terminates with *you know,* which implies to the therapist that behind this discourse marker there is much more that needs to be verbalized. For the client, however, its function might only be indexical of newly disclosed emotionally significant material or a sign of resistance to further disclosure. Yet, these functions are rejected by the therapist who redefines its role by stating, *No, I don't know,* and in this way tries to elicit more therapeutically relevant material (cf. Hutchby 2002). Why does it constitute a redefinition of the function of the investigated discourse marker? If *you know* functions as an element of high involvement style then it is not responded to cognitively. The therapist's cognitive response, indicating potential lack of knowledge or experience in this area, triggers further verbalization as the client resumes elaborating on his disturbing experience.

The interactional resumption of self-expression by the client (facilitated by the therapist) and the avoidance of a situation in which the therapist verbalizes for the client (cf. Rogers 1942) allow the client to be fully in touch with his/her emotional states. This is particularly crucial if one of the goals of psychotherapy to achieve awareness of one's emotions is to be realized (cf. Labov and Fanshel 1977).

The client's elaboration starts with the so-called initial response token (*oh*) which as explicated by Jefferson (1988: 428) can mark "serial shifting from distance to intimacy". The discussed example reveals how *oh* marks the beginning of further verbalization of the 'unexpressed'. One element of the verbalized experience, namely the fact of being constantly criticized becomes then one of the core issues that the therapist and client work on in this particular session. This specific way of handling clients' *you know* by the therapist starkly differs from its treatment in an ordinary conversation premised on symmetrical interactional roles and pursuit of intimacy (Drew and Heritage 1992). *You know*, which abounds in ordinary conversations, tends to function as a discourse marker (cf. the discussion above) and not a cognitive entity in this type of interaction. Its cognitive framing may lead to a serious break in pursuing conversational self-expression, changing a conversation into a question-answer framework resembling an interaction of a more institutional character. As Lakoff (1973) observed, a sense of rapport, so salient in an ordinary conversation, is achieved by being understood without saying what one means. It may also be why clients in psychotherapy – typically well-socialized into an ordinary conversation – tend to rely on *you know* at moments of self-revelations. They look for (finally) being understood. Yet, the therapist, with his unexpected *I don't know* withholds the sought affirmation and instead invokes a more confrontational stance towards the client, directing him/her in this way back into the self-disclosure.

Extract 6 features a similar strategy wherein the client's *you know* is responded to by the therapist with, *No, I don't know*, which leads to further verbalization:

Extract 6

1	T:	Go ahead, you were saying?
2	C:	No::, then I think if I actually <u>saw</u> someone <u>really</u> do something that would
3		impress me, **you know.** (1.0)
4	T:	No, **I <u>don't</u> know.**
5	C:	>Oh<, if it was <u>really</u> reaching out, it would be easier not to reach out, the
6		cynical voice sort of says (0.5) but when it's really recognizable pain
7		and >kind of< doing something really ↑useful practical about it, reaching
8		out to this person. I think there is <u>no</u> question that there is real,
9		genuine content as opposed to put on, >pretend<. I <u>know</u> there is a part of
10		me that always says 'pretend', 'put on'.

The therapist considers the client's *you know* to be 'therapeutically incomplete', i.e., there is more material behind *you know* that needs to be released. In order to bring it out, the therapist rejects the function of *you know* as an involvement strategy and provides a cognitive response to it, stressing the negative *don't*, which in turn triggers elucidation from the client.

The therapist's cognitive reframing of clients' emotional non-referential appeals ('No, I don't know + what' or 'What don't you know' [analyzed below]) can also be interpreted as instances of 'other-initiated repair' or 'next-turn repair initiation' (Schegloff 1981). This constructional format is positioned immediately after the trouble-source took place (here the client's *you know* is problematic from the perspective of identifying the therapeutic matter by the therapist). The emerging trouble, however, needs to be approached in the specific context of psychotherapy. Before the therapist proposes and (re)formulates the therapeutic matter (cf. Hutchby 2002), it needs to be brought out, i.e., verbalized, by the client. Thus, the repair concerns on the one hand, the fact that the client has not fully revealed therapeutically-relevant experience, while on the other, it appeals for personal framing and understanding of verbalized categories.

In the verbalized material, opening with the initial response token *oh*, the client expands on the theme of 'pretending', which is further topicalized in the course of the session. The therapist's response in Extract 6 slightly differs from the one in Extract 5 as he does not specify what needs to be identified or focused on, yet in this way the agency of the client is maintained as he is given a choice as to what needs to be further disclosed.

Tsui (1991) discusses a variety of functions that can be ascribed to the utterance *I don't know* other than a statement of inability to deliver information. The author has singled out six such functions: avoiding assessment, prefacing disagreements, avoiding explicit disagreement, avoiding commitment, minimization of impolite beliefs and marking uncertainty. Tsui (1991) concludes, however that the central meaning that unites all instances of occurrence of *I don't know* is a declaration of insufficient information. It seems then that the utterance *I don't know* can occur in a variety of conversational contexts and its function will often be defined by the specific aims of the speech event and also by the specific interactional sequence in which it transpires. For instance, this type of 'disclaiming knowledge utterance' as used by the clients at the end of their self-disclosing talk in their interactions with the psychotherapist might function as an involvement strategy in this highly intimate context. Indeed, Gerhardt and Stinson (1995: 625) conclude that a client's *I don't know* functions as a "part of the patient's involvement in the reflexive task of self-investigation". Hutchby (2002: 150) provides a detailed overview of the phrase concluding that "it is not necessarily, and certainly not only, a report on the mental 'state' of 'lacking knowledge'. Rather, considered within the context of talk-in-interaction, it has to be analyzed for the kinds of interactional work it is doing in the sequential places in which it is produced" (cf. also Tsui 1991: 609).

Therefore, in line with Hutchby's postulation, what is the interactional work performed by the *I don't know* phrase in the context of psychotherapy sessions? At first glance it seems that *I don't know* is applied by clients for the effect discussed by Potter (1996), i.e., to "inoculate the speaker against possibly negative inferences that might be drawn on the basis of what has been said" (Hutchby 2002: 150). Let us analyze the following example wherein the client's *I don't know* is followed by the therapist's *What don't you know?* which leads to further verbalization:

Extract 7

```
1   C:   Wh (h)en I see th (h) em going cr (h)azy, you know, when my mother would
2        go crazy, she was crazy ALL THE TIME, >it wasn't like she could take her
3        time off<,  I >mean< I understand people are healthy and giving themselves
4        permission, but still seeing ↑craziness is (0.5) is (0.5) scary, you know, (1.0)
5        what if I say the wrong thing, I don't know. (1.0)
6   T:   What don't you know?
7   C:   I don't know how to handle it. >I feel like< I wanna fight it back and get
8        myself in real trouble...
```

I don't know closes the client's intimate, yet as it becomes clear a bit later (line 7 and on), partial self-disclosure. Gerhardt and Stinson (1995: 625) demonstrate that *I don't know* tends to occur at moments of elaboration and self-disclosure on the client's part, although the phrase looks like a disavowal of what has just been revealed. At the same time its function may overlap with the one proposed by Potter (1996). Both of these interpretations would be applicable if it was not for the therapist's upcoming contribution. This cognitive contribution (*What don't you know?*) as an interactional reference to *I don't know* elicits more talk, i.e., disclosure from the client. It also reframes the client's talk as *he* becomes the agent by giving voice to his real anxiety and concerns. Consequently, it can be claimed that a psychotherapist's *What don't you know?* takes on a cognitive meaning triggering verbalization of the yet 'unexpressed' from the client.

In Extracts 5, 6 and 7 the clients' *you know* or *I don't know* are sequentially placed at the end of the information units and there is no further verbal material that follows them. A therapist's response to the clients' *you know* or *I don't know* allowing them to resume the process of self-disclosure in the course of therapeutic interaction would be a marked strategy in the context of an ordinary conversation. Such cognitive treatment of involvement strategies invokes a confrontational stance which an ordinary conversation with its focus on intimacy and symmetry discourages.

The extract below is another exemplification of the therapist's successful redefinition of the function of the client's *I don't know* as a marker of being involved in self-reflection into a cognitive entity:

Extract 8

```
1   T:   Did you know that today you'd be ta::lking about your relationship with
2        your mother? (2.0) Did you plan this?
3   C:   No, (.) but I had this feeling of ↑rejection, I don't know.
4   T:   What don't you know?
5   C:   I'm, I'm thinking about (.) my other relationships a::nd how I was (.)
6        choosing a partner who was  like my ↑mother in that way or my
7        father (1.0) °maybe°, I know it's >difficult for me to talk about it< but
8        I do know that I have strong feelings and sometimes I can't sort
9        them out.
```

If the client's *I don't know* were to function as an indication of inability to supply the requested information, it would be placed at the beginning of the client's turn (line 3). *I don't know* – occupying the whole of client's turn in line 3 – could be interpreted as a strong implicit disagreement[76] (cf. Pomerantz 1984: 74; Tsui 1991). The utterance however is tagged to the preceding statement. The vague function of the utterance in line 3 is taken advantage of by the therapist who treats the client's *I don't know* as disclaiming-knowledge utterance. This handling of *I don't know* by the therapist solicits from the client more self-disclosure.

Not all of the therapist's attempts to redefine the function of the clients' *I don't know* in order to bring out more self-disclosing material are successful. The extract below presents how the client rejects the therapist's attempts to solicit more elaboration:

Extract 9

```
1   T:   What else are you angry about?
2   C:   (.) I'm angry that she had to die at this time (.) you know.
```

3   T: <u>No</u>, I don't know, <u>tell</u> me about it.

4   C: <u>Anyway</u> >as I was saying< I've been really compulsive ↑lately and getting

5   <u>tired</u> of working...

The therapist regards the client's statement in line 2 to be of profound importance to the therapeutic work. Yet, in his professional view, it is incomplete as there is nothing revealed about the specific reasons behind the client's anger or how it got manifested, etc. Thus in order to retrieve this information the therapist seeks to elicit the missing aspects by attempting to redefine the client's use of *you know* from its discourse marker function to a more cognitive one. This effort, however, falls through. The client starts her turn in line 4 with 'anyway' signaling that she is ignoring the invitation to elaborate on her anger and instead retreats to topics mentioned earlier. Thus the interactional meaning of 'anyway' that emerges from this context is to indicate the change of the conversational agenda. 'Anyway' is an item that prefaces a new aspect of the client's talk. This decision is respected by the therapist who allows the client to evade further disclosure. This is, however, also an extremely important piece of information for the therapist as the client signaled that there is an unresolved issue in her life that brings discomfort and anger. As evidenced in line 4 above, the client is not ready yet to address it. However, as Ferrara (1994) has observed in psychotherapy, if something carries importance for the client, it will resurface.[77]

Finally, the therapeutic *I don't know* with the function of resuming client's self-disclosure can be contrasted with the same utterance with the function of signifying an inability to deliver information.

Hutchby (2002) states that *I don't know* in the tag position, produced at the end of a knowledge claim, differs from the same utterance's use in a stand-alone turn (for example as a response to an invitation), which structurally occupies the whole turn rather than being tagged. More importantly, *I don't know* as a response to the previous turn's substantive action is a manifestation of its cognitive character, as exemplified below:

Extract 10

1   T: Is that <u>distraction</u> from loneliness?

2   C: Well, **I don't know** because >I haven't thought about it but<

3   T: // Something I

4   made up?

5   C: No, I think it certainly makes sense.

The client's *I don't know* above constitutes a response to the question; additionally its cognitive character is reinforced by providing an explanation for the lack of knowledge.

The function of the utterance *I don't know* is unmarked when it is produced "in reply to an information question when the speaker is unable to supply the requested information" (Tsui 1991: 607).

Sometimes the inability to supply the requested information is additionally reinforced by placing the same utterance *I don't know* at the end of the turn, as exemplified in the Extract 11 below:

Extract 11

1 T: So <u>you</u> think this is a <problem in you> and not our sensitivity?
2 C: **I don't know** if there is a connection, (.) **I don't know**.
3 T: But <u>you</u> think the problem is in your own <u>denial</u>.
4 C: I <u>don't</u> really know.

However, as evidenced in the corpus of the psychotherapy sessions, the utterance *I don't know* does not always constitute a response to a cognitive claim, but is tagged to the client's (partial) self-disclosure.

A therapist's responses (*No, I don't know; What don't you know?*) function as self-disclosure triggers. Thus while the clients produce *you know* or *I don't know* as non-referential, non-cognitive entities and involvement strategies, the therapist approaches them cognitively in order to bring out therapeutically relevant material from the client. In other words, the therapist redefines the interactional function of client's discourse marker *you know* and the utterance *I don't know* from noncognitive into a cognitive claim. This material can then be critically approached in joint effort by the therapist and client in order to facilitate the client's self-transformation.

3.3.4 Repetition

Another strategy used by the therapist to foster self-expression is the use of repetitions. Tannen (1989) distinguishes between four functions of repetition in a conversation such as: production, comprehension, connection and interaction. The last function indicates the importance of repetition at the interactional level of talk where it may accomplish social goals pursued in a conversation or help to manage the business of conversation.

Tannen (1989) further divides repetition into self-repetition and allo-repetition (the repetition of others). Furthermore, she places instances of repetition on a continuum ranging from exact repetition to paraphrase. As Wong (2000: 408) aptly states, repetition constitutes a strategy to which participants in a conversation must display some orientation. Thus researchers should describe what repetition accomplishes in a conversation. Ferrara (1994) has stated that repetition is a crux of interactive nature of discourse in psychotherapy and made a distinction between two main types of rejoinders to statements in the psychotherapy setting: *echoing* and *mirroring* – on the basis of the criteria of syntactic form, function and originator.

Echoing, as Ferrara explains, is client-generated and takes clausal rather than phrasal form. By echoing the therapist's utterance with the same intonation pattern, the client demonstrates emphatic agreement with it. The therapeutic dimension of echoing lies in the fact that by identifying with the therapist's insightful interpretation of his/her experience, the client claims it as his/her own (1994: 115). As Ferrara (1994: 115) explains: "it is in fact therapeutic to be understood so thoroughly by another that you can emphatically agree with statements they make about your life".

Mirroring, on the other hand, involves the therapist's partial repetition of the client's utterance. By repeating the client's word or phrase viewed as salient to the therapeutic process, the therapist, according to Ferrara, indirectly asks for its elaboration. Ferrara underlines that her definition of mirroring (and echoing as well) involves falling – never rising – intonation (1994: 124). According to Ferrara, mirroring constitutes an indirect appeal for elaboration and characterizes many types of consultations where one interlocutor (here a therapist) attempts to facilitate another's talk (here a client's) by attentive listening. So the difference in the function between echoing and mirroring lies in the fact that while the first one directly signals understanding between the therapist and the client and indirectly creates empathy, the latter indexes an appeal for elaboration of the statement.

Repetition in the context of investigated psychotherapy sessions, leading to the client's verbalization of distressing experience or knowledge, is therapist-generated (cf. the concept of mirroring, Ferrara 1994). What differentiates the instances of the therapist's repetitions from instances of Ferrara's mirroring, however, is that the therapist does not always rely on falling intonation. In fact, the extracts discussed below demonstrate how both rising and falling intonation of the therapist's repetitions trigger self-disclosure from the clients.

The abundant examples of repetition found in the psychotherapy corpus, except for unmarked functions in the production and comprehension of discourse, play a very important role in creating interpersonal involvement (the function of connection), which in turn leads to a client's self-disclosure. The analyzed instances of repetition exemplify the so-called synchronic repetition.[78]

Let us consider the following extract:

Extract 12

1   C: >Yeah, sure<, there are 2 of them. One is like >keeps asking me< you know,
2   I'm your <u>super</u>man and for the first time I answered <u>yes</u>, but when it's
3   an endless question I say: what do you <u>want</u> from me? or I don't answer;
4   (0.3) it's my <u>father</u>, very sad, depressed alcoholic and the other one is like
5   uhm, (2.0) just **a fake**.
6   T: **A ↑fake**
7   C: <u>Yeah</u>, like this guy,> you know<, just that comes to my mind, somebody
8   wearing the clothes of a superman but you know <u>exactly</u> that he is <u>not</u>
9   a superman, it's just <u>pretending</u>.

In the above example, the client is talking about the great disappointment of not having had a good father-daughter relationship in her life and its grave consequences in her adulthood. This emotionally charged disclosure ends with the word 'fake'. It is, however, carefully hedged by 'uhm' and 'just' with a two second pause between them. The word 'fake' is then picked up by the therapist and repeated with rising intonation. Bolinger (1982) suggests that rising intonation is a signal that the information unit has not been completed. Consequently the therapist's repetition can be construed as an indirect appeal for the explanation of the word, yet not in terms of its semantic content but, more importantly what it signifies to the client. As a result, the client continues with the personal elaboration on what being 'a fake' entails. The therapist's repetition in excerpt 12 seems to have accomplished two goals at the same time. On the one hand, the client resumed an act of self-disclosure but at the same time the repeated word ('fake') has been topicalized by the therapist. The personal elaboration constitutes another example of the verbalization of the previously unexpressed.

In another example the therapist comments on the client's visible sadness. This comment is followed with the client's remark, which is then repeated by the therapist and followed with the client's verbalization:

Extract 13

```
1   C:   Do I always look sad?  Does it show so much?
2   T:   NO, not when you're dealing with something, (0.2) but you were sitting here,
3        and there was sadness in your eyes. 'Does it show so much?' >No<,
4        most of the time you're smiling and looking very pleasant but I've been
5        observing your eyes and there was sadness (2.0) there seemed to be like
6        a secret sadness.
7   C:   >Uh huh<, it can get quite extreme.
8        (3.0)
9   T:   ↑Extreme sadness
10  C:   Yes, °I had very long periods of very strong depression° (.) and that takes
11       us to the first thing I mentioned to you on the first day…
```

The therapist's initial turn ending with a very personal observation of the client's 'secret sadness' receives only minor expansion from the client. However, the additional client-proffered qualifier of the sadness ('extreme') is also picked up by the therapist. The repeated phrase 'extreme sadness', again with rising intonation, encourages the client to personalize this concept thus verbalize the emotional states embedded in the phrase. This repetition plays a substantial interactional role as the client now continues disclosing therapeutically relevant issues. The instance of repetition exemplified above also constitutes a case of collaborative production of talk since the word 'extreme' has been originally uttered by the client and the word 'sadness' by the therapist, who then combines these two and uses the phrase as a verbalization trigger. Such collaborative production contributes to creating a connection between talk participants. Sacks (1992 Vol. I: 58) proves that through collaboratively completing another person's sentence, interlocutors: "have a way of proving to the person they're talking with that they're hearing and understanding what he's saying". Although in the above instance neither therapist nor client complete each other's statements, they collaboratively construct the act of verbalization.

In the following extract, the therapist summarizes the experience presented by the client, which is elaborated on with her confessing 'and I should not exist'. This painful one sentence confession is then repeated by the therapist. This time, however, there is no rising intonation assigned to the repetition, yet it still triggers verbalization from the client:

Extract 14

1	T:	So the script does <u>not</u> only say 'there is still something <u>wrong</u> with me' but
2		also 'something <u>is</u> wrong with me and <u>I don't matter</u>'.=
3	C:	=**And I should not exist.**
4		(1.0)
5	T:	**And I should not exist.**
6		(1.5)
7	C:	Everyone else is <u>more</u> important, everyone else's <u>needs</u> are more important…

In Extract 14, the therapist provides an immediate and concise summary of what the client has disclosed so far. This summary, however, is additionally advanced by the client's flat assertion 'and I should not exist'. It is vital to underline that this thought has not been previously presented by the client but is now contributed by the client to complete the therapist's statement. The therapist validates this completion by repeating it, which triggers further self-expression from the client. The repetition prompts the client to continue her elaboration on what the script prescribes for her. All of the verbalized material – elicited by the therapist who relied on repetition – is further approached by the therapist and client working towards a therapeutically relevant outcome, i.e., the client's self-transformation.

In Extract 15 the therapist does not consider the client's revelation to be complete. Similarly to the examples discussed above, this is indexed by the therapist's repetition of a key word uttered first by the client. This strategy aims at eliciting more self-disclosure from the client by re-focusing the client's narration on one aspect of the disclosed experience. The repetition constitutes an indirect appeal for the personal framing of 'paradoxically':

Extract 15

1	C:	I <u>understand</u> that now. I like to think I've come quite far from where I
2		was and I've strengthened the the healthier part of ↑me (.) I guess at
3		the beginning that part needs ↑validation, >sort of< 'you are OK, you
4		are doing all right'(.) and there is also a part of me that wants to push
5		that away again **paradoxically**.
6	T:	**↑Paradoxically**
7	C:	<u>Yeah,</u> >when we push away the very things that we want< (1.0). It's
8		like when somebody is nice to me, when X said the other day 'Can I
9		give you a kiss?' I just <u>immediately</u> thought: why would she <u>do</u> that?
10		What for? I haven't done <u>anything</u> to deserve it, or I must have
11		somehow earned it.

The repeated word in line 6 in fact resumed the self-narrating stance and has been topicalized at the same time.

Extract 16 contains some interesting work performed by the therapist and client in a joint effort of resuming client's self-disclosure:

Extract 16

```
1   C:   They were weak, (.) too weak to protect me. I remember running around
2        in the garden, she was chasing ↑me and my mother was just standing
3        there (.) watching my grandmother, she was TERRIFIED of my grandmother
4        and my ↑father was nowhere, he was in the house, he coul::d have come out,
5        he could have said 'stop this crap, there is nothing wrong with HIM' but he
6        never did (2.0) >and it was the same with my mom's family<, she was
7        physically abused, she was sexually abused by her father's brother and
8        no one stepped in to help her and and she would tell me these ↑stories that
9        she was sexually >abused and raped and beaten< and all that kind of
10       stuff.=
11  T:   =It was none of your business.
12  C:   It was none of my business, it was too much.=
13  T:   =None of your business to know.
14  C:   Yeah, yeah, and she she was very abusive of ↑me and my father was gone
15       for the day and I was left with this psychotic woman (.) and there are
16       lots of blanks, I don't really know what happened, I have strange memories
17       (1.0) sometimes I think there is a possibility that I was sexually abused
18       by ↑her and there is just this sense of not being protected by anybody,
19       certainly not men in my life, (3.0) letting me down, letting other people down.
```

Initially the client offers a disclosure of his observations, experiences, feelings and regrets concerning an overwhelming family situation. This is a highly emotionally charged account which the client ends with 'and all that kind of stuff'. This phrase used at the end of the client's (lengthy) turn implies that there is more to be revealed as far as the situation at home is concerned. Trailing off with 'and all that kind' seems to be the client's way of dealing with what would otherwise be a very traumatic account (cf. Antaki, Barnes, and Leudar 2005a). This phrase, however, is not addressed (i.e., repeated) by the therapist even though it seems to be a perfect candidate to act as a verbalization trigger. The therapist instead offers a very emphatic comment to the proffered disclosure (line 11). It seems, then, that in the therapist's view or professional vision (cf. Hutchby 2004, 2007) it is more therapeutic (i.e., here emotionally healing) to reassure the client of his view on the family situation. The therapist's reassuring statement gets expanded by the client in line 12 with the qualifier 'too much' and then slightly modified by the therapist in line 13 with the verb 'to know'. This modified repetition triggers more self-disclosure from the client regarding his abusive childhood. It is interesting to notice that the same phrase ('it was none of your business') has been used by the therapist to underline his sympathy and reassurance towards the client and then used to prompt the client to continue self-narration.

Extract 17 below exemplifies the therapist's failed attempt to induce more self-disclosure from the client by resorting to his personal reference ('strange'):

Extract 17

1	T:	<u>Now</u>, I <u>don't</u> understand the way we began here (.) with my concern that you
2		get some medical attention in case it is a heart condition, would she have
3		done that? Would she have put some energy and said I'M concerned about
4		this, <u>do</u> something about it?
5	C:	No=
6	T:	=<u>So</u> what was it like for <u>you</u> when I did that?
7	C:	It was a **strange** feeling=
8	T:	=**Strange**=
9	C:	=Yes=
10	T:	=**Strange good or strange bad?**
11	C:	Goo::d.
12	T:	Can you tell me <u>more</u>?
13	C:	But I was a little bit <u>confused</u> because you were talking about my <u>heart</u> and
14		I have <u>never</u> made that that connection…

In line 9 the client merely acknowledges the therapist's repetition and does not return to self-narration. This kind of conversational behavior requires from the therapist to minimally elaborate on the repetition ('strange good or strange bad?') still in very vague terms as a way of providing the client with an opportunity to give voice to his personal framing of 'strange'. Since this trigger falls through as well (the client approaches the therapist's statement as a question to be answered), the therapist resorts to asking a direct question (line 12) which, in turn resumes the client's self-disclosure. This example also nicely depicts how the direct question 'can you tell me more?' indexes the function of the therapist's repetition of the client's word or phrase. Repeating the client's word in line 8, the therapist focuses the client on the particular aspect of his experience that should be expanded on in the session and thus enables the client to resume and then pursue self-disclosure. It is important to underline the therapist's attunement as manifested here by the 'no gap no overlap' strategy when attempting to orient the client inward.

Repetition in the context of psychotherapy constitutes one of the strategies employed by the therapist to trigger more self-disclosure from the client. It needs to be underscored that even though psychotherapy functions as a place where talking about oneself is considered necessary (cf. Farber 2003), clients nevertheless/still might feel uncomfortable articulating certain thoughts and feelings and (traumatic) experiences to their therapeutic partner. Or, typically clients offer partial self-disclosures of certain emotions or experiences, revelations considered to be therapeutically incomplete by the therapist. At such moments it is extremely important to resume the client's interrupted disclosure but remain within his or her local conversational frame. Repeating a client's word or phrase from his/her previously disclosed account often enables the therapist to put the client back on their self-disclosing trajectory. Needless to say, this is not a random repetition. Rather, therapeutically relevant material that gets repeated in the therapist's professional view will bring out personal framing of the word/phrase.

The personal framing then takes the form of (further) self-disclosure. Unlike in Ferrara's mirroring, which is characterized by the falling intonation, the therapist's repetition in my corpus takes different prosodic and grammatical forms from a single word repeated with rising intonation (e.g., Extracts 12, 13, 15) to a declarative statement (e.g., Extract 14).

To sum up, the self-disclosure triggers used by the therapist in the above-discussed extracts (and these extracts are representative of the whole corpus) do not carry any propositional import. This is to say that these triggers do not proffer any new information that the client is not familiar with. Rather, the therapist – in order to elicit further self-disclosure from the clients – relies on their own verbal contributions. In the words of Schegloff (2001) what is 'getting done' by the therapist's reliance on some of the clients' verbal input is the facilitation of self-disclosure in this particular here-and-now. Thus the therapist's local interactional work enables him to have clients volunteer more personal information.

3.3.5 'Fishing' for self-disclosure: Information-eliciting tellings and reformulations

Buttny and Cohen (1991) state that a common structural feature of the discourse of psychotherapy is the three-part sequence; that is (1) the therapist asks a question to which (2) the client provides a response and finally (3) the therapist offers an assessment or comment on that answer. Buttny and Cohen provide the following example:

T: For a while?=
C: = Yeah
T: How long?
C: For about a year and a half
T: That's sweet of you!=

(Adapted from Buttny and Cohen 1991: 71)

The last line, as Buttny and Cohen (1991: 71) expound, "provides a slot for the therapist to display expertise and also maintain conversational control". The three-part sequence is also a characteristic of a typical institutional exchange (cf. Mishler 1984).

Hak and de Boer (1996), however, in their paper on formulations make a clear distinction between the three types of interviewing characterizing medical, psychiatric and psychotherapeutic contexts. Unlike Buttny and Cohen (1991), they refer to the medical interview as a type of investigatory or interrogatory type from which they exclude the psychotherapeutic interview. The psychiatric interview is classified as an exploratory type, where the physician's formulations are used to explore the patient's experiences. Psychotherapeutic interviewing is discussed as an example of *collaborative* interaction where the course of the interview is contingent on the patient's decisions, i.e., his/her confirmations or disconfirmations (Hak and de Boer 1996: 94). According to Hak and de Boer (1996) the key difference between the psychiatric and psychotherapeutic 'first encounter' interviews consists in the fact that in the first type the physician does not rely on a formulation-decision pair to formulate the professional problem definition. In the psychotherapeutic interview, on the other hand, the formulation-decision pair constitutes the main interactional device used for formulating the therapeutic relevant issue. I will come back to the issue of formulations further in the discussion.

Sacks (1992 Vol. I: 49–56) demonstrates that the power of the question-answer sequences lies in the fact that the questioner (here the therapist in his/her institutional identity) gets the right to speak in the next turn follow-ing the answer and in that turn he or she may produce a follow-up ques-tion.[79] That type of organization of exchange, however, does not lend itself to facilitating a client's self-disclosure as in this type of interaction clients (may) feel pressured to provide the 'right' response to the therapist's in-quiry instead of being encouraged to freely express the concerns and thoughts that they would otherwise have problems to topicalize during a session. This type of exchange would be better identified as 'leading the witness' than labeled as aiming at eliciting a client's unabashed *self-*disclosure since he/she would receive direct prompts (therapist's questions) to which he or she would provide the answers (or not). Under the interac-tional circumstances of the question-answer framework, the client would be denied the opportunity "to express freely the emotionalized attitudes which are basic to his adjustment problems and conflicts" (Rogers 1942: 172). The therapist, then, needs to utilize a more *indirect* way of inquiry which aims at drawing forth a client's true self-disclosure.

Pomerantz (1980) demonstrates how in ordinary conversation an inter-actant may solicit information in an indirect way by relying on the so-called 'side' tellings, instead of asking a direct question. The following well-known example nicely illustrates this strategy:

A: Yer line's been busy.
B: Yeuh my fu(hh)! ·hh my father's wife called me...

                              (Adapted from Pomerantz 1980: 189)

In the above example, person A makes an assertion of a type 2 knowable[80] that concerns a situation which constitutes type 1 knowable for the recipi-ent. In other words, person A makes an indirect attempt to have person B divulge information that she/he knows intimately. Pomerantz (1980) refers to these information-eliciting tellings as 'fishing' devices since they consti-tute an attempt to have a co-interactant disclose the relevant, sought-after information. Indeed, side tellings can be construed as indirect triggers that grant conversational space to an interlocutor in order to facilitate the pursuit of the subject/issue in his/her own direction.

Bergmann (1992) found 'information-eliciting telling' to be a prominent feature of psychiatric talk and discussed its use by psychiatrists during in-take interviews. In this context, side telling (often comprising litotes[81], mitigators and euphemistic descriptors), as discussed by Bergmann, indexes discretion. By relying on what Bergmann (1992: 155) calls 'discreetly exploring utterance', the candidate patient is solicited to give voice to private problems and personal feelings, e.g.:

(1)
    Dr.F: I (just) got the information, (0.8)
            (that you're) not doing so well.

(Adapted from Bergmann 1992: 138)

(2)
    Dr. F: I can see (from) your face that the:- (1.0) mood (.)
            apparently is not ba:d.

(Adapted from Bergmann 1992: 139)

(3)
            You sound kind of depressed.

(Adapted from Bergmann 1992: 143)

As the author explicates the psychiatrist's 'side tellings' include a report about the recipient (the candidate patient), strongly indicating: the derivative character of the psychiatrist's knowledge (Example 1 above), psychiatrist's knowledge as a product of one's observation (Example 2), and formulation of the referred-to facts as a consequence of outward appearance (Example 3). In fact, a psychiatrist's information-eliciting tellings frame his/her knowledge as fragmentary and uncertain (*I just got the information, I can see from your face, You sound...*). Yet, Bergmann comments on the candidate patients' *readiness* for proffering information or confessions, thus producing disclosive talk following the psychiatrists' information-eliciting tellings.

It seems that being faced with incomplete or confusing information about them, people project an urge/need to clarify their personal details. After all, in this particular context they presume to have the upper hand, i.e., an authority to declare what constitutes the truth and what should be rejected. This is in line with Labov and Fanshel's (1977) comment on an individual being an expert at his/her emotions or personal experience in an ordinary conversation, on which the psychiatric intake interview is also premised. This strategy can be particularly salient in the context of asymmetrical interactions (e.g., psychiatrist – candidate patient) as 'information eliciting tellings' can be used by the psychiatrist to empower (even though sometimes in an illusory way) the patient by providing him/her with an opportunity to relate to the proffered report.

In discussing the usefulness of indirectness in facilitating candidate patients' disclosures, Bergmann points to the following: by relying on litotes (thus avoiding direct reference), the psychiatrist creates the possibility for the co-interactant (candidate patient) to offer authentic description and show openness and honesty. Mitigators, on the other hand, enable one to stave off a possible disagreement from the co-interactant. Bergmann (1992: 155) concludes that these discreetly-exploring utterances facilitate authentic descriptions from candidate patients since "this way of prompting implicitly assures them that whatever they are going to disclose will find understanding and affirmation". In Bergmann's view indirectness involves empathy and that is why this type of utterance tends to be applied in numerous approaches to psychotherapy, enabling the clients to reveal those aspects of their lives that are usually kept hidden.

As Bergmann observes, information-eliciting tellings indeed feature prominently in the interaction between the psychotherapist and client (cf. also Buttny 2004). This conversational/interactional practice proves to be a very useful strategy in facilitating clients' self-disclosure in the data under analysis. Self-disclosure is a process that in the context of the psychotherapy tends to be to a great extent facilitated by the accompanying attuned and involved psychotherapist. Yet, there are some differences between information-eliciting tellings used in the context of the psychiatric intake interview and the context of the psychotherapy session. Let us consider the following example:

Extract 18

```
1   C:    I'm afraid to reveal how °I feel° (.) >I'm afraid people will think that
2         I'm weird<, many times I was really really sad at work (.)  but I
3         didn't allow myself °to cry.° (3.0)
4         >But I cry when I drive to my work all the way< and then once I get to work
5         I put on a mask >or something<, I'm sad and very sca::red inside but I'm so
6         afraid to show it.
7→ T:     <I'm guessing that the problem isn't in the showing it, the problem is in
8         the ridicule or the rejection from the other person.>
9   C:    Yeah, (.) and I was bullied at school (.) and I was trying to hide it for many
10        years with the >drugs, alcohol and tablets<, I haven't been drinking for
11        9 years now but I'm so:: °scared°, I, I don't go into the kitchen at work,
12        >you know<, I don't want anybody to see my feelings and cry...
```

In the extract above the client's self-disclosure concerns his inhibitions in revealing feelings in private but mostly in social situations. The therapist resumes the client's self-disclosure by making a mitigated assertion (lines

7–8) based on what has been heretofore verbalized by the client. The therapist 'fishes' (cf. Pomerantz 1980) for the client's account i.e., his further self-disclosure by offering an observation based on already-disclosed material by the client. What distinguishes the information-eliciting tellings proffered by the psychotherapist in the analyzed context from the criteria proposed by Bergmann (1992) is that they contain no element signifying any derivative character of the psychotherapist's knowledge. This is to say that the proposed information-eliciting telling in the context of psychotherapy is utterly based on information collected during personal meetings with the client (the psychotherapy session), not granted by a third party. This fact greatly contributes to creating intimacy and trust between the interactants, which in turn promotes the client's self-disclosure. The client may remain assured that he/she is attentively listened to as the therapist in his inquiry relies on the contributions proffered by the client.

Another characteristic of the information-eliciting tellings in the context of psychotherapy is that a therapeutically relevant aspect of a client's talk is singled out by the psychotherapist in an attempt to solicit further self-disclosure from the client (lines 7 and 8 above). It is the psychotherapist's choice as to what aspect of the client's narrative should be focused on, yet it should be then verbally pursued/elaborated on by the client. Thus the psychotherapist's proffered information may attempt to refocus the client's perspective. For instance, in the extract above the 'information-eliciting telling' aims at shifting the client's focus from his inhibition about manifesting certain emotional states to the potential social consequences of such conduct, i.e., possible rejection and ridicule. This is a very tentative telling, inviting the client to follow this particular thematic link.

What is referred to above as information-eliciting telling (lines 7 and 8), i.e., a strategy to "prompt the recipients to volunteer information about themselves" (Buttny 2004: 46), strongly resembles one of the most inventive practices in psychotherapy, i.e., (re)formulating (Davis 1986) or reframing (Buttny 2004) or, more generally, *formulating* a client's problem by a therapist.

Reformulation, as it has come to be known in the studies on interactions in psychotherapy, allows the therapist to *propose* to the client an alternative version of his/her talk which lends itself to further therapeutic intervention/work.

According to recent studies, formulations have a role both in fact-taking as well as in delivering interpretations on the client's problems or experiences (cf. Antaki, Barnes, and Leudar 2005a; Vehviläinen 2003). Davis (1986) claims that the therapist's formulation manifests his/her actual listening to the client's revelations and understanding the situation. Pudlinski

(2005) investigating caring responses to troubles tellings on a peer support line found formulations to be one of eight methods that call takers use to express sympathy or empathy. Davis (1986) suggested three stages of the reformulation process: firstly, the therapist defines the problem, secondly, documents it, and finally, pursues consent from the client. The therapist's formulation – by singling out a certain aspect of client's input – sets it as a new topic for conversation.

Researchers within the CA field – following the study by Heritage and Watson (1979) – see formulation as a practice that functions as a conversational adjacency pair. This is to say that, for instance in the context of a psychotherapeutic interaction, the therapist's formulation should be ratified by the client with a strong preference for agreement. Formulation then occasions a reaction from an interlocutor (here a client) who is privileged to accept or reject it (Vehvilläinen 2003). This is referred to as formulation-decision pair (Heritage and Watson 1979). Buttny (2004: 57) presents the following adjacency pair format:

1. therapist's ascription of other → clients' confirm/disconfirm
2. therapist's recommendation → clients' accept/reject

As far as the form of the speech activity of formulation in psychotherapy is concerned, Buttny (2004: 45) underlines that they should be carried out with 'professional cautiousness' (cf. Drew and Heritage 1992).[82] Thus a therapist's reframing should come out as rather tentative and opening the conversational space for the client's contribution and possible revision. On the other hand, however, there is a strong indication in the therapist's turn that what is proffered by them essentially derives from the client's talk. As Buttny (2004: 47) sums up, therapists tend to qualify and/or mitigate their descriptions and thus frame them as tentative by "expressing uncertainty, downgrading their epistemological status, or drawing on publicly available facts". In this way formulations[83] seem to be a more efficient means than direct questions to pursue information from the client as formulations to a great extent, give the client back his/her own personal data. As far as the functions of formulation are concerned, researchers agree on their transformational aspect, i.e., selecting – out of the client's own account – an element that should be specifically (and ideally) pursued by the client as this will bring him/her closer towards a therapeutically-oriented direction. This 'transformation' ideally should be accepted by the client (the preferred action).

Antaki and colleagues (2005a) position formulation not as performing any therapeutic intervention, e.g., re-focusing the client's story, but as a practice which is applied to clarify the client's account in order to collect factual, recordable data. In order to find out whether the therapist's statement functions more as an information-eliciting telling (triggering self-disclosive talk from the client) or a formulation (transforming the client's talk in a way that is adequate for therapeutic work), it is imperative to investigate what such a statement accomplishes in the 'here-and-now' contexts (cf. Schegloff 2001).

Now, returning to the above extract, does the therapist's description in lines 7–8 function more as an information-eliciting telling or as a (re)formulation? As evidenced in lines 9–12, (and discussed above), it does trigger more self-disclosure from the client. As for the criteria for a (re)formulation (which significantly overlap with the criteria for information-eliciting tellings), the therapist's statement includes one aspect (out of two) of the client's previous contribution. Thus, the therapist considers pursuing topic of the consequences of social ridicule more therapeutically relevant than having the client continue with the behavior description.

Since the therapist's version of the client's problem should be framed as tentative, the therapist's formulation starts with 'I guess' providing interactional space for further (possible) revision from the client. Secondly, in line with the premise that a (re)formulation calls for confirmation or rejection, the client opens his 'decision' with the acknowledgement 'yeah'. It is noteworthy however, that following the acknowledging 'yeah', the client discloses more personal material, which documents the therapist's formulation (cf. Davis 1986). Consequently, it can be claimed that the therapist's statement in lines 7–8, elicits more talk from the client and thus functions as a self-disclosure trigger; it also, however, succeeds in reformulating the client's therapeutic focus. Thus, the therapist's conversational practice achieves two important aspects of the therapeutic agenda: the client (readily) self-discloses and the self-disclosure is refocused more towards a therapeutically-oriented direction. It needs to be underlined that a client's self-disclosure often constitutes a result of a psychotherapist's information-eliciting telling (lines 10–11 below) followed by additional verbalization triggers (lines 13, 15 below):

Extract 19

1	T:	Welcome X.

2   C: Hi. (2.0) So >I'm just thinking< in terms of the discussion about <u>script</u> that

3   (4.0) I, I guess I sort of feel:: the <u>pull</u> towards the script when I'm ↑here,

4   (2.0) °I think°. One of the things I find <u>difficult</u> is being in the group,

5		>interacting with the group< and finding a place in the group, feeling
6		a sense of <u>belonging</u>, feeling a sense of value (.) but then I <u>also</u> know that
7		>pretty< soon I start giving off messages: >don't come too close, don't
8		get too close< and I can see:: people start picking up on them and (.)
9		sort of getting away from me.=
10→	T:	=Well, there must have been a time in your life when 'don't come too close'
11		was <u>so</u> essential.=
12	C:	=Oh, <u>yeah</u>.
13→	T:	You want to <u>tell</u> me about that?
14	C:	Mhm.
15→	T:	It must have been quite <essential.>
16	C:	Well, (.) I think it was for me being <u>alone</u> and <u>safe</u>, not being with people
17		who would be hurtful and (.) you know, who would have upsetting
18		interactions with people and <u>fighting</u> most of the time…

In the extract above the information-eliciting telling (lines 10–11) comprises one aspect of the material revealed by the client (the 'don't come too close' theme).

Both extracts (18, 19) demonstrate how important it is in the context of psychotherapeutic inquiry to *enable* the client to self-disclose in order to receive the authentic personally-framed description even in the face of seeming resistance. The psychotherapist insists on the client to pursue the brought-up issue by providing additional prompts until the client resumes. There may often be some resistance from the clients to the (painful) process of self-scrutiny. Yet the fact that the therapist presents an exploring utterance as coming from the client's own narrative makes it much harder to resist or even reject (cf. Antaki 2002: 425). In the above extract, the therapist needs to do additional interactional work (lines 13 and 15) before the client resumes his story. It is noteworthy, however, that these prompts (lines 13 and 15) – by not contributing anything new in terms of content – index the function of the initial information-eliciting telling. That is, the client is strongly encouraged to elaborate on the theme of what was 'essential'. And, as already discussed, there is a strong emphasis on the client to unfold, i.e., verbalize parts of his/her interior life which are usually hidden or denied. The therapist's claim in lines 10–11 also, generally, meets the criteria set for a (re)formulation as it attempts to refocus the client's talk on the origins of the problems. Thus, instead of contemplating the present situation, the client is solicited to concentrate his narrative on past experiences. By stressing 'so essential' the therapist seems to imply that being alienated could be one of the survival strategies used by the client in the midst of family fighting. It is worth underlining how the therapist starts the (re)formulation with 'well' in line 10, an item that recurrently prefaces problematic utterances (Pomerantz 1984). Indeed the therapist wants to engage the client in sharing some traumatic experiences. The client provides a confirmation to the formulation with the acknowledgment token 'Oh, yeah' in line 12 but no further self-disclosive talk.

The therapist's prompts or postpositioned queries (cf. Buttny 2004) exemplify how the client's statement is not merely used to receive the acceptance but to get the client involved in presenting his experiences. Instead of employing the seemingly more efficient strategy of asking direct questions to get the client's account of his survival strategy, the therapist solicits the client's elaboration in a more indirect way. The *indirect* or tentative postpositioned queries in the data under analysis differ, however, from those found by Buttny (2004) in his corpus. As exemplified above, the therapist in the data under analysis often indexes certainty of his queries (the verb 'must', Extract 19, line 15). This may signal the therapist's *therapeutic* (i.e., professional) recognition of the client's situation. The reliance on such certainty indices: 'there must have been a time...', 'it must have been essential', however, seems a potentially risky interactional move in view of the fact that formulations should be performed with a certain delicacy or professional cautiousness (Drew and Heritage 1992). After all, they only propose a version of the client's talk pending the client's approval or at least compliance. A client's opposition to or rejection of a therapist's claim (dispreferred action), if reoccurring, could lead to some serious damage in the therapeutic alliance between the therapist and client.[84] On the other hand, Tannen and Wallat (1987) remark that professionals (here the psychotherapist) can strategically direct talk through the capacity to identify topics as relevant or irrelevant in the here-and-now context.

In the extract above, the therapist's attempts to engage the client with the therapist's alternative version are carried off as the client in the end resumes his self-disclosure in the thematic direction proposed by the therapist. The indirect or tentative character of the therapist's pursuit of the client's involvement manifests itself, in the extract above, in the persistent use of prompts aiming at elaboration of the answer. The therapist's statement (lines 10–11) functions as an information-eliciting telling as the interactional work undertaken by him makes the client continue his self disclosure. At the same time, however, the statements take on the function of (re)formulation as the client accepts the suggested transformation of his story.

The extract below aptly illustrates how the psychotherapist's information-eliciting telling (line 4) induces the client to verbalize certain feelings and attitudes herself:

Extract 20

```
1   C:   °I felt very protected° when X said that she wanted to work and you said
2        'Y also asked'. It's something I am not accustomed to and (.) that's not
3        the first time it happened with you (.) and it always affects me.
4→T:     <I'm curious why, how that is not part of your daily life experience.>
5   C:   It isn't.=
6→T:     =Yeah, I hear you and believe you.
7   C:   Mhm.
8→T:     And that's sad because I would like it to be your daily experience.
9   C:   I've learnt very much not to ask what I want because I always draw back, (.) I am
10       withdrawn I think and I don't need
11  T:                                     // Now, (.) are you talking about your
12       marriage (.) or are you talking about growing up or both?
13  C:   >I have a wonderful husband<, I like him very much, (.) I respect him very
14       much. I can trust him. We've been together for X years now. He is
15       a wonderful father, he is honest, and yet there is a problem between us (.)
16       because of the accident...
```

In line 4 the therapist encourages the client to reflect on why she is not used to being responded to by other people. This remark derives from the client's account and constitutes an interpretation of the client's disclosure in lines 1–3. The therapist refrains from suggesting a possible list of explanations. The information-eliciting statement (line 4) opens with a pre-questioning 'I'm curious' to which the client does not proffer an answer. The client, however, ratifies the therapist's formulation by expressing acceptance. In the second attempt of encouraging the client to verbalize her story (line 6) the therapist only underlines his siding with the client in admitting the existence of a problem and resists offering any new contribution. This is to say that the therapist does not speak for the client. The third attempt undertaken by the therapist (line 8) is responded to by the client, thus the process of client's self-disclosure is resumed (lines 9–10 and 13–16). The three attempts made by the therapist aim at enabling the client to explore therapeutically relevant matters with the therapist actively facilitating the process. What makes this statement an information-eliciting telling, in addition to its 'personal character report' is its potential tentativeness

indexed by a pre-questioning token ('I'm curious'), and the use of anaphoric 'that' (line 4) instead of naming the problem.

The therapist's professional expertise embedded in his information-
eliciting tellings aiming at the client's self-disclosure constitutes a product of
his observation and impressions based on what the client has revealed so far.
Lines 6 and 8 of the exchange also manifest the therapist's resistance to suggesting any reasons for the client's distress as his role here is to facilitate the
process of client's self-discovery by firstly self-disclosing. The therapist succeeds in transforming the client's initial contribution from her recounting a
single event to interpreting this event as an instance of her daily routine (formulation). The client's initial ratification is not followed by any further self-
disclosure, thus extensive interactional work is undertaken by the therapist to
facilitate more elaboration. This takes again, as in Extract 19, the form of
postpositioned queries which do not carry any new propositional input but
clearly recognize the client's emotional state (line 8). The therapist's intervention in lines 11–12 in the form of interruption constitutes an attempt to
narrow down the account of the client, who at this point seems to have di-
verged from the accepted (re)formulation. Beginning from line 13, the client
starts pursuing the version of her problem formulated by the therapist.

In Extract 21 the client reflects on handling the uncomfortable situation
of accepting her husband's 'outside marriage' relationship with a woman
and his two sons:

Extract 21

1	C:	Nevertheless, I, I have a very <u>good</u> relationship with the children. They come
2		to our <u>home</u> we make <u>excursions,</u> (.) we go to lunch together on Saturday and
3		last month
4→	T:	// And in your heart? You were <u>talking</u> about your behavior.
5		<What's your heart like being with these children?>
6	C:	I'm ve::ry hurt, I can manage, I can take <u>many</u> things and my intelligence says
7		it's the best thing that you can do, (2.0) °but my heart is not in this project°,
8		<u>not</u> when I'm with the children, I like them.
9	T:	How old are they now?
10	C:	X and Y.=
11→	T:	=So you've been doing this a lo::ng time.
12	C:	More or less I make an occasional orientation. He asks me, he telephones
13		me, he asks me 'Can I come with you?' or 'Can I take a test with you?'
14		and he he has <a lot of> <u>trust</u> in me and when I'm with <u>him</u>, it's
15		like another person, like a relative...

The client is initially very much oriented to pursuing the theme of being successful in managing a difficult personal situation, i.e., she is concentrated on the intellectual aspect(s) of the situation while the emotional part of it is left out by her. In lines 4–5, the therapist attempts to refocus the client's account to the more 'feeling-based' aspects (formulation). This attempt takes the form of interruption. In fact, the client partially reorients her account (lines 6–8). Towards the end of the statement in line 8, she comes back to highlighting her adjustment, underlining her relationship with the children. In line 11, the therapist professes an 'information-eliciting telling' deriving from the information provided by the client (line 10). The telling's anaphoric 'this' (line 11) frames this statement as tentative and in this way provides the client with conversational and 'thematic' space to pursue 'this' herself (cf. Pomerantz 1984). The client has been invited to continue with her personal story.

In another extract the therapist approaches a situation in which the client experiences emotional difficulties to give voice to traumatic feelings:

Extract 22

1	C:	I can't talk ((CRYING)).
2	T:	Mhm, (.) don't sob, >let this cry come< out right out of your guts, all the::se
3		years trying to stop the crying, <just let it come>, (.) just open your mouth
4		and °let it come.° I'll be right here with you, just let yourself go crazy.
5	C:	Oh, yes.=
6→	T:	=Yeah, (2.0) it must have been hard keeping a::ll this inside.
7	C:	But (.) I had to talk to another therapist about it but (.) it is still difficult,
8		you said yesterday 'who would die if you let those tears come?' and I think
9		it is ↑me because when they come, (.) there is no normalcy, I'm right into
10		a black hole and there is no life (.) and no energy…

The therapist in lines 2 through 4 encourages the client to break out of the emotional shell and share her innermost feelings with the therapist ('just let yourself go crazy'). It is noteworthy that the therapist initially remains within the communicative frame of the client. This signifies the therapist's respect for the client's suffering. In line 6 the therapist proffers information-eliciting telling based on his *in situ* observations. This side telling comes out as tentative since the therapist does not name the 'what' the client has kept unrevealed. This is to say that the client is in this way encouraged to reveal the experiences that have been kept encapsulated and isolated. In other words, the client is given autonomy in how the indirect 'all this' (line 6) will be approached and pursued. Yet at the same time the use of the verb 'must' can be read as the therapist's confirmation of the client's emotional suffering and as a prompt to talk about it. By making an emphatic comment in the form of information-eliciting telling the therapist provides the client with an opportunity to break through the protective shell and self-disclose. The client indeed gradually starts a long process of coming-out of the emotional shell and sharing by way of disclosing very intimate aspects of her life.

The therapist's statement in line 6 can also be interpreted as an instance of formulation. It does refer to an element of the client's talk – concealment of true emotions. Its tentative status, as commented above, is retained by the unspecified 'this'. Again the therapist's statement (line 6) defines the problem (the case of reformulation) but the problem needs to be documented by the client who is solicited to self-disclose. Beach and Dixson (2001) observe how formulations testify to an empathic ability to understand another's difficult situation and the feelings connected with it, and thereby contribute to subsequent disclosures of subtle personal material. This is the function of the therapist's formulation in line 6. The therapist underscores the client's emotional suffering and in this way encourages subsequent disclosure(s).

Interestingly, the information-eliciting tellings in the context of psychotherapy manifest different evidentiality, mainly marked by verbs (e.g., modal auxiliaries and verbs of cognition). Thus, on the one hand, there are quite strong tellings produced by the therapist, as presented in the first set representing some examples from my corpus:

1. *Now, you **must** be angry about **something**.*
2. *You **must** be more angry **than** I even imagine.*
3. *You **know** a lot about giving up, **don't you**?*
4. *You **know** that loneliness.*
5. *It **must** have been hard keeping all **this** inside.*

These psychotherapeutic information-eliciting tellings comprise information about the client and that information is derivative of his/her disclosive talk. These statements make strong claims to the clients' knowledge. Nevertheless each of the prompts has certain incompleteness or tentativeness embedded. For instance, in example 1 the word 'something' remains undefined. In example 2, the comparative form calls for more elaboration, while in example 3 the question tag calls for ratification and elaboration. In example 4, the anaphoric pronoun (*that*) refers to the client's personal experience of loneliness. This is the loneliness that the client has partially revealed. In example 5 (discussed above) the tentative status of the claim is maintained by the undefined 'this'. These statements induce the client to at least ratify their propositional aspect, i.e., to confirm them or reject them. In fact, the clients do not always provide *yes* or *no* answers to the proffered tellings, confirming or rejecting them but rather provide more self-disclosive talk, further elaborating on the proposed themes.

On the other hand, however, there are also exploring utterances with verbs indicating much less certainty about the expressed claim as presented in the second set:

1. *I'm **guessing** that the problem isn't in the showing it, the problem is in the ridicule or the rejection from the other person.*
2. *OK, I **wonder** how much of it has to do with not having a partner to engage you in talking about your feelings.*
3. *I **suspect** you have gone through a good part of your life denying that you need it.*
4. *I **suspect** this rage still exists and has turned against you.*

Although different in their grammatical form from the first set of tellings presented above, these statements also invite the clients to relate to the propositional content in terms of expressing their views and/or experiences of them. In fact, as far as their form is concerned, they resemble more formulations than the statements in the first set. Thus, the therapist is attempting to refocus the client's story and possibly engage him/her in expanding on the suggested reframing. The (re)formulations take on a very tentative form as indexed by 'I'm guessing', 'I wonder', 'I suspect'.

Both forms (presented in set 1 and set 2) used by the therapist as 'information-eliciting tellings' strongly hint at the therapist's professional expertise in *reading* the clients' communicative input. Yet both sets of tellings contain some undefined elements (set 1) or they invite speculation (set 2). In other words, they invite the client to clarify, i.e., to confirm and preferably to upgrade the therapist's interpretation.

What the therapist proffers to clients is only a B-event in Labov and Fanshel's (1977) terms. This is to say that the therapist has less right to know and tell than the client for whom his/her personal experience constitutes an A-event. To put it another way, the 'information-eliciting tellings' proffered by the therapist make as much as and merely a claim to the client's territory of information (cf. Kamio 1997). The information the therapist wishes to obtain belongs to the client's internal experience (Kamio

1997: 18) and can only be accessed and recounted by the client. By relying on certain indices of tentativeness, the therapist signifies that this information resides in the client's realm of knowledge.[85]

A statement offered by a therapist to a client, whether labeled information-eliciting telling or reformulation has the potential to facilitate a client's self-disclosure, which constitutes an important step in the process of self-transformation. As for the function, information-eliciting telling aims at soliciting more self-disclosive talk from the client. As Antaki and colleagues (2005a) state sometimes a therapist's statement does not need to perform any therapeutic intervention. Indeed, often clients appreciate the fact that somebody (here the therapist) is at last willing to hear their stories and is genuinely interested in their experiences. Thus, information-eliciting telling provides client with the conversational space to reveal their hearts, and the therapist with a possibility to collect more information. The main function of reformulation, on the other hand, is (preferably) to prompt the client to confirm or accept the alternative version of his/her problem suggested by the therapist. Thus a therapist's (re)formulation attempts to refocus a client's perspective in order to shift it towards a therapeutically-oriented direction.

An information-eliciting telling does not require the client to refocus but rather to proffer more personal data. However, as the above discussion has evinced, clients often react to a therapist's statement by not only accepting or rejecting it but also offering more talk in the direction suggested by the therapist. In view of that, it can be claimed that often a single statement not only elicits more talk from the client (the function of information-eliciting telling) but also the ensuing talk documents the formulation suggested by the therapist. Thus information eliciting tellings and reformulations in the context of psychotherapy often share the function of facilitating client's self-disclosure. Consequently it is often impossible to tease out these two similar strategies even taking into account the interactional context in which they transpire. As far as the tone of formulation is concerned, this therapeutic version of the client's problem needs to be designed as tentative. Information-eliciting tellings, as the data show, often combine indices of tentativeness with some markers of certainty. In this way the therapist may manifest his attunement ('It **must** have been hard...') with the client but at the same time, by leaving some aspect undefined or unspecified ('...keeping all **this** inside'), encourages the client to define and specify *this* by drawing on his/her personal experience. Both speech activities are based on what the client has revealed so far.

Another important feature that accompanies the use of either information-eliciting telling or (re)formulations by the therapist is postpositioned query. As Buttny (2004: 57) explains, even though the basic adjacency pair structure in the (re)formulation prevails, occasionally the therapist's ascription/recommendation is followed by postpositioned query. In his data, by relying on postpositioned queries, the therapist pursues the client's responses. In this way the client is able to co-construct the suggested alternative version and get involved in the interaction. Buttny's (2004) data feature queries in the form of direct questions or various particles (e.g., *yeah*, *uhm*, *hmm*). In the data discussed above, the therapist also relied on postpositioned queries. The queries used by the therapist glossed the original information-eliciting telling. The therapist admitted the client's acceptance of his claim but nevertheless ceaselessly solicited documenting the client's proffered 'yes'. Thus it can be claimed that the function of postpositioned queries can be indicative of whether the therapist's statement is geared more towards refocusing the client's story (formulation) or it seeks more self-disclosure from the client (information-eliciting telling). Yet, as the analysis has proven, often the therapist's statement offering an alternative version of the client's problem is accepted by the client, who then additionally provides more self-disclosive talk. Thus the statement fulfills two functions.

The question remains why the therapist relies so extensively on tentativeness in soliciting self-disclosure from the clients. Or in other words, why is it more *therapeutic* to be more indirect than straightforwardly direct in addressing/confronting the client? In my view the key notions in the therapeutic aspects of information-eliciting telling are autonomy and symmetry. These tellings on the one hand, comprise very intimate facts from a client's life, but on the other include certain indices of vagueness, i.e., indirectness. By providing the clients with the chance to shed some light on the vague or incomplete aspects, the therapist enables them to be agents in the interaction. This is to say that the clients, due to the indirectness, can pursue the theme, i.e., to dispel vagueness in their *own* way. This is how their autonomy gets manifested in the interaction with the therapist. At the same time, however they can give voice to their problems, i.e., to continue self-disclosure. In this way it can be claimed that both parties – therapist and client – equally benefit from it: the former is able to hear the client's story and formulate therapeutically relevant issue(s) while the latter feels autonomous. The client is in charge of how 'all this' (Extract 22, line 6) will be put in words and what words will be chosen to pursue the description. By being offered an indirect version of their problems, the clients are put in the position of authority to (re)assess the therapist's claim. This brings about a sense of (interactional) symmetry to the client-therapist interaction. Even though the therapist remains very much in charge of the therapeutic agenda, the client becomes empowered to rectify the therapist's claims.

It needs to be underlined that the clients of psychotherapy often lack these two important assets, i.e., autonomy and symmetry (of relationships) in their ordinary lives. They frequently miss out on those aspects in their daily interactions and maybe this is why they very spontaneously respond to the therapist's tellings soliciting their stories in a mild and unimposing way (cf. Bergmann 1992). It might be new territory for them that they are willing to explore. As already indicated, psychotherapy is a place where a sense of personal coherence can be constructed and maintained. A therapist's information-eliciting tellings with their embedded indirectness provide clients with an opportunity to explore their personal coherence. In sum, the client's (resumed) self-disclosure constitutes an effect of joint interactional achievement of the therapist and the client.

3.4 Concluding remarks

Irvin D. Yalom (1989), in one of his many outstanding accounts of his psychotherapeutic work with clients, states the following: "patients, like everyone else, profit most from a truth they, themselves, discover" (1989: 111). Clients' self-disclosures in the therapy room exemplify their strenuous efforts to progressively disclose and, in effect, come to terms with their anxieties and traumas in order to live their lives more fully.

Self-disclosure features, to a different extent, in numerous psychotherapy approaches. This discussion, unlike more psychologically-oriented studies, focused on how clients' self-disclosure is an interactional achievement and how it is facilitated by the psychotherapist's situated (interactional) strategies. This is where psychotherapeutic self-disclosure departs from the same practice but applied in contexts other than psychotherapy. The psychotherapist's *presence* – evident in his choice of communicative strategies – promotes clients' narrative expressivity which in turn contributes to enhancing their self-awareness. The taught/instilled self-awareness helps clients to face potential difficult experiences in real life. In psychotherapy, unlike in other social contexts, it is the client who is granted extensive clinical and conversational space to disclose (and not the therapist). This is very different from an ordinary conversation where one interlocutor's disclosure should ideally trigger revelations from other interlocutors, thereby constructing conversational symmetry.

In this sense, the interaction between the client and psychotherapist can be construed as asymmetrical since the psychotherapist remains in control of the flow of interaction, yet it is the client who should benefit from it. In the context of psychotherapy, the therapist's interactional and communicative strategies create a channel for clients' verbalization and self-discovery in an atmosphere of trust and confidentiality. The therapist's interactional work brings out the clients' agency. Their personal experiences, authentic views and opinions are encouraged to surface. Therapist's strategies refocus their discourse on the so far denied personal *I* and move their disclosures away from intellectual to emotional aspects of their experience. What needs to be underlined is that in triggering clients' self-disclosure, the therapist extensively relies on the client's own contributions. The therapist *listens* and observes not only what the client says but how he/she conveys it verbally (and non-verbally). The therapeutic power of self-disclosure also derives from a willingness of the other person (here a psychotherapist) to unconditionally accept the proffered narratives. The non-judgmental environment constructs intimacy and closeness.

One issue that remains to be tackled in the concluding section is why and how the interactional and communicative strategies applied by the psychotherapist function as therapeutic aspects of communication. First of all, it needs to be underlined that there are different dimensions of what 'therapeutic' entails. In the long run therapy aims at changing the client's life qualitatively, but the long-awaited change is brought about in small stages; a key stage is to have the client self-disclose. Thus, self-disclosure is therapeutic as it allows the client to reveal and face anxieties and traumas by *sharing* them with an involved listener without (maybe for the first time) risk of social ridicule. Through self-disclosure clients are also encouraged to give vent to often hidden and unexpressed emotional states. They are provided with an opportunity to explore different aspects of their lives without any fear of losing face. Self-disclosure is brought off in this specific context with extensive facilitation by the psychotherapist. As indicated above, a strategy is therapeutic at this particular stage of the psychotherapy process if it *facilitates* a client's unrestrained free expression.

The current discussion has focused on five such strategies (the use of *you know/I don't know*, repetition, information-eliciting telling and reformulation) which allow the psychotherapist to promote clients' verbalization and often, at the same time achieve other goals (cf. reformulations). As already underscored above, these strategies constitute an expression of the therapist's involvement, attunement and empathy to client's personal expression (cf. Erskine, Moursund, and Trautmann 1999). And (good) therapy cannot be carried off without an involved, attuned and emphatic psychotherapist. This particular affective stance (of involvement, attunement and empathy) manifests itself in the psychotherapist's communicative strategies in his interactions with the clients.

Yet, there is nothing *intrinsically* therapeutic about the above discussed strategies applied by the psychotherapist. In fact, the use of a cognitive response *I don't know* to an interlocutor's discursive *you know* in an ordinary conversation may be perceived as disruptive to the pursuit of intimacy which constitutes one of the most important premises of an ordinary conversation. Disrupting the interlocutor's appeal for intimacy and/or involvement by responding to *you know* cognitively might seriously affect the relationship between the interactants in a conversation.

Although psychotherapy is significantly based on the premises of an ordinary conversation, its goals are not identical with those of a conversation. In psychotherapy, the therapist needs to make sure that his communicative and interactional strategies enable the client to give full voice to his/her experience while the established therapeutic alliance between the participants ensures confidence in what the therapist proposes. It needs to be acknowledged that there may be other strategies used in different psychotherapy approaches which manage to encourage clients' disclosures equally well. Thus, a certain function can be linguistically or communicatively realized by a number of different strategies which must be relevant to the context and goals of the communicative situation. This allows for the conclusion that to label a certain feature of language or communication as therapeutic (or any other), one needs to look into its function(s) rather than its form. Investigating the function of a certain form, so in other words: what it does in a certain context, requires examining a broader interactional context in which it occurs. Before naming a certain linguistic or communicative feature therapeutic, first and foremost its function needs to be specified as one serving any of the goals of psychotherapy.

To apply Ochs' (1992) line of reasoning, no feature of language or communicative strategy directly and exclusively indexes therapeutic function(s). Ochs, in her discussion on indexing gender in language, explicitly states that a certain form can index certain stances or acts. They, in turn, may help to constitute female or male gender identity in the specific *local* context. Thus, for instance, a question tag may index a state of uncertainty or the act of requesting confirmation/clarification/feedback. As Ochs explains, these contextual features may index female identity in the local context. It seems that in Ochs' investigation the defining criterion of whether a certain feature will be perceived as typically male or female is its *local* perception, understood in terms of local speech community norms and expectations. The features labeled as therapeutic discussed above may also index other stances or acts. Yet their therapeutic stance is brought out by the therapist with his *local* work which is performed in a specific interactional context. In this way the therapeutic aspect of a certain language form or communicative strategy must be achieved. To paraphrase Ochs, the relation between language form and the therapeutic function is non-exclusive since a form does not pragmatically presuppose therapeutic categories, and it is constitutive, as first of all language forms or communicative strategies index social meanings (e.g., being involved, attuned, empathic and understanding), which in turn constitute therapeutic meaning in the specific interactional context.

Following Cameron's (2000a: 157) interpretation, it can be claimed that the therapist's communicative and interactional strategies applied in interactions with clients embody certain beliefs and values as norms of talk. Namely, as the Chapter has sought to evince, one of the therapeutic discourse norms follows that certain feelings and emotions should not be merely felt but *disclosed* to an empathetic and understanding listener (the therapist).

Communication of emotion is another endemic constituent of psychotherapy. Similarly to the interactional phenomenon of self-disclosure, communication of emotion has received meticulous attention in the professional literature. Yet, what these discussions have significantly left unattended is how this communication is realized at the level of discursive and interactional detail.

Chapter 4. Communication of emotion

...the problem in therapy is always how to move from an ineffectual intellectual appreciation of a truth about oneself to some emotional experience of it. It is only when therapy enlists deep emotions that it becomes a powerful force for change.
(Yalom 1989: 35)

4.1 Introductory remarks

Psychotherapy constitutes one of the few social contexts in which experiencing, expressing, describing, and constructing both one's positive and negative emotions is highly encouraged, appreciated and expected. Indeed, emotional experience seems to function as the most salient and recognizable characteristic of this unique social context (cf. Gaik 1992; Besnier 1990). This may be due to the fact that, as Lupton (1998: 99) states, "emotions are conceptualized as 'building-up' within the body, as subsequently creating tension and pressure which may lead to internal damage if they are not released". Uninitiated clients seeking psychotherapeutic assistance often do so merely in the hope of some sort of emotional relief, which should ideally take place in the safety of a relationship with another person (the therapist). This chapter presents how emotions feature in the process of psychotherapy.

Communication of emotion constitutes one of the fundamental discourse norms of psychotherapy. The all-encompassing term (*communication of emotion*) is to indicate that aspects of constructing, *doing*, experiencing, describing, and eliciting, as well as validating one's emotions occupy the primary position in the interaction between the therapist and client. This is an indispensable element of the psychotherapeutic endeavor without which its participants are not able to reach their independent and common goals. There are however, clear expectations and an ensuing division of emotional labor between the participants of the psychotherapeutic undertaking as to who should encourage emotional expression and, in turn, who should project it. Emotions in psychotherapy manifest themselves in a multitude of ways; thus the strategies used by the therapist to prod the clients to emotional experience, as well as the clients' communication and construction of emotions will be covered in this chapter.

The presentation commences with the concept of emotion as envisioned by social scientists, and the psychotherapists' perspective on the role of emotions in the process of psychotherapy. The discussion then proceeds to data analysis where different aspects of emotional display and work transpiring in interactions between therapist and client will be dealt with.

4.2 Emotion in socio-psychological perspective

Oatley and Jenkins's (1996: 122) survey of the literature on emotions concludes that emotions "are the very center of human mental life".[86] At the most basic level of functioning, emotions are "an adaptive form of information-processing and action readiness that orients people to their environment and promotes their well-being" (Greenberg 2004b: 3).

The definition of emotion proposed by Campos and colleagues (1994: 285) highlights its role in social relationships since emotions: "establish, maintain, change, or terminate the relation between the person and the environment on matters of significance to the person". This aspect points to their function as a foundation of social life as the plans they trigger to a great extent involve other people. Berscheid (1987) points to the commonly accepted assumption among scholars and lay people alike that interpersonal relationships constitute the most frequent contexts in which people experience emotions.

Psychotherapists also highlight that emotions nearly always arise in the context of social relationships (cf. Moursund and Erskine 2004). Parkinson (1996), underlining the highly salient social aspect of emotions, claims that interpersonal factors tend to be the main cause of emotion, making people engage in social encounters or pull out from them. In fact, emotions prioritize certain kinds of social interaction, for example they can prompt cooperation or conflict.[87] Minimizing unpleasant and maximizing pleasant affect constitutes a driving force in human motivation and action. It is also worth underlining that emotions stay closer to evaluation of the significance of things relevant to a person than to their truth or rationality (Greenberg 2004b). Emotion influences modes of processing and guides attention, in addition to enhancing memory. Greenberg (2004b), in advancing the thesis that emotion can often precede cognition, points out that neuroscience has proven that emotion is an indispensable foundation for a number of cognitive processes, predominantly decision-making (cf. Bechara et al. 1997; Damasio 1994).

Even though psychologically-oriented studies on emotion make and retain a clear distinction between such concepts as emotion, feeling, mood, attitude, and affect, in linguistics, *affect* tends to function as a kind of all-encompassing term. It often functions as a generic term in reference to feelings, moods, dispositions and attitudes associated with a person or situation (Ochs and Schieffelin 1989). It may subsume not only traditional psychological notions of emotion, mood and attitude but also "notions related to interactional linguistic phenomena such as masking, hedging, undercutting, and so forth" (Caffi and Janney 1994: 328). Ochs (1989) states that in linguistic studies the term *affect* is preferred over *emotion* since *affect* relates to expressed emotional dispositions as well as the part of emotion that is expressive and experiential.

There are two main tendencies in the humanities and social scientific literature in which emotions have been conceptualized and studied. Lupton (1998) labels them 'emotions as inherent' and 'emotions as socially constructed' perspectives.

Emotions as inherent[88]

Within this perspective it is assumed that there is a set of basic emotions with which all humans are born (Lupton 1998).[89] Consequently it follows that emotional states are not learnt by an individual but rather inherited. Lupton enumerates the focuses of the research within this perspective:

1. identifying the anatomical or genetic basis for the emotions,
2. showing how emotions are linked to bodily changes,
3. seeking to explain the function served by inherent emotions in human survival and social interaction,
4. identifying which emotions are common to all human groups.

(Lupton 1998: 11)

This approach is strongly influenced by Darwin's theory of emotions (1872). This theory conceptualizes emotions as primitive states of physiological arousal involving innate instinctual drives (Lupton 1998: 11). Darwin believed that emotions were crucial to survival as they constituted reactions to threats and dangers and they also signaled future actions or plans. 'Evolutionary psychology' has reformulated Darwinian focus on survival and emotions are seen as "total body reactions to the various survival-related problems created by the environment" (Plutchik 1982: 548). Cognitive theories positing that some emotions are universal and have their basis in physiology – yet identifying the extent to which emotional behavior is influenced by judgment and assessment of the context – are also classified in this perspective. Thus cognitive theorists look into "the interrelationship between bodily response, context, and the individual's recognition of an emotion" (Lupton 1998: 13).

Emotions as socially constructed

In this perspective, emotion has its existence only in relation to social and cultural processes, i.e., "it is always experienced, understood and named via social and cultural processes" (Lupton 1998: 15). Hence emotions are learnt responses and behaviors.

Scholars working within this perspective aim at "identifying and tracing the ways in which norms and expectations about the emotions are generated, reproduced and operate in specific sociocultural settings, and the implications for selfhood and social relations of emotional experience and expression" (Lupton 1998: 15). Within this framework strong and weak versions can be singled out. According to the weak version there is a limited range of 'natural emotion responses' that are biologically conditioned and thus exist independently of sociocultural influences and learning (Armon-Jones 1986: 38). The strong version of this approach, on the other hand, conceives of emotion as an irreducibly sociocultural product. Emotion within this version is wholly learnt and constructed through socialization. Harré, among the more pronounced representatives of the 'strong' version, claims that in fact there is no such a thing as an emotion. In his view one can feel emotional and display his/her judgments in an appropriate bodily way (Harré 1991). What is more, one 'does' – rather than 'has' – emotion: "to be angry is to have taken on the angry role on a particular occasion as the expression of a moral position" (Harré 1991: 142–143).

Pavlenko (2005) proposes 2 key paradigms in the research of language and emotion, which derive from distinct views on the relationship between language and emotions:

1. Within the first one, referred to as *communication of emotion*, language and emotions are conceptualized as largely separate phenomena. This view postulates a one-to-one correlation between emotions as inner states and their perception, interpretation and expression. As Pavlenko states, scholars working in this framework tend to be involved in a search for verbal and non-verbal cues to preexisting emotions and in an

attempt to integrate them in a more or less coherent way (e.g., Scherer 1986; Planlap and Knie 2002; cf. also Bloch 1996).

2. The second paradigm, referred to as *discursive construction of emotions*, concentrates on rhetoric alternatives available to speakers within and across languages and speakers' communicative intentions. Emotion terms and scripts are involved in the ongoing negotiation of meaning in the context of emotional, social, and power relations (e.g., Lutz and Abu-Lughod 1990; Irvine 1990; Ochs and Schiefflin 1989).

In fact, the perspective of discursive construction of emotions underlines the constitutive role played by language. In this respect it falls into the framework of poststructuralism which views discourse as constructing reality, knowledge, experience, identity, and social relationships[90] (Lupton 1998: 24). Within this perspective, the words used in reference to emotions are seen as "coalescences of complex ethnotheoretical ideas about the nature of self and social interaction, and as actions or ideological practices serving specific ends as part of the creation and negotiation of reality" (Lupton 1998: 25). Therefore language plays a central role in the construction and experience of emotions while the physical adjuncts of emotions are viewed as incidental to the emotional state. Hearn (1993: 148) states that emotions do not happen 'automatically' but rather they have to be *'done'* [emphasis original]. Whalen and Zimmerman (1998: 158) advocate considering the interactional context in which emotion occurs: "the study of the social construction of emotion is anchored in the interactional matrix in which the expression occurs: its form, its placement, its response and the organizational and interactional origins of its accountability". Additionally, Whalen and Zimmerman conceive of emotions as subject to social definition. Yet, as Pavlenko (2005) asserts, these paradigms (*communication of emotion* and *discursive construction of emotions*) may be compatible as scholars working on communication of emotions also admit that speakers use emotion categories to accomplish social goals while researchers of discursive construction of emotions recognize the embodied nature of emotional experience (cf. Lutz and Abu-Lughod 1990) and the role of conventionality in affective displays (cf. Arndt and Janney 1991).

To sum up, emotions are a constitutive part of human life. They comprise a very significant material in the exploration of an individual's concerns (Frijda 1988: 352). Consequently, if a recognition and interpretation of an individual's and others' emotions fails, he or she may seek psychotherapy to experience some sort of emotional relief. Emotions constitute a significant object of work and reference in the process of psychotherapy.

4.3 Emotions in the process of psychotherapy

As Greenberg and Paivo (1997) state, emotional arousal occupies the most prominent role in the interaction between a client and psychotherapist. Numerous approaches to psychotherapy share the dictate of affective system as critical both in understanding as well as changing human experience and behavior. Emotions offer a rich source of information about people's situational reactions and this fact is particularly applicable in the context of psychotherapy. The communicative climate of psychotherapy primarily provides the client with an opportunity to experience emotions[91] (cf. Orlinsky and Howard 1986; Lambert and Bergin 1994; Czabała 2006) and, as a result, one of the most essential tasks for a psychotherapist is to validate the client's emotions and work with them directly in order to promote a qualitative change in one's life.

Greenberg and Safran (1987, 1989) recognize a correlation between the level of emotional experience during a psychotherapeutic session and the actual positive outcome of psychotherapy. They observe that the higher the level of emotional experience, the more benefits the client gets from the psychotherapeutic endeavor. Frank (1961, 1974, 1977) points to two 'emotionally-oriented' aspects of the process of psychotherapy that lead to positive effects experienced by the client. One of them is inducing the client's emotional arousal during a session. The second constitutes the client's undergoing corrective emotional experiences in the dialogue and therapeutic alliance with the psychotherapist.

A long-awaited qualitative life change in the effect of psychotherapy is contingent on the recognition and acceptance of one's *real* emotions as they reflect one's needs and constitute an important source of information for a therapist. Greenberg (2004a: 1) calls this "a special form of information processing, crucial to survival and adaptation". Here, an improvement of one's mood and discernible changes in one's behavior take place only upon the voicing of once-buried emotions. Yet, Greenberg (2004b: 9) stipulates that expressing emotions in psychotherapy does not consist in the mere venting of emotion but rather "expressing strongly experienced emotions in therapeutic environments rather than constricting them". Additionally, a client needs to realize the underlying message of one's own emotional experience and use it in a constructive way (Greenberg and Paivo 1997: 5).

Elliott (1984) enumerates the 'emotional' elements of the process of psychotherapy, such as: revealing and getting over emotions, confidence, a sense of emotional relief, a sense of being understood, and invoking hope. Lazarus (1989) underlines the role of emotional experience in the psychotherapeutic process by stating that the main aim of psychotherapy relates to the achievement of balance between one's convictions, experienced emotions, and behavior. Psychotherapy constitutes a specific social context in which less dominant (i.e., hegemonic) discourses can (re)surface. This can be achieved by realizing true feelings and emotions a client holds towards significant people in his/her life in the safety of the therapeutic alliance. This in turn enables the client to improve interpersonal relationships as well as having a beneficial effect on his/her health (cf. Lupton 1998; Czabała 2006).

Greenberg (2004b), in his *Emotion-focused therapy* (EFT), conceives of emotion as a basis in the construction of the self and self-organization. He relies on a dialectal-constructivist view (cf. Greenberg, Rice, and Elliott 1993; Greenberg and Pascual-Leone 1995, 2001) to explicate how people not only have emotions but also constantly make sense of them: "in this view personal meaning emerges by the self-organization and explication of one's own emotional experience and optimal adaptation involves an integration of reason and emotion" (Greenberg 2004b: 3). The ongoing process of making sense of experience is manifested by being aware of bodily-felt sensations and articulating them verbally – in this way constructing new experience. Emotional experience – except for being generated by highly differentiated structures – is also substantially shaped by a person's life experience and the culture[92] he/she is immersed in, in what emerges as an 'emotion scheme'.[93] A person's emotional core derives from his/her early experiences with others (Stolorow 1992). A client's emotion scheme constitutes the main target of the therapist's intervention and therapeutic change, thus emotion coaching occupies a central role in therapy. In this process, clients are helped to recognize and understand, channel, and modify their emotional experience, i.e., emotion coaching involves 3 emotion processing principles: increasing awareness of emotion, enhancing emotion regulation, and transforming emotion (Greenberg 2004b: 8). Emotion coaching is based on a collaborative relationship and its aims of accepting, utilizing, and transforming emotional experience are contingent on an atmosphere of safety, empathy and validation established by the therapist. As Greenberg (2004b: 6) states "in this type of relational environment people sort out their feelings, develop self-empathy and gain access to alternate resilient responses based on their internal resources". Emotion coaching involves two stages: *arriving* and *leaving*,[94] the first of which involves 4 steps aiming at increasing awareness and acceptance of emotion:

1. It is important to help people become aware of their emotions.
2. People need to be coached to welcome their emotional experience and allow it (this does not mean that they must express everything they feel to other people but rather acknowledge it themselves). People also need to be coached in skills of regulation if needed to help them tolerate their emotions.
3. People need to be helped to describe their feelings in words in order to aid them in solving problems.
4. They need to be helped to become aware of whether their emotional reactions are their primary feelings[95] in this situation. If not, they need help in discovering what their primary feelings are.

(Greenberg 2004b: 7)

The prescribed steps clearly designate the interactional status of the psychotherapist in the first phase (*help people...*) whose role is to interpersonally and interactionally facilitate the process of becoming aware of one's emotions and then accepting them. The therapist should help the clients to label their emotional states and discuss with them what it is like to experience certain kind of emotion (Greenberg 2004b: 7). An emotion needs to be felt if its verbal articulation is to emerge important.

The second phase, *leaving*, involves 4 more steps, these focusing on aspects of emotion utilization or transformation:

1. Once the person has been helped to experience a primary emotion, the coach and person together need to evaluate if the emotion is a healthy or unhealthy response to the current situation. If it is healthy it should be used as a guide to action. If it is unhealthy it needs to be changed.
2. When the person's accessed primary emotions are unhealthy, the person has to be helped to identify the negative voice associated with these emotions.
3. The person is helped to find and rely on alternate healthy emotional responses and needs.
4. People need to be coached to challenge the destructive thoughts, in their unhealthy emotions, from a new inner voice based on their healthy primary emotions and needs, and to learn to regulate when necessary.

(Greenberg 2004b: 7)

The second phase also features the therapist as an active agent in promoting a client's *leaving* destructive emotions. Once the client has accessed emotional experience, he/she needs to approach it cognitively as information. Emotion is intimately connected with meaning and for an emotional change to take place it needs to be accompanied by a cognitive change (Greenberg and Paivo 1997). It should be stressed that "putting emotion into words" (Greenberg 2004b: 9) enables the clients to incorporate it into their conscious and conceptual understanding of self and the surrounding world.

LeDoux (1998) draws attention to the role of the amygdala[96] in the process of transforming emotions. The amygdala constitutes the center of the emotional brain (cf. LeDoux 1998; cf. also Jamison 2004), interpreting whether incoming sensory information poses a threat. The amygdala creates emotional memories "in response to particular sensations such as sounds and images that have become associated with physical threats" (Greenberg 2004b: 4). Thus if a client suffers from depression for instance, his/her amygdala reactions to the harmless reminders of past experiences need to be transformed so that they are not perceived as a return to the old failure or trauma. Yet these emotional interpretations formed by amygdala are in fact quite difficult to change (LeDoux 1998). LeDoux (1998: 265) explicates that from this perspective therapy "is just another way of creating synaptic potentiation in brain pathways that control the amygdala". Although the current discussion will exclude the aspect of the neurological changes and processes occurring in the process of psychotherapy (for a discussion see LeDoux 1998), within this perspective psychotherapy is interpreted as "a process through which our neocortex learns to exercise control over evolutionarily old emotional systems" (LeDoux 1998: 21).

The context of the psychotherapy session, as amply demonstrated by psychological and psychotherapeutic literature (cf. the discussion above), constitutes one of the settings in which emotions are a key topic. According to Besnier (1990: 432), representing a more anthropologically-oriented view, the focus on affect in the context of the psychotherapy session takes a number of forms: "the therapist focuses the patient's attention on the affective dimension of the encounter itself or of narratives provided by the patient, emotion-labeling, emotion term glossing, and negotiations of the meaning of emotion terms". Emotions then constitute the primary focus of psychotherapeutic work in two ways. Firstly, unlike in other social contexts one interlocutor (client) is explicitly asked and prodded by another one (therapist) to discuss how she or he is doing/managing emotionally 'here-and-now'. Thus the client's emotional state becomes the subject matter of the interaction transpiring between him/her and the therapist. Secondly, it is assumed that the client's distress can be understood by accessing the real emotions accompanying it even when the client remains unaware of or simply wishes to deny these emotions as this has constituted one of the client's survival strategies. What remains to be analyzed is how the emotional work gets done in the actual interaction.

4.4 Expression, construction, and experience of emotion in the psychotherapy session

> *Emotions are notoriously difficult to verbalize.*
> *They operate in some psychic and neural space*
> *that is not readily accessed from consciousness.*
> *Psychiatrists' and psychologists' offices are kept*
> *packed for this very reason.* (LeDoux 1998: 71)

Such ubiquitous features of the human experience as anger, sadness, shame, anxiety, hurt, and fear can be much more effectively acknowledged and coped with when shared with a sympathetic and empathetic listener who is also able to offer sensitive support. A client entering a therapeutic alliance with the psychotherapist has an opportunity to make new sense of old experiences and emotions in the company of an involved listener who facilitates this difficult and often painful yet, ultimately, liberating process. Yalom (1989) asserts that an indispensable condition for successful psychotherapy, understood in the current discussion as a truly qualitative change of the client's life, is its enlisting of deep emotional experience. Scholars investigating the conversational practices in psychotherapy within the Conversation Analysis perspective (cf. Peräkylä and Vehviläinen 2007) have similarly identified 'recognition of the client's emotion' as a candidate for a common practice in different psychotherapeutic schools and protocols. Emotions and emotional work feature in various forms in psychotherapeutic interaction. Clients are instilled to enhance their emotional awareness as well as experience regulation and transformation of their emotions; they are also encouraged to reflect on their experience. The therapist, a significant agent facilitating the client's processing of emotions, undertakes a variety of emotion-regulating/supporting interventions. This entails significant interactional effort from both the client and therapist. As a result of joint interactional effort undertaken by both parties, emotional work is in fact *performed* through the use of and reliance on certain communicative strategies.

Here, different aspects of emotional work performed by the therapist and client will be discussed. Before investigating actual psychotherapeutic exchanges for their emotional aspects, a few theoretical precepts on which the analysis will be grounded are needed.

The unique context of psychotherapy potentially offers numerous examples of emotional communication, i.e., spontaneous externalization of internal affect (Arndt and Janney 1991); this type of communication seems to be particularly applicable to the client who often through psychotherapy (initially) seeks just an opportunity for some kind of release of emotional tension. It seems that a client's emotional communication is made possible/ facilitated to a great extent by the psychotherapist whose aspects of emotive communication significantly contribute to building and maintaining an emotional bond, i.e., therapeutic alliance with the client (Moursund and Erskine 2004). A therapeutic relationship between the client and psychotherapist based on understanding and trust provides the client (maybe for the first time in his/her life) with a sense of security that favors (emotional) spontaneity. Within this sheltering context, the psychotherapist's emotive expression is often intended as a communicative act addressed to another person, i.e., the client, rather than being just a reflection of an underlying mental state. Thus the therapist becomes a unique facilitator of the client's (un)restrained emotional expression. It has been determined that emotional expression can be facilitated or inhibited depending on the type of emotional stimulus as well as on the nature of the relationship between the parties.

The analysis to follow will predominantly be based on the 'discursive construction of emotion' and will only sporadically draw on the 'communication of emotion' approach (cf. Pavlenko 2005). While the spontaneous, externalization of internal affect seems to lend itself to the latter research paradigm, and the psychotherapist's emotive choices and strategies could well be analyzed by drawing on the first research framework, the current analysis – unlike a number of psychological studies – will not consider the expression of emotion to function as a straightforward trace of an underlying psychological state. In the 'discursive construction of emotion' paradigm, language plays a pivotal role in the construction of emotion; in other words, within this perspective emotions are *done*.

Sarangi (2001: 46) draws attention to the function of language in "one's articulation of feelings and in one's understanding of the meanings of such feelings". Words constitute the feelings of emotions and within this perspective language does not function merely as a means of expression but it has the potential to become the experience itself. Although psychotherapy does not always aim at the experiential aspect, for emotions to be fully recognized and processed by the conscious mind, they first need to be verbalized. As Sarangi (2001) asserts, it is through the use of words that pain, hurt, and fear, for example, become realizable and – in the long run – understandable.[97]

It is also assumed that even in such a sheltered and secure – albeit highly emotionally-charged – setting as a psychotherapy session, clients are not always ready or willing to produce uninhibited emotional expression but are frequently capable of suppressing or intentionally misrepresenting their true emotional states. In the words of Erskine and Moursund (1988: 43), "it has long been known that clients bring to therapy both openness to work and resistance to change". Although they do possess emotive capacity (cf. Caffi and Janney 1994) to describe all their emotional experiences, clients regularly engage in a desperate emotional survival strategy by making willful and concerted attempts at wiping their traumatic life experiences from the record. Consequently, not verbalizing one's negative emotions is a conscious move not to deal with them only to risk resuscitating *almost* forgotten loss, fear, humiliation, abuse, etc. The mere context of a psychotherapy session alone does not in itself inspire a client to immediately drop his/her protective and emotionally defensive behavior and spontaneously verbalize real (negative) feelings. This again frequently requires extensive interactional work on the side of the psychotherapist to let the client's real but at the same time less socially acceptable emotions (re)surface for psychotherapeutic work. These emotions often concern the client's current or previous significant others.

The security of the therapeutic alliance with the psychotherapist gradually helps clients to re-focus their personal accounts from intellectually-oriented (facts-oriented) to emotionally-focused. Thus the embedded emotional metamessage of intellectually-oriented account (cf. Besnier 1990) is not pursued by the psychotherapist but rather the client's *explicit* description of his/her emotional states is strongly preferred. This is to say that in psychotherapeutic interaction the theme to be pursued is not any longer how the client perfectly adapted to the situation he/she did not approve of, but rather the focus is on how she/he *really* felt about particular circumstances.

4.4.1 Topicalizing 'feelings-talk'

In their interactions with clients, therapists attempt to focus interlocutors on the emotional aspect of their experience(s), i.e., to reflect on what emotional state(s) accompanied a certain dysphoric event. This often entails interactionally refocusing the client's account from intellectual or fact-oriented to a more emotionally-focused one. Therapists commonly treat the client's prior talk as occasioning an inquiry about his/her feelings. Let us analyze the following exchange between client and therapist exemplifying therapist's numerous contributions (lines 2, 4, 6, 12–14) aiming at topicalizing the 'feelings-talk':

Extract 1

1	C:	There was <u>no</u> empathic understanding where I was (.) not at all.=
2→	T:	=Ok, <so it's the lack of empathy that's really significant here.>
3	C:	The <u>lack</u> of relationship.
4→	T:	What are your fee:lings with this?
5	C:	On the day?=
6→	T:	=<u>No</u>, right now! °Are you crying inside?°
7	C:	>Right now I feel a bit dead.<
8	T:	'Cause we've been talking in a very <problem-investigating way.>
9	C:	Mhm (.) I'm still stunned 'cause I don't <u>know</u> what to believe until I can (2.0)
10		I'm not sure he is willing to speak to ↑me but I would <u>like</u> to talk to him and
11		make some sense.
12→	T:	Now, I'm trying to figure out what would happen if you really got pissed!
13		<u>Really</u> pissed off and wrote him a ↑letter and say 'the way you ended with
14		me is a:bsolutely <u>inappropriate</u>'.
15	C:	Mhm.

The extract above presents the client grieving over the very abrupt termination of the sessions with another therapist. In line 1 the client offers her position on how she felt about the situation, to which the therapist provides a gist formulation (cf. Heritage and Watson 1979; Hak and de Boer 1996). Interestingly, this contribution is produced at much slower rate than surrounding talk indicating its interactional significance and thus calling for the client's orientation. In this way the therapist is also taking an opportunity to make the client concentrate on the theme (no empathic understanding) which she has introduced herself. The client orients to it in line 3 yet correcting the therapist's formulation by referring to the lack of therapeutic alliance as the main obstacle in the relationship. The therapist is aiming at topicalizing the theme of 'lack of relationship' by inquiring about the feelings that accompanied it (line 4). This 'feelings-talk' is further topicalized and the discussion begins to revolve around the client's actual feelings about the unfair and inhumane treatment she received from her former therapist (line 6). Interestingly, the therapist in his turn in line 8 makes a clear point of the transitional moment of the session in which 'feelings-talk' becomes topicalized and the fact-oriented discussion is dropped.

Extract 2 features an exchange in which the client is recalling the precious moments from the life of her terminally-ill daughter by addressing her directly:

Extract 2

1   T: Yeah, °just elaborate on that wait° <tell her the story in that sentence.>
2   C: It was a <u>really</u> good decision to have you ( ), then I was waiting for your
3   movements and watched for a sign of life (1.0) this girl was insi:de me.
4   Although I wanted to hold you in my arms, I almost <u>didn't</u> want you to
5   be inside my body.=
6→T: =Tell her how <u>wonderful</u> it was.
7   C: >It felt like I really needed you at that time.< I had other children <u>too</u> but it
8   was something that words can't be put to (.) having you: inside me (2.0)
9   something I hope you'll know one day.
10 T: <u>Yeah</u>, say that sentence again.=
11 C: =Something that I hope you'll know one day.=
12 T: ='Cause tell her the impo:rtance of it to the next and the next generation
13   of women.
14 C: Because it's a la:nguage that can <u>only</u> be spoken between one woman and
15   another woman who knows this thrill, who knows the looking (.) just the
16   look in the eyes of another who is carrying a baby, it's the <u>biggest</u> and
17   the most <u>wonderful</u> gift to be able to hold it.

The client's extended turn in lines 2–5, is framed by the therapist's contribution (line 6) as very emotional as the client is elaborating on her experience of awaiting the birth of her daughter. In fact, the therapist in line 6 picks on the emotional metamessage in order to topicalize 'feelings-talk'. This type of prompt aims at eliciting from the client elaboration on her turn in lines 2–5 with the focus on its emotional aspects. The client orients to it by admitting that 'words can't be put to' this experience (line 8). In line 10 the client is asked to repeat a part of her statement. The repetition (line 11) constitutes a highly emotional moment in the interaction as her terminally-ill daughter does not stand a chance of experiencing this precious moment. Thus the interactional function of the repetition was to provide the client with the opportunity to reinforce the emotional experience and then work with it in the company of an empathic and involved recipient (the therapist), i.e., in the safety of the therapeutic alliance. Similarly, the therapist's prompt in lines 12–13 attempts to elicit more 'feelings-talk' from the client who orients to it in lines 14–17.

In Extract 3 the therapist seeks to elicit the client's confirmation of her prior turn in which she stated her wish to be dead:

Extract 3

1	T:	You hope to be dead?=

1   T: You hope to be dead?=

2   C: =Yeah (1.0) I can handle my life a:nd I think I've done a very good job

3   functioning, adapting, being good whatever my role is and, no, I wish

4   I had never been <u>born</u>, °it could be over°. No:, I can't complain, I have

5   a good life, >you know< (.) I'm not <u>tired</u>, I just don't want to exist,

6   that's all.

7   T: And before your husband picked another woman

8   C: // Oh, that's

9→ T: // D'you

10   remember the time you were excited about being alive (.) those first

11   couple of years?

12 C: It was very much <u>below</u>, it didn't come out even when X was born (.)

13   the same day I was so sick, my heart stopped beating, I was unconscious

14   for some days and when I woke up, the first words I said was 'why didn't

15   I die?' and my >daughter was born and I love her.<

16→ T: Did <u>you</u> feel that way before you met your husband?=

17 C: =Yes, not very consciously, I didn't put it into words, fee:l, that's the right

18   word. I was lonely, I didn't want to be here...

The therapist's echoing question (line 1) does not trigger 'feelings-talk' from the client, i.e., rather than delve into the emotional justification of this 'wish', the client elaborates on the intellectual aspects, i.e., adjusting to life circumstances. Thus in her extended turn (lines 2–6) the client testifies as to how well she has been functioning in life judging by intellectual perspective and/or general societal standards. The emotional load of the therapist's statement in line 7 – as well as his interruption in lines 9–11 – strongly indicates that the priority in the client's response should be given to 'feelings-talk'. These are very sensitive and intimate statements which call for emotional rejoining. Yet, the client's response in her extended turn, lines 12–15, only partially relates to her actual feelings. The therapist, however continues orienting the client to 'feelings-talk' with the question in line 16. This turn, in fact, triggers more emotional account from the client (lines 17–18).

Extract 4 is a continuation of the session with the same client:

Extract 4

1   C: We stayed married, he is living with me and he has another family >and he

2   is happy with that< (2.0) he thought everything would be so:lved by having

3   only more <u>children</u> and he became frustrated but
4   T: // Does he <u>father</u> those children?
5   C: <u>Yes</u>! He is very responsible. >He is an excellent father< and he is tender and
6   he could never aba:ndon them, <u>no</u>, I wouldn't allow it.
7→   T: What's it like for <u>you</u> though, to have him commi:tted to that other woman?
8   C: I know her (.) she is not educated at <u>all</u>, >only a few years of school.< They live
9   in very low standard but he is <u>very</u> responsible.=
10   T: =Does he pay the rent?=
11   C: =<u>Yes</u>, e:verything, they are dependent on him
12   T: // °But he keeps them lower class°=
13   C: =Yes, (.) so I can manage this (.) I have to say I find it just that they are <u>not</u> at the
14   same level (2.0). Nevertheless, I, I have a very <u>good</u> relationship with the
15   children.They come to our <u>home</u> we make <u>excursions</u>, (.) we go to lunch together
16   on Saturday and last month
17→T: // And in your heart? You were <u>talking</u> about your
18   behavior. <What's your heart like being with these children?>
19   C: I'm ve::ry hurt, I can manage, I can take <u>many</u> things and my intelligence says
20   it's the best thing that you can do, (2.0) °but my heart is not in this project,°
21   <u>not</u> when I'm with the children, I like them.

In lines 1–3 and 5–6 the client refers to her specific marital situation where her husband is involved with another woman and takes care of their two children. She does not however, make a reference to how she feels about this (presumably uncomfortable) situation. Instead she focuses on the intellectual, i.e., how both she and her husband accommodated to the circumstances. While it might be assumed that in the psychotherapeutic setting, clients would find it easier (than in other everyday contexts) to fall into openly expressing their painful experiences and crushing disappointments, it follows from the data that the 'feelings-talk' needs in fact to be actively facilitated by the therapist. This is to say that often the therapist must rely on the client's prior talk as occasioning a question about feelings. Accordingly, in line 7, the therapist attempts to refocus the client's account by taking up the issue of the client's emotional attitude to her husband's unfaithfulness. This highly emotionally charged question, although direct, fails to elicit any genuine 'feelings-talk'. If any emotion is present here, it would seem to be pride that the errant husband is 'very responsible' (lines 5 and 9). Interestingly, the therapist's question in line 10 creates further space for the client to continue her disclosure of her adjustment to the unfortunate circumstances (lines 11, 13–16). The therapist's interruption in line 12 does not manage to re-orient the client's account to a more emotionally-oriented one. In lines 13–16, the client continues presenting her personal situation devoid of an emotional stance. A three-part list (line 15; cf. Potter 1996) can be observed in her account which symbolically refers to the typicality of the referred to situation. The client's account gets interrupted by the therapist in line 17. The interruption aims at re-orienting the client's story into a more emotionally-oriented one. This time the therapist manages to elicit from the client how she actually feels about the untoward situation. The client immediately responds to therapist's direct query by distinguishing between her emotional attitude and the 'intellectual' adjustment (lines 19–21).

Extract 5 opens with the therapist's question concerning the near-fatal accident that the female client experienced when she was a young girl:

Extract 5

1	T:	°How were you saved?°
2	C:	<u>She</u> jumped in, two men jumped in, someone a:ll the way to the bottom (.) it
3		was very deep, cliff-like, >cliff, no shore< just (.) and according to <u>her</u> they
4		were able to find me and get me up and one guy was a fireman, .hhh he
5		revived me.
6→	T:	Were you <u>angry</u> that you didn't know this a lo:ng time.
7	C:	(.) Well, it's like I ↑knew it but I didn't >you know< I just had this
8		information, you know, ((your mother tried to drown you, your mother
9		tried to drown you IRONY)), OK, like why are you <u>telling</u> me that?
10→	T:	<Now> it sounds like you're angry at your father?=
11	C:	=Yeah, why are you <u>telling</u> me that? What is the pu:rpose of telling me that?

In lines 2–5 the client describes how she managed to survive the terrible accident. In the previous session however, the therapist found out that her mother did not rush to save her daughter and as a result the client nearly drowned. The fact-oriented account offered by the client is responded to by the therapist with a question (line 6) re-orienting her account into a more emotionally-oriented one. The therapist attempts to topicalize how the client feels about knowing that her mother did not help her. This is clearly a threatening topical re-orientation. The emotional burden of the question is indicated by the hedged onset of the client's response (line 7). In the second part of the response (lines 8–9) the client relies on irony in order to verbalize the shocking information ('your mother tries to drown you'). The therapist continues with attempting to elicit more feelings-talk from the client in line 10. The attempt begins with a marker 'now' indicating a slight re-orientation of the therapist's questioning. The question's mitigated character is also accomplished by the phrase 'sounds like'. The client orients to this question by providing an agreement to it and expressing her thoughts on it (line 11).

In Extract 6 (lines 1–2) the therapist attempts to topicalize the client's feelings about not being appreciated by others in her life:

Extract 6

```
1→T:    So what's it like for you going through life with so many people
2       not appreciating your pro:cess?
3   C:  It's kind of (.) why.
4→T:    <Can you describe what's that like?>
5   C:  (2.0) Well, that I was sort of the ↑oddball and
6→T:                                     // And oddball which
7       celebrated?=
8   C   =Oh, no!
9→T:    °Sometimes being the oddball is a good thing.°
10  C:  Yes, that's true, sometimes it has been (.) maybe in college
11      sometimes, but, well (.) the o:ddball, >is the one you focus
12      on< and kind of beat up and in a way attempt to get it to stop.
13  T:  So in you:r case the oddness of ball is not appreciated?=
14  C:  =Oh, NO! No, no, it still isn't!
```

The therapist's initial question does not receive feelings-oriented response (line 3) but rather an incoherent response where the function of the questioning 'why' can not be specified. Consequently, the therapist rephrases his initial question (line 4) again attempting to focus the client's account on her feelings towards the situation. In her slightly delayed response (a 2 second pause), the client labels the perception of hers by others. The therapist's interruption in line 6 and his statement in line 9 attempt to pursue another (related) aspect of the client's experience. The statement manages to elicit from the client more feelings-oriented account of being perceived an 'oddball'.

To sum up, the therapist's topicalizing or giving priority to 'feelings-talk', albeit met with mixed success (Extracts 3, 4, 6), gradually socializes clients into one of the common practices of psychotherapy, i.e., recognition of a client's *real* emotions and feelings. By topicalizing 'feelings-talk' the therapist draws attention to the client's feelings and this in turn quite often triggers an emotional response (Extracts 1, 2, 5; cf. also Davis 1986). The ability to talk about one's emotions, both positive and negative ones is a very important step towards accomplishing a qualitative change in life.

4.4.2 Constructing a client's less socially-acceptable emotions

Psychotherapy aims at removing the client's suffering resulting from his/her negative emotional states and from the inability to influence his/her own life. It is a process in which the techniques used by the psychotherapist enable the client to regain an understanding of his/her emotions and sometimes even freedom from them. This in turn lets the client realize the causes of his/her ineffective behavior and consequently take control of his/her life (Czabała 2006).

This section features excerpts of the psychotherapist's interactions with the mother of a terminally-ill young woman. Facing the harrowing reality of an inevitable future, the client experiences pain and suffering on a daily basis. The sadness and despair she brings to the therapy room over the illness of her daughter are well recognized and acknowledged by her. What remains left untackled by the client in the interaction with the psychotherapist are *her* negative emotional states very much linked to bearing with her daughter's changeable moods and volatile acting. In the extracts below, the client is constructing her suffering and emotions connected with the tragic situation while the psychotherapist manages what aspects of her pain and suffering should surface, and thus be talked about during the session.

In Extract 7 she expands on the cheerful personality of her daughter even in the face of the tragedy:

Extract 7

```
1    C:   …and even in those dreadful moments (.) we've laughed after night's drain.
2→  T:   <What's it like for you when you hear her laughter?>
3    C:   For a few minutes while the laughter is being laughed (.) when the laughter is
4         happening, it feels as if everything was normal.=
5    T:   =Normal.
6    C:   Just for a few minutes.
7    T:   And when she was little (.) did she la::ugh?=
8    C:   =Everybody said when X is around everybody feels better.
9→  T:   Did that include you?
10   C:   Yeah.
11→ T:   So:: this is a child whose laughter contributed to your feeling be::tter.=
12   C:   =And when I said she was born to make o::ther people feel better it
13        sounds like a terrible burden for a child but it was never hard work for
14        her (.) it was so spontaneous, so
15→ T:                              // Was that ever a requirement of yours?
```

16   C: Umm (1.0) I don't think I <u>needed</u> her to be like that and umm sometimes (.)
17   the other side of her is that giving so:: <u>much</u> in her relationships is that she
18   has been and often is extre::mely demanding wanting >more and more and more.<

Throughout the session the client extensively focuses on her daughter, elaborating on how both of them are (effectively) coping with the difficult situation. She is looking for opportunities to share the precious, fleeting moments of her daughter's life. This is the purpose of her therapy session that she has explicitly expressed. Yet, as the client's story evinces, *her* sense of existence, her agency has been set aside during this difficult time of her daughter's illness, and the psychotherapist is attempting to retrieve it by refocusing the client's narrative on her emotional states. This very much echoes one of psychotherapy's precepts, assuming that even though emotional arousal is already very much experienced by the client in the session, the hidden negative experiences and (negative) feelings connected with them need to be voiced.

The psychotherapist's question in line 2 aims at re-orienting the client's account from the narrative about coping with the situation by the client and her daughter (line 1) to the client's emotions only. She is prompted to reflect on her feelings accompanying her daughter's laughter. In line 8, however, she drops the individual emotional focus initiated by the therapist. This gets repaired by the therapist in line 9 yet still fails to elicit any emotional talk from the client as it receives only minor acknowledgement (line 10). The psychotherapist continues focusing his contributions on the client's emotional state by summarizing her previous thought and again concentrating on the client herself (line 11). It is noteworthy how she rejects this re-orientation by providing in her turn a seeming continuation of the therapist's comment, starting her contribution with the conjunction 'and', (line 12–14) linking it syntactically with the therapist's turn. What makes an appearance of a single turn co-constructed by two interlocutors is also the fact that the client's turn is latched onto the therapist's.[98] The client continuously staves off the therapist's attempts to reflect on *her* emotions solely concerning the situation and focuses instead on her daughter and other people's emotions.

The therapist's attempt in line 15 to elicit from her more individually-oriented emotional talk (finally) succeeds as the client begins to talk about the negative feelings concerning her daughter's personality (lines 16–18). This attempt takes the interactional form of interruption as the therapist cuts the client off in the middle of her account not letting her continue with the story. This interactional move evinces that the therapist considers it more therapeutically relevant for the client to put herself as the main character of her story. The shift, away from the focus on the emotions connected with the client's daughter's terminal illness to the concentration on the emotional experience of the client alone, gradually begins to elicit the client's (hidden) negative feelings. The psychotherapist's perseverance in refocusing the course of the interaction on the client's *I* constitutes a chance for this mother to voice all of her emotions, including uncomfortable ones linked to taking care of the terminally-ill daughter.

In Extract 8 the client continues sharing her private story of suffering with the therapist:

Extract 8[99]

```
1   C:   Well, (1.0) when we're in a really difficult phase and I >wanna< say to
2        her 'Is there anything else I can do? Can I do something to make it
3        more bearable?', she says: no::, just stop, just carry on being, you know (2.0).
4→T:     What happens inside of you when she says it?=
5   C:   =>I want to be worth it< my head knows this, my head knows I can't take
6        the pain, the humiliation, the depreciation that she is going through, which
7        I WANT TO, I WANT TO, you know, I (0.5) can't.
```

Lines 1–3 show how the client, despite the therapist's numerous attempts, is not able to solely focus on *her* feelings and emotions only. In reflecting on harrowing experiences, her account tends to feature her daughter as well. Painful as the situation is, the therapist wants the client to remember about her as a whole person who has, even in view of such a tragedy, every right to (especially in the context of the psychotherapy session) focus her narrative on herself and her emotions, even those aspects which might appear socially less acceptable. Line 4 features such an attempt to re-orient the client's account to her emotions. The therapist's 'what happens inside of you when she says it' creates interactional space for the client to respond to it with the preferred action of providing details of the *real* emotional state. In lines 5–7 she reiterates the emotional hopelessness of the situation: the enormous extent to which she longs, in vain, to help her daughter bear the pain.

In Extract 9, the psychotherapist is attempting to anchor this part of the interaction around the theme of her daughter being *demanding*, which the client has previously pointed out:

Extract 9

```
1   C:   ...some day it makes her sad (.) the other she says she is gla:d the puppy
2        is independent.
3→  T:   <You said earlier that she was demanding.>
4   C:   Yes.
5→  T:   Will you tell me about that?=
6   C:   =Yes, yes (.) I used to pick up the courage to go and pick her up from nursery
7        ↑school because the minute we got out she would be 'can we do this, can we
8        go there' and then we would do this after that, and it was all (.) you know,
9        >keep going, keep going, keep going.<
10→ T:   There must have been times when you really wished she had stopped that.
```

Constructing the interaction around the theme of 'demanding' could potentially elicit from the client some negative feelings concerning the duties of taking care of her ill daughter. Needless to say, in face of genuine tragedy such emotions are extremely difficult to voice. Yet they do exist and they are real. Consequently, they need to be addressed in the process of psychotherapy, which is grounded on recognizing and coming to awareness of one's emotions, even the most socially unacceptable. The therapist's reference to the client's daughter being demanding receives only a minor acknowledgement (line 4) without the client's further pursuit of it. The therapist however, presses the client to expand on it (line 5). The offered account is not focused on the client's emotions linked to her daughter's demanding character but rather on how the client coped with it. Line 10 illustrates how the therapist's strategy to elicit more emotion-focused response failed. The therapist's turn in line 10 attempts to re-orient the client's account into an emotionally-oriented one that underlines her agency. This type of eliciting strategy conveys a sense of certainty ('there must have been') difficult for an interlocutor to reject.

Far from merely acting as an empathic observer, the psychotherapist, in interacting with the client, attempts to significantly shape and control what emotions the client reveals via strategic prompts. In this way the psychotherapist's active interactional involvement enables the client to verbalize emotions which do not always conform to societal expectations. Here she testifies to her inner emotions as if addressing her daughter directly:

Extract 10[100]

1	C:	You know (.) I always hate to make an appointment to see <u>you</u>. >Do you
2		remember the barbecue you cooked for me last week?< you set it on a wooden
3		table in the garden and the table caught fire and we had to throw our wine
4		over it quickly. In <u>fact</u> I didn't think it was a particularly goo::d
5		coming home barbecue 'cause there weren't any sausages.=
6→	T:	=Yeah, <now> (.) let her see what other resentments you have (.) because
7		you've been telling her all the <u>good</u> stuff, let's exa::mine the <u>resentments</u>
8		and the <u>anger</u>.
9	C:	Oh, X, °just shut up for five minutes°, with X I sometimes had tough days too.=
10→	T:	=And you failed ↑to=
11	C:	=And you don't always <u>realize</u> that you said 'don't tell me anything about
12		them', I ca:n't cope with anything more (.) then I feel angry and I want to say
13		'and all I do for you and you just can't listen to me for five minutes'.=
14→	T:	=And the real message to you ↑is=
15	C:	=The <u>real</u> message is I want you to si:t in front of me and <u>listen</u>.
16→	T:	>Keep going,< tell her what o:ther things you don't like.
17	C:	Sometimes I don't like the way you're going up with Dad, °seems to be at my
18		expense sometimes,° I fee:l hurt and he joins in with his jokes about me and I say to
19		you 'I feel <u>hurt</u> X' and you say >'Oh, that's just Dad, Mummy, you should know him
20		by now, you've been with him long enough.'< Why do you <u>always</u> take his side?=
21	T:	=Make that a statement.
22	C:	I don't want you to take his side (.) sometimes I want you to be on mi:ne, umm, what
23		else do I get pissed off at? (1.0) pet spills.=
24→	T:	=<u>Yeah</u>, tell <u>her</u> about that tone in your voice!
25	C:	Well, it's <u>your</u> pet, I know I bought it for you but it's your pet
26→	T:	// And I don't ↑like
27	C:	But I don't like being called up every five minutes to take the dog to the next vet's
28		appointment and then I have to foot the bill as well (.) Sometimes, sometimes I feel
29		like you take advantage of me, you know that I'll <u>always</u> be there and sometimes
30		you just go to the edge.=
31→	T:	=And these last weeks of your life I don't ↑want=
32	C:	=Any of that happen.=
33→	T:	=Then name it, I don't ↑want

Extract 10 depicts a continuation of the session with the same client, yet at this stage of the interaction, the therapist's persistent interactional work results in the client's being less timid about verbalizing her negative emotions accompanying taking care of her ill daughter. The context of psychotherapy facilitates the client's awareness of her *real* emotional states which, up to this point, have been significantly stifled. The authentic emotions are often quite contrary to what the dominant discourses of society bolster and perpetuate. For instance, the dominant discourses of femininity and motherhood in particular, do not allow for any kind of negative feelings towards children (cf. Coates 1997).[101] Thus a mother referring to her children negatively is perceived as breaking the expectations/standards of a 'good mother'. In the interaction under analysis, the client positions herself as mother of a terminally-ill daughter who devotes herself (also emotionally) to her child regardless of how her daughter may act toward her. Such positioning aligned with the dominant discourses of motherhood rejects any negative attitude towards the child. In the context of psychotherapeutic interaction these dominant discourses can be challenged and/or subverted.

The facilitation of the client's emotional expression is fuelled by the therapist's involvement as well as by his interactional strategies. In lines 1–5 she is much engaged in voicing some of her resentments concerning her ill daughter's behavior toward her. This represents a remarkable progression from the early stages of the session when the client thwarted almost any of the therapist's attempts to re-focus her account on herself and her emotional states. Interestingly, in all of her turns in Extract 10, at the behest of the therapist, the client addresses her daughter directly with her painful emotions while the therapist facilitates the dialogue.[102] The address in lines 1–5 is quite relaxed and even humorous towards the end. Therapist latches his prompt in lines 6–8 prodding the client to continue with voicing her negative feelings, e.g., her anger. A noteworthy point is that the therapist relies on the inclusive form 'let's' thus underlining his presence and also assistance in the client's expression of the negative emotions. In line 10 the therapist offers the client a prompt directly addressing the client's daughter that could either be repeated by the client and in her turn completed with the information, or just completed by the client, in this way forming a co-constructed turn by both interactants. It needs to be underlined that the therapist's prompt in line 10 constitutes a very strong assertion ('you have failed to'). The client continues with presenting her negative feelings but the prompt gets mitigated in line 11 into 'and you don't always'. The client, supported by the psychotherapist, talks about feeling hurt and ridiculed. In lines 27–30 she expresses her anger at being somehow obliged to tend her daughter's puppy dog. The therapist (line 24) draws attention to an aspect of prosody ('tell her about that tone in your voice') and uses it as a prompt for the client to voice her annoyance. The therapist remains very much in control of the interaction; e.g., in line 26 he attempts to re-direct the course of the client's emotional expression into a new aspect of her negative emotions. This is interactionally realized by the therapist's interruption 'and I don't like' with rising intonation indicating the incomplete status of the information unit. She opens her response to it with the therapist's 'don't like' followed by her resentments. The second part of the response (lines 28–30) constitutes a very explicit expression of being mistreated by her daughter. This expression is hedged with the adverb 'sometimes' (used twice). It seems that such a hedging makes it easier for the client to express her negative emotions. In line 31 the therapist orients the interaction to a very difficult point for the client as she is prompted to talk about what she would like the last weeks of her daughter's life to be like in terms of the quality of their relationship. The therapist's turn in line 31 forms a syntactically complete unit with the client's previous turn and in this way makes it easier for the client to complete the prompt (line 32). Thus lines 27–32 could form one turn as they constitute a complete syntactic and information unit.

The psychotherapist's interactional work promoting the client's agency by focusing on her real emotions enabled the client to give voice to the feelings that have been up to now stifled and kept hidden. As a mother of a terminally-ill daughter she instantly shares with the therapist her recognized (and socially acceptable) emotions of sorrow and despair linked with the condition of her daughter for which the therapist offers his support.

More importantly, however, in the psychotherapeutic interaction there is ample clinical and interactional space for her (or any other client's) negative emotions which clients tend not to reveal but nevertheless possess. It is the psychotherapist's task to help the client voice them. These negative emotions also constitute an aspect of the client's suffering and need to be expressed. It needs to be underlined that the therapist's focus on the client's agency in expressing her emotions as well as facilitating the client's negative emotions aims at retrieving this woman as a whole person. This is to say that in the struggle with her daughter's illness she has lost other aspects of her identity, besides being a mother. Psychotherapeutic work makes it possible to regain these lost aspects of self by emotional expression of both positive and negative feelings.

In the words of Greenberg (2004b), the client needs to *arrive* at her (hidden) negative emotions first in order to *leave* them for the benefit of her psychological well-being. Czabała (2006) states that by revealing to the therapist the negative feeling towards certain significant others, the client experiences neither rejection, condemnation, nor censure. Perhaps these negative emotions were kept well hidden precisely to avoid societal disapprobation for deviating from an established norm.

4.4.3 Non-verbal communication of emotion: Aspects of 'silence' and 'crying'

Among the various aspects of non-verbal communication, silence and crying appear to function as the most significant means through which clients are able to manifest and/or voice their emotional states and/or release them. Although such aspects of non-verbal communication as *silence* and *crying* that occur in the interaction between the psychotherapist and client might lend themselves best as manifestations of the client's inner states,[103] the discussion to follow will consider them from an interactional perspective, as features of social interaction (cf. Whalen and Zimmerman 1998). Discursive psychologists have evinced that displays of emotion can accompany particular activities, e.g., managing issues of blame and responsibility (cf. Hepburn 2004; Buttny 1993; Edwards 1997, 1999). Thus avowals of emotion do not need to project the speaker's underlying emotional state but may be involved in different activities (Hepburn 2004). The current discussion will then concentrate not on *silence* and *crying* as interactionally facilitated and invoked by the therapist, but rather will attempt to describe at what moments of psychotherapeutic interaction they transpire. The question will also be addressed what function they perform in this specific setting. Unlike the previous discussion, the focus here will be placed on the client and his/her display of emotion manifesting itself by silence and/or crying.

Under less control than the verbal messages, non-verbal signals tend to be more representative of true affect and attitudes (Philippot, Feldman, and Coates 2003; cf. also Argyle et al. 1970; Richmond and McCroskey 2000) and non-verbal behavior is a constitutive part of the emotional response.

Silence – indispensable for successful communication in certain everyday contexts (cf. Jaworski 1993) – emerges as an accepted and expected part of therapist-client interaction. Jaworski (1993) asserts that silence requires the active involvement of the participants as well as a lot of filling in of information in order to be understood and adequately interpreted. Different forms of pauses transpire regularly in speech, playing a number of functions, such as cognitive, discoursal and stylistic. Silence is an established technique in psychotherapy (cf. Cook 1964) even though the 'talking cure' association might imply its irrelevance or even rejection. Levitt (2001) states that what distinguishes psychotherapy from an ordinary conversation is that while in the first context sustained pauses are rare, frequently indicating discomfort, in psychotherapy shared silence is an expected aspect of interaction.[104] Trad (1993) presents the 3 most significant purposes of using silence in the context of psychotherapy: to share interpersonal experience, the client's use of silence in order to promote self-revelation, and the use of silence by both parties involved as a means for self-reflection.

Scholars investigating aspects of silence in the context of psychotherapy session have relied predominantly on the content-based analysis eliciting retrospective comments either from therapists or clients about the role and use of silence in their own interactions (cf. Ladany et al. 2004; Levitt 2002). As Hill and associates (2003: 514) assert, "the data might reflect general attitudes towards using silence rather than the actual behavior in specific situations". In other words, silence as a significant communicative resource in psychotherapy has not been examined from more discourse-analytic or interactional perspective. Nevertheless, these studies have generated certain important conclusions.

Hill, Thompson, and Ladany (2003) looked into therapists' reliance on silence during a psychotherapy session. The conducted survey revealed that therapists used silence first and foremost to facilitate reflection, encourage responsibility, promote expression of feelings, avoid interrupting session flow, as well as promote empathy.[105] Additionally, therapists pointed to experiencing silence during therapy as enhancing the therapeutic alliance. The study also reported that during the silent periods, psychotherapists tend to observe clients, contemplate therapy, as well as convey interest. The authors conclude that this indicates that these silences can be regarded as 'pregnant' rather than 'empty' (Hill, Thompson, and Ladany 2003: 521).

Levitt (2002) on the other hand, examined clients' experiences of silence in psychotherapy by means of interpersonal process recall (IPR).[106] The clients identified obstructive pauses, facilitative pauses as well as neutral ones. The study focused on the obstructive silence, i.e., moments in which clients diverge from the process of therapeutic inquiry, as these are related to interpreting silence in psychotherapy as aspects of a client's resistance or regression. The category of obstructive silence was further subdivided into disengaged pauses and interactional pauses. Clients referred to availing themselves on disengaged pauses when they wanted to avoid painful emotion or when they felt withdrawn from the interaction itself. As Levitt (2002: 231) states, "clients often reported feeling uncomfortable with the topic at hand and would either pause to find a way to halt the exploration or to shut themselves down emotionally". These pauses transpired when clients were moving in their accounts towards anxious content. Interactional pauses, on the other hand refer to the moments in which "the client's focus shifted from the therapeutic discourse to either the therapist or the therapist-client interaction" (Levitt 2002: 234). The clients accounted for the interactional pauses in terms of the demands of interpersonal communication, the safeguarding of the relationship with the therapist as well as confusion about therapist comment or activity.

Moments of silence in the following extracts are represented with timed pauses. In Extract 11, the client is talking about her inability to ask for affection in her life, dating back to the period of childhood:

Extract 11

```
1    T:   The baby needs the attention mo:re than you do now.
2    C:   I don't have any memories (.) any, of my parents telling me that.=
3    T:   =Mhm.
4    C:   I think when I was Y years old >I was already telling this to myself<
5         without anybody telling me
6    T:                              // Yes, a lot of those things are self-generated,
7         they don't come from parents, kids figure them out themselves.
8→   C:   That's right, (5.0), what came to my mind was what you said ye:sterday
9         >that< being all alone >sort of fits with that<, or it's kind of 'why ask?' because
10        I'm alone anyway (.) or something like that. I ask because I'm alone and
11        other people are more needy, >I mean< I can make the whole combination
12        of arguments 'why not ask?'
13   T:   <If there is a guarantee> that you will receive absolute, one hundred percent
14        guarantee, then (.) would you ask?
15   C:   No, probably I would be afra:id because it's not just the asking (1.0) it's
16        what would I get? >I mean< what's the quality of what I get, that would
17        be the next question (.) and also the next stage of saying: well, I might get
18        something but is this what I want? It would be more confusing.=
19   T:   =So you might get something that is not the quality that you ↑want
20   C:   Mhm, this is exactly what happened when I was thinking about wanting to be
21        held (.) yes, to be held, but (.) but in a way it's a very big source of confusion
22        for me (.) because I'd like to be held and rea:lly be able just once not be
23        responsible for acting this way.
24→  T:   I see tears in your eyes.
25→  C:   Mhm, (9.0), there is a lot of sadness (2.0) but there is also some conflict. I'm
26        touching the place where I wish I hadn't, I don't know how to say that,
27        wanting to give awa:y the responsibility for being held and >at the same time<
28        I know this is not possible and I want to be responsible for what happens to
29        me (.) it's like touching something in a very cautious way.=
30   T:   =Like a child needs the other person to initiate with enthusiasm.
31   C:   Yeah.
32   T:   A sense of vitality in reaching out to you.
33   C:   Yeah.
```

The therapist's interactional position in lines 1, 3, 6, and 7 remains facilitative as his comments convey to the client a sense of being actively listened to (line 3) and a sense of validation (lines 6–7). The first significant pause (5.0) in the client's turn takes place in line 8. The pause precedes the client's intimate revelation. This is to say that what follows the pause is the client's disclosure of some truth about herself. Interestingly, the client's disclosure contains a number of hedges (e.g., 'sort of', 'kind of') which index the highly emotional aspect of the proffered material. A noteworthy point is that the client immediately orients to the therapist's comment in lines 6 and 7 ('that's right') yet introduces a moment of silence before elaborating on the agreement. Thus it can be claimed that the client has the knowledge of how to elaborate on her immediate agreement (this constitutes her A-event knowledge) and the pause signifies that what follows constitutes highly emotional disclosure. Another important moment in the interaction takes place in line 19 when the therapist offers a (re)formulation which the client extensively documents (preferred action) with further intimate revelation. This particular disclosure is responded to by the therapist with a comment (line 24) which underlines his interactional presence as well as attentive listening. This remark additionally emotionally enhances the already quite expressive stretch of the interaction. Again the client orients to the remark by acknowledging it. This acknowledgment is, however, followed by a long pause (9.0), after which the client embarks on elaborating on her doubts, expectations, and uncertainties regarding her innermost feelings (lines 25–29). Thus, the two pauses used by the client appear immediately prior to her revealing highly intimate personal material. As far as their interactional function is concerned, they index the client's ensuing statements as emotionally marked.

In the next extract the client is attempting to inform the therapist about the event she would like to devote the session to:

Extract 12

1	C:	There <u>might</u> be a block because I can find time for other things but not writing.
2		But <u>actually</u> I want to speak today about myself (.) to finish the thing which I
3		haven't been able to finish properly yet.=
4	T:	=What is that thing?
5→	C:	Umm (7.0), it's uh, uh, I was abu:sed as a child and I don't really want to (4.0),
6→		in one way I'm not accepting it <u>totally</u> yet and (3.0) because I can't understand
7		why (.) that it happened. So I have done a <u>lot of</u> work with it but I feel I
8		haven't finished it because still, what ha:ppened was that I got a lot of anxiety

9		and I couldn't handle it so I was escaping it. But I <u>do</u> know that I haven't
10		finished it properly (.) but I <u>really</u> want to do that.
11	T:	Now, can you feel what your spine is doing and what your left shoulder is
12		doing?=
13	C:	=For the moment?=
14	T:	=While we were talking.

In lines 1–3 the client points in a very indirect way to an issue that she would like to work on with the therapist. Since the speech event of psychotherapy is premised on the principle of transparency of meaning, the therapist (line 4) is attempting to elicit from the client what constitutes the problem, i.e., define the general 'thing' in terms of the client's personal experience. In her extensive turn (lines 5–10), the client is referring to the traumatic situation she has experienced. In line 5, the revelation of a dysphoric situation (sexual abuse in the family) is hedged with 'Umm' and preceded by a lengthy pause (7.0), and an interjection of hesitancy (the patterned disfluency 'uh, uh') at the outset of the disclosure. In lines 5 and 6 other pauses (4.0 and 3.0) function as pre-disclosure markers. The pauses embedded in this stretch of talk (a single turn) interactionally mark a highly emotional aspect of the client's experience to be revealed.

In the extract that follows, the therapist's first two turns address the client's experience:

Extract 13

1	T:	You know a <u>lot</u> about giving up, <don't you?>
2	C:	Yes.=
3	T:	=You're an <u>expert</u> at that (.) or have been.
4	C:	Ye:s, but at the same <u>time</u> I am <u>always</u> fighting but I haven't been fighting in
5		this area. I've been fighting in the wrong way, >I heard that angry cats are
6→		getting scratches< you know, a:nd (5.0) I think I have been driving people
7		<u>away</u> from me (.) because of my anger.
8	T:	I haven't seen <u>any</u> of that today and I'm usually pretty <u>sensitive</u> to the anger
9		that sort of leaks out (.) I haven't seen you do that today.=
10	C:	=No: I think that I'm much calmer today than I've ever bee:n but when I'm
11		talking to you there is <u>still</u> some anger left.

Highly intimate, i.e., emotional experience requires some interactional work to be performed before it gets revealed. Thus, in his turn (lines 4–7), the client is beginning to relate to his 'fighting' personality. Towards the end of the turn, approaching the most salient revelation ('driving people away'), the client makes a pause (5.0) which functions as a pre-disclosure marker. Additionally, the discourse marker 'you know' (line 6) and the evidentiality marker 'I think' function as hedges, seeking support from the therapist and mitigating the upcoming revelation.

The three extracts discussed above (11, 12, 13) demonstrate that typically in the psychotherapeutic discourse (lengthy) pauses tend to precede a client's revelation of highly intimate personal material. Consequently, it can be claimed that they interactionally index therapeutically relevant material to be disclosed by the client. Such silences cannot be interpreted then as aspects of clients' resistance (as the bulk of psychological literature seems to claim; cf. Levitt 2002) but rather as significant interactional strategies. Additionally, their communicative status manifests itself with the therapist's non-orientation to them, which is to say that in these moments of silence the client is in no way prompted by the therapist to return to his/her self-expression. To rephrase Sabbadini (1991) – who says that silence is a space for words that cannot be spoken – silences in the context of psychotherapy communicate that significant, intimate material of high emotional significance is about to be spoken.

Psychological research has typically investigated crying by way of self-report questionnaires[107] (cf. Hepburn 2004). Crying has not been researched from a more interactional perspective that could reveal the actual interactional work crying does or activities in which it is embedded across numerous social contexts. The context of the psychotherapy session is one of the few social settings in which client's crying is not negatively approached or commented on in a way that would make clients promptly cease it. Quite the contrary, crying – in the case of some clients – constitutes an important, healing element of the psychotherapeutic process. Nelson (2005), on the basis of attachment theory, looks into crying not as a means to release emotion but rather as an aspect of connection. This is to say that once conceptualized as emotional connection rather than emotional release, crying can be better understood. Thus crying emerges here as a relationship behavior. Let us analyze the following extract:

Extract 14

1→ C: <u>Yeah</u>, it's hard time, ((it's what I know. You need to help me make my
2   decision. CRYING))
3   T: <I am helping you right now.>
4   C: <u>Yes</u>, yes, you are. You said that you <u>know</u> what I want.

5   T: If I told you what to <u>do</u>

6   C: // I don't want you to tell [me what to do.]

7   T: [you'd be happy.]

8   C: I <u>don't</u> want you to tell me what to do.

9   T: Ok, so we know it (.) If I don't tell you, you will do it a:ll <u>alone</u>.

10   C: >Well< I'm su:re I don't wanna be next year in the same place!=

11→T: =But this is <u>not</u> the same place (.) last year it was >this woman and this

12   woman< now you decide that it's this woman, now what am I gonna ↓do,

13   I am with an infertile woman.

14→C: >That's where I'm at,< after I told X that I was staying with ((Y, she went

15   and got herself pregnant and then had an abortion. CRYING))

16→T: °Tell me about your tears.°

17   C: That could have been <u>my</u> child and he:rs.=

18   T: =And is she a woman you'd want to grow old with and raise this child together?

19   C: <u>Yeah</u>, we could do that.

20   T: But I take it that the purpose of the <u>marriage</u> would be to bring up the child.

21   C: I want to doubt it that it would be as brutal as that.=

22   T: =Ok.

The client shares with the therapist his need and wish to become a father even in view of (obvious) difficulties. In lines 1–2 the client is conveying to the therapist his request to help him take a decision. The last part of the utterance in his turn is embedded in crying. The interaction continues with the client and therapist who remains involved in attempting to present his opinion on the client's issue. In lines 11–13 the therapist is confronting the client with his wish of being a father yet being in a relationship with an infertile woman. The client orients to this utterance by acknowledging the fact and follows with referring to the traumatic situation. The last part of the disclosure in lines 14–15 is embedded in crying. Although it can be speculated that crying in these two turns could project the client's underlying psychological state, one of despair and devastation, this remains highly provisional. From a more interactional perspective the first instance of crying is embedded in informing the therapist to help the client make a decision. It is worth considering how the social meaning of this utterance would differ once crying is removed. In other words, this move can help to interpret the role of crying. It seems then that crying enhances the non-propositional aspect of the utterance, i.e., it appeals for the therapist's understanding and empathy. Thus it upgrades the emotional aspect of the utterance. Crying embedded in the client's utterance in lines 14–15 appears to call for the therapist's understanding and sympathy and/or empathy for the client's situation. Thus both instances of crying add to the emotional load of the clause in which they are embedded. It is interesting to notice how in the psychotherapeutic interaction, unlike in other social contexts, the client's tears (cf. line 16) are topicalized. In this way both therapist and client are able to access the emotional aspect of the experience. In response to the therapist's request in line 16, the client gives voice to his sorrow and misery which, as emerges, his crying has indexed.

Both silence and crying function as significant features of therapeutic interaction. Silence tends to precede salient intimate material to be revealed by the client while crying tends to be embedded in clients' utterances of significant importance for them. Both, then, occur in moments of enhanced emotionality during a psychotherapeutic interaction. These two interactional features, however, receive different interactional handling from the therapist. While silence tends not to be topicalized by the therapist, crying often occasions talk about a client's feelings.

4.5 Concluding remarks

The all-encompassing term 'communication of emotion' as applied to the context of the psychotherapy session refers to a multitude of ways in which the client's *real* emotional experience becomes the focus of the therapist's work. This focus manifests itself in the therapist's strategies aiming at: giving priority to 'feelings-talk' and enabling the client to voice his/her less socially acceptable emotions and attitudes. The conducted analysis also addressed the moments of silence and crying in the client's talk as interactionally marking moments of emotional salience in the client's. What needs to be underlined is that – with the exception of moments of silence and crying – the client's focus on his/her emotional experience constitutes the effect of interactional work involving both parties. This is to say that the therapist's communicative and interactional strategies aim at facilitating the client's (ideally unrestrained) expression of emotion. Rarely do clients entering a psychotherapy room spontaneously embark on an in-depth verbalization of their most painful emotions. Even though the communicative context of the psychotherapy session encourages just such uninhibited expression, it tends to require extensive co-creation by both involved parties.

How, then, is communicating emotions therapeutic? Or, in other words, how do the discussed strategies function therapeutically? *Therapeutic* refers here to recognizing one's *real* emotions in reference to therapeutically relevant situations and/or circumstances. This is to say that a part of the therapist's interactional work is devoted to attempts to re-focus the client's account onto his/her personal true feelings and actual opinions, beyond the constraints of social approbation. Such avowal enables the client to retrieve his/her lost agency and becomes truly curative. 'Feelings-talk', i.e., prioritizing discussion about the client's emotions accompanying a certain situation rather than carrying on (by the client) with his/her adapting to this situation makes it possible for the client to recognize the *real* feelings of hurt and disappointment behind seemingly perfect social adjustment. This strategy enables the client to (finally) bring his/her needs into the foreground where they can be addressed. Such dramatic re-focusing of the clients' accounts on their *real* emotions can only be successful once it takes place in the therapeutic alliance. Finally, moments of silence and crying, embedded in the clients' talk help to interactionally manage moments of emotional salience in the clients' disclosures.

Communication of emotion is the third norm, which along with the transparency of meaning and self-disclosure is essential for a social interaction to be considered a psychotherapy session. This is to say that a successful psychotherapy session should be anchored in these norms. These norms, as the discussion has evinced, are indexed by specific verbal and non-verbal strategies whose therapeutic function (i.e., prodding the client to self-disclose, to focus on his/her emotional state, and to explore the significance of the proffered expression(s)) is brought off in the local interactional context by the interacting parties. This follows the premise that the relation between language/strategy and its (therapeutic) function is not a simple straightforward mapping of linguistic form to function. Rather it is constituted and mediated by the relation of language to stances, social acts and other social constructs (cf. Ochs 1992).

The therapist's work with the client must be embedded in the therapeutic relationship, indexed by the therapist's strategies of emotional support and his full involvement in the client's verbal and non-verbal acts of communication.

Chapter 5. Emotional support

We talked for a while about bad feelings and good ones. I stressed that every person has both, that having bad feelings didn't make you bad. I don't know if these therapeutic platitudes did any good, but by the time Miranda called her, Eggy seemed relieved. I know that what's said is often less important than the tone of voice in which the words are spoken. There is music in dialogue, mysterious harmonies and dissonances that vibrate in the body like a tuning fork. (Hustvedt 2008: 275)

5.1 Introductory remarks

Supportive communication defined as "verbal and nonverbal behavior produced with the intention of providing assistance to others perceived as needing that aid" (Burleson and MacGeorge 2002: 374) constitutes a fundamental form of human interaction. This should come as no surprise since everybody at different points in their lives either seeks or offers his/her support to another person. Supportive interactions are a primary means through which social and personal relationships are created and fostered.

Emotional support conceptualized as expressions of care, concern, affection, and interest mainly during times of stress or upset (cf. Albrecht and Adelman 1987; Cutrona and Russel 1990) has been classified by Cutrona and Suhr (1994) as a type of supportive messages. According to this classification, emotional support involving expressions of care, concerns and sympathy, is contrasted with esteem support (e.g. reassurance of worth), network support (e.g. expressions of connection and belonging), informational support (information and advice) and tangible assistance (e.g. offers of money). Significantly for the current discussion, the classification proposed by Cutrona and Suhr (1994) draws a clear boundary between emotional support and informational support. Indeed the context of psychotherapy session clearly favors the first type of support as in the unique setting the client rather than being specifically told what to do, is to regain self-esteem and/or inner strength in order to sort out his/her personal issues. Psychotherapist's expressions of care and support as well as his full presence with the client extensively facilitate the process. This is to say that in the context of psychotherapeutic interaction, provision of emotional support refers to an activity directed at managing or modifying the *psychological* states of others, addressing, among others, the feelings of disappointments or sadness. In this sense emotional support, to a great extent, functions as comforting strategies focusing "on the management of feeling rather than the treatment of physical or material conditions" (Burleson 1994: 136). If experienced as sensitive and helpful, it can yield numerous benefits for the recipient.

Burleson (1994) describes *sophisticated comforting strategies* (cf. also high person centered comforting messages) as acknowledging, elaborating and legitimizing the feelings and perspective of a distressed person. As Burleson (1994) explicates these strategies contain features that express receiver focus, evaluative neutrality, feeling centeredness, interpersonal acceptance as well as insight and/or understanding. The interactional context of a psychotherapy session where the *intentional* effort is made by one person (a psychotherapist) to assist another one (a client) in coping with a perceived state of affective stress can be regarded as an ideal setting for studying both the content of the sophisticated comforting messages as well as their interactional realization. After all, entering the psychotherapy room, individuals manifest a deep need for quality care and genuine interest from another person. The psychotherapy room offers much space for the clients to deal with their traumas and yet such effort requires top-quality understanding, support and comfort from the psychotherapist.

Burleson (2003: 552) provides a general description of how emotional support can be accomplished, i.e., by "direct expression of affection and concern, invitations to discuss feelings and associated problematic states, statements of encouragement and hope, efforts to assist with problem analysis, offers of information and advice, as well as other verbal and non-verbal behaviors".

Since stressful and traumatic situations often create numerous needs, supportive messages tend to be multifunctional, frequently serving multiple goals. Thus there is a distinction between proximal (immediate) and distal (long-term) objectives as well as those instrumental and relational in character (Burleson 1994). The first distinction seems to be particularly applicable to the messages of emotional support offered by the psychotherapist in his/her interactions with the clients. It can be assumed that the therapist's emotional involvement in the clients' disclosures in the therapeutic here-and-now gradually leads to clients' enhanced coping capacities outside the therapy room.

Burleson (2003) states that emotional support can be best understood as specific lines of communication consisting in listening to, empathizing with, legitimizing, and actively exploring another's feelings (cf. also Burleson 1984). This is particularly important in view of the fact that the descriptions of emotional support discussed in professional psychotherapy handbooks (stocks of interactional knowledge, Peräkylä and Vehviläinen 2003) are often very general and vague, lacking a detailed description of the actual interactional realization of emotional support. Consequently, there is a need for concrete specification of how the emotional support can be expressed and conveyed without reducing it to a few static phrases (cf. Burleson and MacGeorge 2002).

What remains to be investigated is what communicative and interactional strategies are drawn on to convey a sense of emotional support to the client in order to comfort him/her[108], as well as how the psychotherapist's emotional presence for the client is accomplished in the midst of therapeutic interaction.

5.2 Strategies of emotional support

The psychotherapist's provision of emotional support to the client is crucial for the establishment and maintenance of the therapeutic relationship (or working alliance) between the psychotherapist and client and generally, the quality of a therapist's emotional support is greatly responsible for the success of psychotherapy. The quality of the therapeutic relationship and, consequently, the psychotherapist's emotional support is related to his/her personality traits as well as the communication skills of the therapist (Wynn and Wynn 2006; Burleson 2003).

Certainly the psychotherapist in his/her work with the client draws on selective emotional support strategies depending on a number of variables, the most significant of which appear to be the client's personality type and the sort of problem the client wishes to deal with. It seems however, that the main and/or essential skill upon which other emotional support strategies are based is the expression of empathy.

Psychotherapists regard empathy as a central aspect of the process of cure in various types of psychotherapy (cf. Wynn and Wynn 2006) and Carl Rogers (1951) listed it as one of the three necessary conditions for therapeutic growth. The psychotherapists, Moursund and Erskine (2004: 88) refer to empathy as "the most common descriptor of what happens in psychotherapy" and the therapist's empathic ability as his/her 'stock-in-trade'. They also specify that – to have a therapeutic effect – empathy must be *conveyed* to the client and not just experienced by the therapist.

Empathy as featuring in the context of psychotherapy can be construed from a more conversation analytic perspective as "a multiphased process, involving a sequence of experiences, including the therapist's 'resonation' with the patient's experience, the therapist's expression of empathy, and the patient's reception of it" (Wynn and Wynn 2006: 1386; cf. also Barrett and Lennard 1981). A noteworthy point of this definition is that it underlines the position of the client who needs to 'receive' an empathic comment, i.e., to validate it.

Pudlinski (2005) draws a line between empathy and sympathy in the sense that, while the first concept relates to resonant feelings and under-standing/knowing, the latter is based on congruent feelings and relating. He discusses eight methods for expressing empathy/sympathy to troubles tell-ing on a peer support line: emotive reaction, assessment, naming another's feelings, formulating the gist of the trouble, using an idiom, expressing one's own feelings about another's trouble, reporting one's reaction and sharing a similar experience of similar feelings. Bachelor (1988) offered a system of categorization for the analysis of empathy in psychotherapy and distinguished between cognitive empathy, affective empathy, sharing em-pathy as well as nurturant empathy.[109] Wynn and Wynn (2006) investigated the instances of these types of empathy (excluding the nurturant type) in actual psychotherapeutic interactions. They demonstrated how the three types of empathy singled out by Bachelor (1988) are interactionally achieved. They described empathy as comprised of at least "a therapist ut-terance with an expression of empathy, followed by a patient's receipt of the therapist's expression of empathy" (Wynn and Wynn 2006: 1394), em-phasizing that a potential lack of the patient's receipt is actually oriented to by the interactants and may even lead to signs of conversational failure.

In the analyzed corpus of Integrative Psychotherapy sessions, the therapist exhibits four main types of emotional support which I label as: emotive ex-tension of the client's account, emotive reaction, validation, and mirroring the client's experience. These expressions need to be deeply embedded in the interactional context, i.e., they have to be aligned with the client's turn(s) to perform empathy, i.e. to manifest resonant feelings and understanding as well as validated by the client[110] (cf. Wynn and Wynn 2006). All of the psycho-therapist's expressions of emotional support presented below are positively oriented-to by the clients. In this way the clients co-construct the functions of these expressions as empathic.

5.2.1 Emotive extension of the client's account

The interactional strategy of extension as applied by therapists in their in-teractions with clients constitutes an understanding and paraphrasing back what the other speaker (here the client) has said and presumably means (Vehviläinen 2003; cf. also Peräkylä and Vehviläinen 2007). As Vehviläinen (2003: 582) states, by extending another person's account one is able not only to manifest his/her understanding of the talk but also "to talk from within the same world". Additionally, an act of extension evinces that the speaker possesses "the relevant knowledge [...] to provide the lo-cally relevant continuation of the thought" (Vehviläinen 2003: 582). Ex-tracts 1 (lines 6 and 8) and 2 (line 5) display the psychotherapist's expressions of empathy as they extend the emotional aspect of the clients' disclosures. The therapist's unsolicited comments in fact reinforce the emo-tional content of the client's account. A noteworthy point is that the thera-pist relies on the knowledge that the client has already shared or at least hinted at. The therapist brings the emotional aspect into play by making the client's affective reaction significant. Explicit recognition of one's feelings comforts a person (Zimmerman and Applegate 1992). Since most emo-tional information is conveyed by means of metamessage (cf. Besnier 1990), the therapist's expression of empathy attempts to interactionally un-pack it. The therapist tunes into the client's emotional content and she rati-fies the attunement by providing her comments following the therapist's expression of empathy:

Extract 1

1	C:	...and I think the most impo:rtant one is going <u>back</u> and seeing the cubicle and
2		taking me out of it, also (.) I had a ↑fantasy that I was there to be killed so any
3		of the staff in uniforms, well a:ny of the nursing staff or medical staff were to kill
4		me (.) and the o:nly people who were not there to kill me were the people who
5		brought in sou:p and bread and butter and (.) >they were important to me.<
6→	T:	But <u>nobody</u> in there with <u>you</u> (.) nobody to <u>play</u> with you.=
7	C:	=<u>No</u>, not emotionally.
8→	T:	<u>Nobody</u> to stroke you.
9	C:	I wasn't allowed toys because toys carried infection and what I lo:ved before
10		and love now were animals...

Extract 1 (in which the client reflects on her childhood memories of being kept in a glass cubicle for health reasons) features the strategy of emotive extension in which the therapist's comments upgrade the client's account (cf. Peräkylä and Vehviläinen 2007). This takes the form of extreme case formulation (Pomerantz 1986) as the therapist relies on the extreme term of 'nobody' in both of his turns (lines 6 [twice] and 8). It needs to be underlined that such extreme case formulation requires an orientation from the interlocutor (client) with the preferred action of agreement. Taking into the account the 'drama' of the extreme case formulation, such extension can only be performed once the truly therapeutic alliance has been established between the interacting parties. Otherwise the therapist risks the client's disavowal and even withdrawal from the further interaction. The therapist's emotive extension as evidenced in lines 6 and 8 is, in fact, oriented to by the client. Following the therapist's emotional alignment, the client provides and an agreement to it (line 7) and further elaborates on her affective state.

In the extract that follows, the therapist's emotive extension takes the form of substituting the client's proffered lexical item for a more extreme one:

Extract 2

```
1   C:    And I found a piece of paper and I just wrote >dear God, please help her< and
2         in that mo:ment I felt as if I wouldn't know happiness again a:nd that something
3         so so terrible has ha:ppened that I wouldn't laugh again (.) and it felt as if my
4         heart was broken.
5→T:      Broken is probably too simple.=
6   C:    =Shattered.
7   T:    ↓Shattered, is that what you wrote on the piece of paper?
```

In line 5 the therapist attempts to emotionally upgrade the client's account by suggesting a more dramatic or extreme term to be used to name her feelings. The client instantly orients to the therapist's challenge by offering a more extreme adjective ('shattered') to name how she felt when she found out that her daughter was diagnosed with a terminal disease. The adjective offered by the client is then used by the therapist to construct the next turn (line 7) and in fact build a part of the interaction around it.

In both Extracts 1 and 2, the clients' ratification of the therapist's expressions of empathy is immediately oriented-to (as represented by the interactional strategy of latch). In this way the therapist and client have co-constructed a single turn, which manifests the clients' identification with the therapist's expressions.

The therapist's emotive extension does not always take the form of extreme case formulation:

Extract 3

1	T:	°And how <u>long</u> do you go into the depression?°
2	C:	Several months on medication.
3	T:	Can you work during that period of time?
4	C:	<u>No,</u> I can't (2.0) o:ften I can't even get out of bed.=
5	T:	=And can you stand the light or: do you have to block off the light?
6		Does it have to be dark?
7	C:	I prefer it. I try to function so <u>nobody</u> realizes what's going on (.) it's <u>easy</u> for me.
8→	T:	>You're trying to keep a smile like that< and people can't see it.
9	C:	It's ea:sy.

In line 7 the client states that she maintains the appearance of normal functioning during a period of severe depression. The therapist in his following turn, line 8, provides an emotive extension of the client's previous statement by contributing the image of the client masking her destructive mood from other people by hiding behind a smile. This extension, however mild, conveys the potent metamessage of 'speaking from the client's experience'. The client orients to the extension not by mere 'yes' or 'no', i.e., acceptance or rejection but rather by echoing the already stated (line 7) easiness of such acting. This, at the same time, constitutes the client's acknowledgment of the therapist's emotive extension.

The therapist's emotive extension constitutes elaboration on the client's previous account either by upgrading the emotional aspect of the client's experience or by echoing its emotional load. In either case, the therapist conveys empathic understanding of the client's emotional trajectory.

5.2.2 Emotive reaction

The extracts that follow exemplify the therapist's expressions of emotional support taking the grammatical form of interjection (*what* +; *how* +*)* which is emotionally aligned with the client's previous turn. In fact, the emotive reaction constitutes the emotional sum-up of the client's previous turn in which he/she talks about his/her real but traumatic experience of being, functioning, and managing to survive in the world. In Extracts 4 and 5, the clients ratify the therapist's expression by building their next turn on it. In psychotherapy, clients tend to reveal experiences that have either never been verbalized before or, if verbalized, failed to elicit an empathic response from another interlocutor (Pawelczyk and Erskine 2008) and those emotive reactions offered by the psychotherapist are extremely important in reassuring the clients that the therapist is an interested, involved and attuned listener:

Extract 4

```
1    C:    It is always spontaneous, >even her doctors said so.< (.) When she was first
2          diagnosed, she was in hospital in X, and her doctor loved her and she
3          loved him >easily, openly and freely< without any difference or fear and
4          when we had to move back to X, we had our last visit and he said he would
5          never forget her (.) and we cried (.) but he never has, he writes to her.
6→T:       Hmm, what a wonderful doctor!
7    C:    And he was a wonderful doctor and because X is so good with people, they
8          can't do enough for her (.) e:verybody wants to give her something
9          >you know< and that's why she's been on so: many trials.
```

In Extract 4 the therapist's topically aligned reaction in line 6 reflects the client's emotional attitude presented in lines 1–5. The therapist's emotive reaction is oriented to by the client (lines 7–9) who ratifies the therapist's expression and then re-orients her account to her daughter.

In Extract 5, the therapist's emotive reaction can be observed in line 5:

Extract 5

```
1    T:    Well (.) yeah (.) any move creates a crisis in probably anybody's life, packing up
2          and moving and getting re-established, <but I wonder if he's in more crisis than
3          you even know> and I don't know but
4    C:                                    // But he wasn't even willing to see me.=
5→T:        =How pa:inful!
6    C:    And I really don't know what I should do: <I don't know> but he wouldn't
7          tell me when he was coming back or where his address would be.
```

The therapist's formulation in line 2 gets interrupted by the client (line 4). This interruption is emotionally aligned to by the therapist in line 5 by focusing on the emotional aspect of the client's experience. Similarly to Extract 4, the emotive reaction is ratified by the client by providing further disclosure.

In Extract 6, the therapist's empathic interjection is validated by the client's minimal acknowledgment ('yeah'):

Extract 6

1	T:	Would you <u>tell</u> me what was going <u>on</u> at school?
2	C:	Oh (.) I was an oddball, too, everybody treated me like that >kids, teachers<
3		and going back from school was scary too a:nd I even remember from
4		my earliest memories 'you are disgusting, you're awful, you're the worst
5		thing' (2.0) my mom was envious of <u>everything</u>.
6→	T:	<What destruction to a child! What cruelty!>
7	C:	Yeah.

The client's highly personal disclosure in Extract 6 (lines 2–5) receives the therapist's supportive expression in line 6. The proferred emotive reaction following the client's disclosure underlines the therapist's understanding and sympathy to the client's plight.

All the emotive reactions proffered by the therapist signify his presence and attentive listening to what the client is attempting to convey. Moreover, they are very feeling-centered, not only accepting the client's suffering but foregrounding it. In this way the therapist's emotive reactions function as instant comforting strategies aiming at alleviating or lessening the client's emotional distress here-and-now. Yet in the long run, exposure to such explicit recognition of their feelings can help the clients cope with distressful situations in the future (cf. Burleson 1994).

5.2.3 Validation

In Extracts 7, 8 and 9 the therapist's expression of emotional support follows the clients' accounts of highly traumatic or abusive situations they have found themselves in. The excruciating aspect of each situation is brought out by the clients' own references to their emotional states in the described situation (Extract 7: 'I'm profoundly shocked', 'I felt downtrodden'), their perception of their social position in the described circumstances (Extract 8: 'I couldn't quite fit in', 'I was an oddball', 'I had no sense how to socialize') or the impact of the situation on their current circumstances (Extract 9: 'I can't forget it or erase it').

In each case, the psychotherapist's expressions constitute (empathic) validation of the client's situation. The therapist's validation legitimizes the clients' feelings and experiences. The proffered validation approves of the client's view of the situation (Extract 7) and attempts to justify (Extract 8) or normalize (Extract 9) the client's circumstances.

In Extract 7, the female client (line 5) echoes the therapist's utterance (line 4) in this way demonstrating agreement (cf. Ferrara 1994):

Extract 7

```
1   C:   But I'm profoundly shocked by the last session that I had in therapy when my
2        therapist suddenly got angry a:nd said that what I wa:nted was warm feelings and
3        (.) he >hadn't any warm feelings to give me< (.) and I felt downtrodden.
4→T:     I can't believe there is anybody not having warm fee:lings for you!
5   C:   I don't understand it myself.
```

In Extract 8, the therapist's justification of the client's perception of his situation (line 7) is extended by the client (line 8) who builds a single turn with the therapist's comment by latching an immediate agreement and adding the third factor ('it was shame-based')[111]:

Extract 8

```
1   T:   Were you the kind of kid that other kids would pick on?
2   C:   Oh, yeah.=
3   T:   =How come?
4   C:   (.) I think because (.) I couldn't, because I was very anxious and I couldn't
5        quite fit in, people >picked that up< and I was an oddball (3.0), yes (.) oddball.
6        I had no se:nse how to socialize because my family wouldn't.
7→T:     Your mom was crazy, the house was chaotic.=
8   C:   =And it was very, it was shame-based.
```

Extract 9 features a painful disclosure of a male client concerning the difficult relationship with his mother:

Extract 9

```
1   C:   It's a situation that comes back to me all the time (2.0) I can't forget it or erase it,
2        it has to do with trust (.) I am a little boy 4 or 5 years old and I have done bad
3        things.=
4→T:     =What bad things?
5   C:   °I didn't clean my room, I didn't eat the food that my mother prepared for me°.=
6→T:     =So what's ba:d about that?
```

7   C: The <u>bad</u> thing is that it should be done when when my fa:ther comes back home.

8→   T: <What is <u>bad</u> about a 4 year old boy who does not want to eat the food?>

9   C: I don't think it's bad.=

10→T: =And what's bad about a 4 year old who doesn't want to clean the room?

11   C: °It's not bad.°

[...]

12→T: So <u>maybe</u> we need to talk about no:rmalcy.

13   C: Yeah.=

14→T: =Because it's pretty no:rmal for a 4 year old to look and certain food

15→   and say I DON'T EAT THAT.

16   C: Yeah.

17→T: And it's pretty <u>normal</u> for a 4 year old <u>not</u> to want to pick up their toys and

18→   not to clean up their room (.) that's pretty normal for a 4 year old.

19   C: Yeah.

Interestingly the interaction in Extract 9 is built around the adjective 'bad' that the client has initially used (line 2). In the course of the exchange, the therapist gradually normalizes and validates the client's behavior as a child. In this way he clearly sides with the client and the way he acted and at the same time questions the mother's conduct. The therapist's expressions of validation (lines 12, 14–15 and 17–18) are preceded by a series of questions (lines 4, 6, 8, 10) which foreground the absurdity of the client's mother's behavior towards her son. In this way, the client becomes assured of the irrationality of his mother's attitude and thus his not being able to 'forget it or erase it' as well as the feelings accompanying it are validated.

Clients readily identify themselves with the empathic comments which approve of their views of the situations in question. Therapist's validation of clients' accounts has a *normalizing* function. This is to say that the clients get reassured by the therapist that their behavior is not crazy or shameful (Moursund and Erskine 2004). Therapist with his validating comments lets the clients know that that their experiences constitute self-protective reaction and "that others experiencing similar life circumstances might well respond in similar ways" (Moursund and Erskine 2004: 121).

5.2.4 Mirroring

Sacks (1992 Vol. II: 260) states that "one best way of saying 'I understand what you say' is to say 'I've been through it myself'". Indeed, one of the emotional support strategies used by the therapist in interacting with clients is directly referencing his own (intimate) experience:

Extract 10

```
1   C:    I rehearsed things in de:tail before something was going to happen (.)
2         I think it >sort of< spills over into my need of trying to control things
3         which are uncontrollable.
4→T:      Well (.) I have me:mories of training myself, with that voice ↑inside,
5         being on a bus going to school, I trained myself with that kind of voice.
6   C:    Yeah, and even co:ming here I packed almost everything just in case
7         anything happens.
```

In Extract 10, the therapist comforts the client by drawing on his experience of 'training' himself as well. By *mirroring* the client's experience in this most direct way, the therapist is able to significantly diminish the client's sense of feeling alienated and at the same time enhance the quality of the therapeutic alliance between them. Additionally, mirroring the client's experience points to fluidity of interactional roles which in turn contributes to a sense of equality so crucial for the therapeutic relationship.

In Extract 11, the therapist attempts to comfort the client by referring to his professional experience (lines 3–11):

Extract 11

```
1   C:    He said that I have this unending dema:nd for warm feelings (.) but then I know
2         he ha::d warm feelings for me.
3→T:      I'm just telling you my experience over here that came to my memory. I had
4         that experience 2 years ago in a workshop with a guy (.) I had this experience
5         last February with a woman who fa:lsely accused me of being moralistic about
6         the affair she was having, a:nd not caring about her at all. And I found myself,
7         ok, you don't accept my caring, you're falsely accusing me, I'm not gonna
8         waste my caring so you know, I know these 2 experiences, one from 2 years ago with
9         a man who was see:mingly insatiable and with the woman who falsely accused me
10        of something (.) and as I tried to explain myself, I couldn't get through, well
11        (.) I don't know if that's
12 C:                              // There is >an element of that< because he a:sked me
13        if I felt his warm feelings and I said I didn't …
```

The client identifies herself with this expression of empathy by taking up the therapist's thread, getting hold of the conversational floor by means of the interruption (line 12).

Although it is generally thought that comforting strategies are "welcome in virtually any circumstances" (Cutrona 1996: 109), the highly emotionally-charged context of psychotherapy particularly encourages such strategies. The discussed ways of offering emotional support by the therapist – by elaborating on the client's story, emotive reactions, siding with the client in his/her conflictual situation, justifying his/her life circumstances as well as mirroring the client's experience – convey to the client a sense of being (finally) understood. This provides clients with the great comfort of being an individual who is being attentively listened to by another person (the therapist) who can correctly *read* the client's situation. This 'correctness' is verified by the clients with their typically latched statements. Even though the sophisticated comforting strategies were originally discussed as applicable to everyday contexts, they emerge as a fundamental interactional tool in the hands of a psychotherapist who, by explicit recognition and elaboration on the client's perspective (cf. Burleson 1994), relieves his/her emotional stress. This experience in terms of proximal objectives (cf. Burleson and MacGeorge 2002) can help the client manage his/her (future) emotional distress in a more satisfactory way.[112]

To conclude, the therapist's expressions of emotional support manifest his involvement in the authentic interaction with the client. This involvement, as an aspect of the relationship between the interacting parties, constitutes one of the indispensable conditions for a potentially empathic comment to succeed. Another one is the client's ratification which should follow therapist's expression of empathy. Thus the sequential environment needs to be considered in assessing the success of an empathic comment (cf. Pudlinski 2005). The four strategies of emotional support applied by the therapist are the consequence of his *active listening* to what the client is communicating both verbally and non-verbally. The interactional practice of active listening is a well-recognized skill for both counselors and psychotherapists[113] (cf. Hutchby 2007; Moursund and Erskine 2004). Hutchby states that in child counseling sessions, active listening plays a crucial role in "the work of inciting the child to communicate about his or her experiences" (2007: 79) and formulating what is regarded as therapeutically relevant. In the discussed context of psychotherapy session, the practice of active listening enables the therapist, first and foremost, to build a therapeutic alliance with the client by interactional tuning into both *what* the client is saying as well as *how* he or she says it. Therapist's strategies of emotional support evidence how the therapist is not only hearing, i.e., accepting what the client is offering but also how he is attempting to identify himself with what the client has been through. Although the psychotherapist's projection of empathy does not by itself remove the client's personal trauma, it provides the context in which clients can explore and seek understanding of their feelings (cf. Burleson 1994: 138). And this may be a new quality in a relationship for some clients. Another novelty concerns the therapist's manifestation of his presence for the client in the therapeutic here-and-now.

5.3 Therapist's emotional presence

Clients' non-verbal cues are frequently brought up and overtly commented on by the therapist in the course of the interaction (cf. the chapter on the *Communication of Emotion*, e.g., 'I see your tears'; 'Tell me about your tears'). Interestingly, clients very often immediately orient to these topicalizations in their next turns.

Clients' numerous projections of non-verbal behavior are used by the therapist to demonstrate (his) emotional presence for the clients. The therapist's emotional presence is performed by his careful observation of the client's various ways of conveying the messages and then (overtly) drawing the client's attention to the observed non-verbal behavior in an attempt to elicit from that client its significance to the discussed issue. This is to say that the therapist listens both to the content of the clients' narratives as well as to *how* the personal issues are conveyed/communicated.

It is claimed here that the therapist's emotional presence (also referred to as *authentic* or *therapeutic*) presence functions as the constitutive feature of the unique alliance between the psychotherapist and the client, i.e., the therapeutic relationship. This *authentic* presence can be observed periodically in friendships but it almost never transpires in the business world. A therapist's tuning into clients' non-verbal cues and their further interactional uptake for therapeutic work are what differentiates a therapeutic interaction from an ordinary conversation. Although the stocks of interactional knowledge of Relationship-Focused Integrative Psychotherapy describe the therapist's presence as a "sustained attunement to the client's verbal and non-verbal communication" (Moursund and Erskine 2004: 121), its interactional realization is not fully detailed.

The qualitative scrutiny of the data reveals two types of projection of emotional presence by the therapist. In the first type, referred to as *client-oriented*, the psychotherapist picks up a client's non-verbal cue (relating to his/her immediate affective or cognitive experience) and the client is asked to account for it.

Let us consider the following extract:

Extract 12

1	T:	So that is a strong woman or a weak woman?=
2	C:	=Yes, that's the question (.) it could be something I learnt from my mother
3		of being <u>strong</u> by being <u>weak</u> bu:t and that also causes a pro:blem as there
4		is not so much social permission for a strong competent woman.
5	T:	So what do you <u>do</u> when you are strong and you are competent (.) and
6		it's not allowed?
7	C:	What do I do then? (4.0) I think I tell myself that it wasn't that <u>good</u>, it's
8		like (.) I diminish myself then.
9→	T:	So you pretend you're not <u>competent</u>, you pretend you're not <u>strong.</u>
10→		What are you smiling at?
11	C:	((SMILING)), Yeah, I do recognize it, from my mother, she can say
12		I don't understand this, I can't do this, I'm not good at this.=
13	T:	=And the truth ↑is=
14	C:	=That she is.
15→	T:	What just happened inside?=
16	C:	=I fee:l the connection, but I wonder <u>also</u> because when she is this ↑way
17		I <u>know</u> she does know a lot about whatever, then I get angry or irritated with
18		her (2.0) why doesn't (.) why does she say she is incompetent and she
19		is NOT. It <u>annoys</u> me and that has been a >sort of a theme< in my life,
20		being angry at women not being accepted so: there are two sides of it
21		and (.) <u>well</u>, I would lo:ve to find my own position.

In Extract 12, the female client narrates her difficulties in asserting her strong femininity. The difficulty is formulated by the therapist in line 1. The formulation is accepted by the client who additionally refers to her mother as the potential source of confusion for her. In lines 7–8, in response to the therapist's question, the client comments on how she deals with her internal conflict. In line 9, the therapist orients to her response by another formulation and by overt commenting on her projection of her smile (non-verbal cue). Consequently, the client is made accountable for the smile. In lines 11–12, the client unveils the significance of the smile which refers to her recognition and acceptance of the therapist's formulation. In line 15 the therapist again takes up the client's non-verbal cue. Interestingly, he makes a claim to the client's internal experience ('what just happened inside') which has not been yet verbalized. The claim is immediately oriented to by the client who reveals the experience. The therapist's references to the client's non-verbal cues (lines 10 and 15) can be construed as markers of his emotional presence for the client. This presence manifests itself in the therapist's heightened awareness of his client's verbal and non-verbal projection of her experience and further elicitation from the client her interpretation of the projected cues. Since, as already indicated, such inquiry rarely transpires in ordinary conversations, the client has an opportunity to experience a new quality of the presence of another interlocutor in an interaction. In other words, the therapist, with his uptake of and reliance on clients' non-verbal signals in their therapeutic work, emerges as a fully involved and interested interlocutor.

In Extract 13, the male client addresses the problem of his inability to recognize his own feelings in his social work:

Extract 13

1   T: Are you feeling <u>anything</u> now? Maybe then you are (.) adjusting yourself
2   ↑maybe (1.0) there is a:lways reciprocity of what we fee::l particularly if we
3   are in a close <u>relationship</u>.
4   C: Sometimes I do feel strong <u>feelings</u> and I can sort them out and I realize that
5   those are the patients' feelings not mine (.) but sometimes I just can't.
6   T: Well,<particularly if you don't have someone who is sensitive to talk to you
7→   about your own feelings> (4.0) What's happening with your body right now?
8   C: I don't know <u>really</u>.
9   T: °You don't know whether you want that sensation to continue or to go away?°
10 C: I don't know if my feet are going to sleep or not.

In lines 1–3, the therapist attempts to explicate the client's problem by constructing the interaction around the theme of a 'close relationship'. Such a theme, however, is not picked up by the client, who echoes his problem in lines 4–5 without orienting to the therapist's formulation. The therapist continues with the theme, yet this time 'close relationship' gets expanded to 'if you don't have someone who is sensitive to talk to you about your own feelings' (lines 6–7). This reformulation is not completed by the therapist as he orients to the client's non-verbal signal (line 7) by asking the client to put into words his internal experience. It seems that having failed to elicit from the client the uptake of the 'relationship' theme (a 4 second pause, line 7), the therapist turns to his non-verbal behavior in order to continue the interaction. At the same time, such an uptake of non-verbal cues by the therapist underlines his involvement and presence for the client. The therapist emerges as a sensitive interlocutor, adjusting to the various channels of communication projected by the client. Such involvement and sensitivity significantly contributes to building and/or maintaining the therapeutic alliance between the psychotherapist and client.

Extract 14 begins with the therapist offering his interpretation of the client's inhibition:

Extract 14

```
1   T:   And what would ha:ppen if you talked about something private like that
2        in front of people you don't know (1.0) you don't do it for an important
3        rea:son. <Can I tell you what I think?>
4   C:   Yeah.
5   T:   The chance of ridicule.=
6→C:    =Mhm.=
7→T:    =What just happened when you said 'mhm'? Did you just remember
8        something? <Have you ever been ridiculed?>
9.  C:   (3.0) °Maybe when I was a child.°
10  T:   Or you remember friends being ri:diculed for telling private things.
11  C:   Maybe (.) but I do:n't have any strong recollection.
12  T:   Maybe more ↑general or not at all?
13  C:   I don't feel that it's very stro:ng but I have another thing (.) when I was
14       a child or >even as a grown up< my mother rejected my opinions when
15       they differed from hers, (2.0) she didn't like them, I could see it in her
16       eyes (.) we didn't talk about feelings in that way at a:ll.
```

In line 4 the therapist's formulation of the client's problem receives a minimal acknowledgement (a minimal response). The therapist's interpretation of the client's minimal response (line 7) evidences that he is listening not only to what the client says but also how she/he does it. Thus in this particular instance, the client's tone of voice is indicative of more experience hidden behind the mere 'mhm' (line 6). By attempting to uncover the client's experience (lines 7–8), the therapist manifests his emotional presence for the client, underlined by his readiness to hear the client's story regardless of how painful and/or embarrassing it might be. Although, in fact, the therapist gradually attempts to unveil the client's experience (lines 10, 12), the client in the end does offer her interpretation of the situation (lines 13–16). Extract 14 evinces how the therapist's full involvement in the client's various ways of message communication enables him to elicit more disclosure and at the same time manifest his emotional presence for the client.

Extract 15 (a continuation of Extract 9) demonstrates the occurrence of the therapist's strategies of emotional support and his projection of emotional presence:

Extract 15

```
1    T:   But then there is something mo:re psychological in the punishment: <wait till
2         your father gets home,> and that is almost to:rture because the child is
3         condemned to fantasy. <So what your father actually di:d when he came
4         home is not as important  as all the fa:ntasy you have that destroys the
5         relationship with him.>=
6    C:   =Yeah.=
7→   T:   =You have just laughed, what happened?
8    C:   I feel a:nger towards my mother, you know, because I think she was doing
9         it 'cause she wanted me to love her and if she lied to my father she thought
10        I would love her.
11→  T:   What a confused woman!
12   C:   I never thought this way about her.
13   T:   It would be very different if she would have said to you <I don't like what
14        you did I'm punishing you right now.>
15   C:   °Yeah.°
```

In lines 1–5 the therapist explains to the client the intricacies of the uncomfortable situation the client used to experience in his childhood. The client minimally responds to the explication (line 6) and produces a shy laughter which is immediately oriented to by the therapist (line 7). The client is asked to account for the displayed non-verbal cue. In lines 8–10 the client verbalizes his own perspective on the uncomfortable situation. The verbalization receives the therapist's emotive reaction (line 11) which at the same time casts a new perspective on the client's trauma. The therapist with his overt comment on the client's projected non-verbal cue is not only able to elicit his view on the situation but also manages to underline his emotional presence by being attuned to the client's various ways of communicating his story. Simultaneously the therapist emerges as an understanding and empathic listener who legitimizes the client's situation.

The therapist's reference to and uptake of the clients' non-verbal cues can be classified as *noticings* (cf. Sacks 1992 Vol. I). Noticings contain an observation of something that is available for both the speaker and the recipient (Sacks 1992 Vol. I: 90–92) and they relate to the immediate moments of experience. Sacks in his discussion on noticings underlined the importance of timed interpretations as well as the topical shift that noticings introduce. In the context of the analyzed extracts, the therapist initiates work with the clients' (inner) immediate experience or feelings in an ongoing interaction. Thus he remains attentive to the client's projected non-verbal messages and attempts to topicalize them for the purpose of further therapeutic work.

The second type of therapist's projection of emotional presence is referred to as *therapist-oriented* to underscore the fact that with such a strategy the therapist draws the client's attention to his own projection of his non-verbal behavior. The therapist's projected non-verbal behavior is a reaction to the client's experience that has been revealed in the previous turn. Let us consider the following extract:

Extract 16

1	C:	But I think I met someone in my life who could <u>understand</u> me.=
2	T:	=That <u>teacher</u>?
3	C:	<u>Yeah</u>, I remember how I was lo:ved.=
4	T:	=<u>Well</u>, that's interesting since you spent so little time with her (.) even
5		now <u>forty</u> years later you remember your little love but you spent so:
6		little time with her, but that was a <u>quality</u> in her, wasn't it?
7	C:	Mhm.=
8	T:	=What <u>was</u> that quality?
9	C:	°She took me seriously.°
10→	T:	You bring tears to my eyes, °she took me seriously°, any other qualities?
11	C:	((SIGHING)) She died 6 months later.
12	T:	So she opened up a little hope, one <u>grown-up</u>, one <u>adult</u> who could po:ssibly
13		take the time to be understanding and then she dies.=
14	C:	=Yeah.

In Extract 16 the male client reflects on his memories of being understood and appreciated by his teacher (and not having such memories regarding his parents). The highly intimate disclosure is interactionally facilitated by the therapist (line 2) who recalls the information offered by the client is the previous session. In lines 4–6, the therapist attempts to elicit from the client the characteristic(s) of the relationship between the client and his teacher. This attempt receives a minimal acknowledgement (line 7), so consequently the therapist poses a direct question (line 8). The therapist orients to the received response (line 9) by underscoring his own non-verbal reaction and drawing the client's attention to it.

Unlike in type 1 (projection) where the therapist overtly addresses the client's displayed non-verbal behavior, in the type 2 (projection), the therapist highlights the significance of the client's verbal message by underscoring his own non-verbal reaction. By overtly commenting on his own reaction to the client's disclosure of intimate experience, the therapist is perceived as an emotionally involved listener.

The two ways in which the therapist manifests his emotional presence for the clients reflect his sensitive attunement to the clients' messages conveyed both verbally and non-verbally. The therapist's uptake of the clients' or his own non-verbal cues is deeply embedded in the local context of the interaction and directly relates to the client's (or therapist's) immediate experience. Such interactional involvement of another interlocutor (i.e., the therapist) constitutes a new quality in the relationship for a majority of clients. The therapist is perceived as strong and allied to the client. The therapist's *authentic being* for the client is an indispensable element in establishing, maintaining and practicing the therapeutic alliance (relationship) between the two participants of the therapeutic interaction.

5.4 Concluding remarks

Emotional support and emotional presence are constitutive elements of the therapeutic interaction and the therapist's reliance on them enables him to perform a number of tasks. First and foremost the strategies of emotional support and emotional presence underline the therapist's full involvement in clients' disclosures of their personal stories. With his active listening, the therapist remains attentive to what the client is communicating verbally and non-verbally, legitimizing and normalizing clients' accounts. Furthermore, the applied strategies make it possible for the clients to articulate their feelings and/or elaborate on why these feelings may be felt. The positive aspects of the therapist's emotional support and presence can be experienced by the clients both in the immediate context of the psychotherapeutic interaction as well as outside it, i.e., in their daily lives. An accepting and relational environment in the here-and-now provides safety leading to greater openness as well as provides clients with the new interpersonal experience of emotional soothing and support that over time become internalized (Fosha 2000).

Conclusion: Reflecting on talk as therapy

> *Effective therapy often seems magical. A life shat-*
> *tering problem is described in the quiet recesses of*
> *a chamber far removed from the site of turmoil.*
> *Questions and answers, stories good and bad,*
> *emotional outbursts, a little silence and perhaps*
> *some tears – all may be present. And then, almost*
> *by miraculous intervention, there is change. The*
> *problem is transformed, seems less severe, or is*
> *possibly dissolved. Yet, we ponder, how was the re-*
> *sult achieved? What is it about this particular con-*
> *figuration of events that brought about change? At*
> *least one central candidate for answering this par-*
> *ticular form of "miracle question" is therapeutic*
> *communication. There is something about the na-*
> *ture of communicative interchange that engenders*
> *change. Yet, to answer in this way is scarcely suffi-*
> *cient. What precisely is it about such communica-*
> *tion that precipitates transformation? What forms*
> *of communication are invited, which are proscribed;*
> *how might we be more effective?* (Gergen, K. unpub-
> lished manuscript)[114]

Psychotherapeutic interaction can be experienced as emancipatory for clients who enter the psychotherapy room in the desperate hope of abandon-
ing life-constricting traumas, revealing pent-up emotions and engaging in
authentic dialogue with an involved and empathetic listener. Talk, then, can
be therapeutic as the unique dialogue that develops in the psychotherapy
room allows the client to become aware of his/her real emotional states,
verbalize troublesome thoughts, and explore and confront personal experiences, and all of this is taking place in the safety of the relationship with the
therapist. This in turn leads to a client's better understanding his/her life
experiences, improved relationships with other people, enhanced self-
acceptance, as well as increased awareness of his/her real needs and desires.
Such a qualitative change in the client's life enables him/her to lead a more
fulfilling and satisfying life.

Undeniably, this process of change is to a large extent facilitated by the
psychotherapist, whose respect for a client's life trajectory instills in

him/her a sense of trust in another human being. This is to say that while providing emotional support and care for the client, the therapist remains in charge of the interaction following his/her interactional project (cf. Schegloff 2007). The atmosphere of trust, as well as the therapist's empathy and understanding, help him/her establish a unique relationship with the client. The safety of this unique alliance encourages open and direct communication without the criticism or censure that the client could possibly experience outside the context of psychotherapy; as Kahn (1991: 1) explains, in the context of psychotherapeutic interaction, "the relationship *is* the therapy".

The current project undertook an examination of the question that Labov and Fanshel, in their 'know that'-oriented study, left extensively unanswered, namely: "how do I do it?" (1977: 28), i.e., how is psychotherapy *done*? The intriguing issue of what makes talk therapeutic receives elaboration in this concluding section.

In order to answer this question, patterns of language use transpiring between the psychotherapist and client have been examined via methods of a discourse analysis framework, broadly defined. The conducted analysis singled out three discourse norms, upon which the speech event of psychotherapy must be based, viz.: *the transparency of meaning, self-disclosure* and *communication of emotion*. These are the defining characteristics of the speech event of psychotherapy. Additionally, the strategies of emotional support and the therapist's emotional presence were discussed as crucial for the establishment and maintenance of the therapeutic relationship. These three norms have then been shown to be interactionally operationalized by a number of both verbal and non-verbal practices. It is claimed that these practices play a therapeutic function by encouraging the client to explore the personal significance of the phrase(s) used, fostering his/her intimate narratives, as well as enabling the client to focus on the emotional aspect of his/her experience. At the same time, however, it needs to be underlined that the function of a particular form is deeply embedded in the context. This is to say that a certain form, be it a language feature or an interactional strategy, can index a number of functions. In order to pin down a form's meaning and function, two types of contexts need to be taken into account. Firstly, a broad one: the socio-cultural context in which the form occurs, and secondly, a narrow one: the local interactional context in which a feature or strategy transpires. As for the broader context, Ochs's[115] (1992) line of reasoning can be applied. To recap, within her indexicality model, a certain language form indexes a particular stance, for example, a question tag constitutes a stance of uncertainty or request. These stances then index a particular social activity. Thus, for instance, in the conducted analysis a therapist's 'what do you mean' following a client's semantically transparent phrase constitutes a stance of mild confrontation, which indexes the social activity of psychotherapy. In other words, a certain linguistic form or interactional strategy is associated with a particular social activity. To refer to Cicourel (1992: 296), "if we do not invoke institutional and local socio-cultural details ... the analysis of meaning is nearly impossible". As far as the narrower context is concerned, the function of 'what do you mean', for instance, must be examined in the local interactional context in which it transpires. Thus the question to be asked here relates to the very interactional detail: what does this question achieve in the local context of the interaction? An investigation of the therapist's 'what do you mean' at the level of interactional detail reveals its function in facilitating the client's access to his/her highly personal story (behind the use of a certain word or phrase) and then sharing it with the therapist. These two types of contexts (socio-cultural and local, interactional) are absolutely necessary to attribute a therapeutic function to a specific language form or interactional strategy. After all, a psychotherapeutic interaction is based on an ordinary conversation, hence 'what do you mean' is not confined to psychotherapy but may occur in other social settings. Consequently, to paraphrase Freed (1996: 67), both setting and associated communicative tasks become an index of a therapeutic style.

The approach adopted for the current study of psychotherapist-client interactions combined a number of methods and methodologies in order to reveal what kind of talk goes in therapy to produce the desired 'cure', i.e., the client's (gradual) accomplishment of life transformation. I deeply believe that only a combination of different context-sensitive methods by discourse analysts researching a professional site, be it doctor-patient interaction, psychotherapist-client interaction or any other, can fully uncover and demonstrate how talk serves to achieve professional goals.

The analyses of psychotherapist-client interactions presented in this book offer a unique perspective of how therapy is accomplished at the micro-level. Thus it has now been demonstrated how *talk is therapy* achieved at the level of interactional detail. To reiterate, in order to find out whether or not a certain strategy takes on therapeutic function (and if so, how), the interactional and contextual details of actual interaction need to be considered. The participants' turn-by-turn engagement in the interaction, their verbal and non-verbal actions and reactions to each other should be further explored to arrive at a complete understanding of how talk realizes therapeutic functions. A fine-grained observational analysis of naturally-occurring talk makes it possible to demonstrate how talk becomes a power-ful tool to effect a change in the hands of a skilled psychotherapist.

What I would like to underscore again is an imperative for the discourse analyst: to avoid the pitfalls of different approaches to fieldwork and ana-lytical paradoxes (cf. Sarangi 2002), one must be present at the research site during the stage of data collection. This is to say that the methodology of (non)-participant observation provides the researcher with a unique insight into the professional and interactional dynamics of the context under inves-tigation. This presence proves crucial not only in the stage of data collec-tion and transcription but also secures the researcher's credibility in terms of his/her relationship with the community under study as well as in terms of the future research findings. This first-hand experience with the investi-gated professional setting can also facilitate more practice-driven findings (cf. Sarangi 2002). Discourse analysts should be aware that they do possess the professional tools not only to describe the verbal and non-verbal prac-tices making up a professional interaction but also to point out the commu-nicative processes that often remain hidden in the interaction between a professional and client.

The current study also draws attention to the psychotherapy session as an interprofessional research site whose verbal and non-verbal practices are of interest both to discourse analysts and psychologists or psychotherapists. The aspect of interprofessionality unequivocally points to some sort of col-laboration that should develop between these two professionals in research-ing psychotherapeutic interaction. Language and communication are potent allies in the hands of a psychotherapist who, nevertheless, always repre-sents a certain psychotherapeutic protocol. The (inter)professional dialogue between a discourse analyst and a psychotherapist can generate a full expli-cation of how the goals of psychotherapy are achieved. In other words, only when discourse-based and praxis-based studies stay informed of each other's research findings can a complete understanding of psychotherapeu-tic practice be accomplished. This understanding is clearly mandated by current social conditions as, increasingly, people the world over are turning to psychotherapy as an acceptable, reliable means to resolve their personal problems as well as to work towards living a more fulfilling life. Moreover, aspects of psychotherapeutic communication are being applied in new pro-fessional contexts, such as the global service sector, where workers are taught to provide customers with (albeit amateur) therapy (Cameron 2000b). This recontextualization of aspects of therapeutic talk enhances its value in current professional and even lay communication. Psychotherapy out-side the psychotherapy room gains importance in the life of an individual as a 'methodology of life planning' (cf. Giddens 1991) as well as an indispensable tool in providing care for customers in the current global economy.

The results of the current study are applicable to the work and practice of psychologists and psychotherapists, showing this community of professionals how the work of a discourse-analyst can be relevant to their own professional concerns and dilemmas as well as contribute to enhancing their own professional reflexivity. This echoes Silverman's (2000, 2001) appeal that academics find common ground among social science traditions for the purpose of advancing disciplines by sharing ideas (cf. also Mullany 2007). Addressing numerous professional dilemmas certainly paves the way for collaboration between discourse researchers and discourse workers.[116] The potential for discourse analytic work in professional contexts presents numerous opportunities of engagement that can only serve to underscore the indispensability of discourse analytic studies.

In the words of the outstanding psychotherapist Ernesto Spinelli:

> ...if therapy can offer anything of significance to the client, it is the possibility of dialogical encounter that will promote honest, if difficult, disclosure of that which is both explicit and implicit, accepted and disowned, in the client's beliefs and values regarding his or her possible ways of being-in-the-world so that these may be confronted as they are, rather than as the client might wish them to be or as the client might wish the therapist (as representative of the world) to see them and, by extension, to see his or her relationally construed self.
>
> (Spinelli 2006: 107)

Spinelli's conceptualization of psychotherapy rejects the suggestion of any magical element being present in a psychotherapeutic interaction. Rather, it testifies to the power of a dialogue with another human being (a therapist) whose communicative and interactional practices enable the client to gain insight into his/her old traumas, confront them anew, and dare to abandon them for the purpose of living a more satisfying life.

Change may itself seem like a magic word and, for uninitiated clients, an unrealistic promise, an unattainable goal. Indeed, change is entirely possible, and well within the reach of clients who resolve to embark on a psychotherapeutic trajectory.

Notes

1. Bertha Pappenheim (also known as Anna O.), an early patient of Breuer and his associate Freud, labeled her treatment a form of 'talking cure' (Russell 1987: 1).
2. There is a distinction between 'client' and 'patient'. 'Client' tends to be used to refer to a person who visits a psychotherapist in his/her private office; 'patient', on the other hand, describes someone who receives treatment while hospitalized or who is seen by a psychiatrist or psychiatric social worker (Ferrara 1994: 35–36; cf. also Kahn 1991: 6). 'Analysand', a psychoanalytic term for a person undergoing psychoanalysis, is used by Ferrara (1994: 36) to denote a subject under long-term psychoanalysis. The current project relies on the term 'client'.
3. The effectiveness of psychotherapy has been empirically proven, cf., Lambert, Bergin, and Garfield (2004); Lambert and Ogles (2004). Lakoff stated the following: "as research has repeatedly demonstrated, across all types of psychotherapy, regardless of method, the results are the same – two-thirds of patients demonstrate some improvement" (1982: 132).
4. The major work that marks the beginning of literature entirely devoted to the discourses of medical encounters is Mishler (1984), cf. also Fisher (1986); Silverman (1987); Todd (1989).
5. Praxis-oriented literature tends to be authored by professional practitioners while discourse-oriented literature by scholars of (socio)linguistic and/or discourse analytic background.
6. C. N. Candlin (2000) defines them as amalgams of ways of talking, valuing, thinking, believing, interacting, acting, writing and reading, together with various props in the world, and each possessing its own construals of reality.
7. C. N. Candlin (2000) talks about reinventing the client/patient in the process via enabling them to become partners in the healthcare process. The 'reinvention' process should include the transferring of partnership practices from certain other healthcare contexts where such a relationship has long been established, shifts from a compliance metaphor to one of concordance between the professional and client/patient emphasizing a sharing of information, responsibility, and agency. As C. N. Candlin (2000) emphasizes, much of the impetus for this social and institutional change follows the doctrine of patient autonomy (cf. Ragan 2000). Fairclough (1992: 201) seriously questions the success of any shift in power: "Democratization in discourse, like democratization more generally, has been a major parameter of change ... but in both cases ... there are questions about how real or how cosmetic the changes have been".

8. However, cf. Braun and Clarke (2006: 84) on researchers never coding their data in an "epistemological vacuum".
9. The school of Integrative Psychotherapy is discussed in the next chapter. Moursund and Erskine (2004: 9) assert that while integrative therapists may differ in their actual work, they still adhere to the observations of proponents of all major schools (cf. also Wachtel 1990). Trömel-Plötz (1981: 243) states that psychotherapists, "no matter how they theorize about their practice, have similar strategies of communication: their therapy-specific interventions show common linguistic properties in terms of how they induce the patients to modify what they are saying, i.e., how they get them to change". See also Bartesaghi (2009: 16) for comments on similarities between schools of therapy.
10. Emphasis mine.
11. Interestingly, Moursund and Erskine (2004: 14) state that a therapeutic relationship "is focused on and has its very existence in a commitment to the well-being of one person, the client". This is, of course, a departure from other types of relationships, e.g., friendships or romantic relationships, which are characterized by mutual benefit of the partners.
12. Farber (2006: 7) attributes it to a reaction to "increasing feelings of anonymity or detachment resulting from the frenzied pace of technology, the perceived lack of a sense of community, and the seeming ubiquity of a shopping mall culture".
13. Gergen (1991) discusses how the concept of self is changing as a consequence of cultural and language changes. As Rose asserts, a number of professions function as experts in "measuring the psyche, in predicting its vicissitudes, in diagnosing the causes of its troubles and prescribing remedies" (1990: 3) and Lupton (1998), in reference to this comment, points to the following professions: psychologists, psychiatrists, social workers, counselors, and probation officers.
14. Cameron (2000a: 3) says that "these experts offer specialist knowledge and guidance on sex, marriage, divorce, bringing up children, and so on, all subjects where in the past people would have acquired knowledge and skill through more informal modes of instruction and through direct initiation".
15. According to Norcross and Freedheim (1992), certain elements of psychotherapy can be found in numerous forms of individual and family counseling, self-awareness programs as well as in treating somatic diseases. They also observe that the therapeutic activity is undertaken not only by psychologists but also by social workers and, as the authors state, by people who do not deal with the professional persuasion of people.
16. Needless to say, the individual approach to a customer is a part of the ideology that can be referred to as 'synthetic personalization' (Fairclough 1989), i.e. "designing discourse to give the impression of treating people as indi-

viduals within institutions that, in reality, are set up to handle people en masse" (Cameron 2000a: 75).

17. Sarangi (2002) identifies power asymmetry, expert-lay knowledge systems, role relationship, place of management and cooperation as major themes.

18. Conversation analysts have also extensively investigated the context of counseling and addiction (e.g. Peräkylä 1995; Silverman 1996); for an account of the history of conversation analysis see Heritage (1984).

19. Subsequent studies in this tradition, e.g. Labov and Fanshel (1977) used the conducted analysis as a frame of reference.

20. His research project was a cooperation between an anthropologist (Ray Birdwhistell) and a psychiatrist (Albert Scheflen) and it started at the end of the 1950s, but the publication of its main results was delayed until the early seventies (Peräkylä et al. 2008).

21. Pomerantz and Atkinson (1984) view ethnomethodological and CA research as sharing the following: "1. The main focus should be on how participants themselves produce and interpret each other's actions; 2. The researcher must treat all the interactional empirical data as unique and different and thus worthy of serious analytic attention; 3. There is a preference of working with naturally occurring interactions, rather than with those associated with experimental situations" (Gale 1991: 287).

22. Qualitative methods have been extensively used in psychotherapy research since the 1980's. The most developed of these are task analysis (Greenberg 1984) and comprehensive process analysis (Elliott 1989; cf. also Madill, Widdicombe, and Barkham 2001). On qualitative data analysis in counseling psychology see Yeh and Inman (2007).

23. The first major study using CA to understand psychotherapy as a particular type of interaction was conducted by Kathy Davis (1986) and took as its topic the therapist's ways of formulating clients' talk (Peräkylä et al. 2008: 19).

24. Cicourel (1992) considers exclusion of extratextual information as one of its main methodological weaknesses. In his view "both immediate and other aspects of context must be taken into account if we are able to understand language and social interaction in everyday life" (1992: 296).

25. Dörnyei (2007: 37–38) lists such most salient features of qualitative research as: emergent research design, a wide range of data, a natural setting, the exploration of the participants' views of the situation being studied, small sample size, and interpretive analysis.

26. Dörnyei (2007: 130) defines this as "a narrative that describes richly and in great detail the daily life of the community as well as the cultural meanings and beliefs the participants attach to their activities, events, and behaviors".

27. As I was not permitted to video-record the sessions, only selected aspects of non-verbal communication transpiring in the therapy sessions under scrutiny are analyzed. In recognition of a potential limitation of my data in this respect, the presented and discussed examples refer to aspects of kinesics, para-

linguistic cues and crying that are overtly commented on by the psychotherapist in his work with the clients. Aspects of silence as represented with timed pauses also feature in the transcripts and their functions are discussed. Still, since psychotherapeutic communication to a great extent does entail reading clients' non-verbal signals, a complete exclusion from the discussion of the functions non-verbal aspects of communication serve in the analyzed context would not adequately address the issue of therapeutic functioning of communication and would, in fact, distort the type of communicative and interactional work that goes on in psychotherapy.

28. See Van Leeuwen (2005) on 3 different models of interdisciplinary research: centralist, pluralist and integrationist.

29. Antaki et al. (2003) refer also to the so-called 'discursive turn'.

30. The concept of 'collaborative interpretation' was discussed by Cicourel (1992) and as Sarangi (2002) states is at par with Garfinkel's (1967) notion of 'documentary method of interpretation'.

31. Goodwin (1994: 626) states that: "the ability to see relevant entities is not lodged in the individual mind, but instead within a community of competent practitioners".

32. Peräkylä and Vehviläinen (2003) evidence a number of studies which have sought such a dialogue, e.g., Arminen (1998), Arminen and Leppo (2000), Peräkylä (1995), Ruusuvuori (2000), Vehviläinen (1999).

33. According to Peräkylä and Vehviläinen (2003: 730–731) SIKs can be classified by: 1. degree of detail in terms of interaction, and 2. degree of penetration into praxis.

34. Sarangi (2002) claims that in certain settings participant observation without becoming involved in the ongoing activity may be problematic for the participants, e.g. in the context of a medical clinic where the participant's observer's lack of involvement in the activities may be of concern for others.

35. Cicourel (1992: 303) also emphasizes the necessity to consult the informants to assess the relevance of the ethnographic information.

36. The long discussion was concluded with an invitation for me to talk with any of psychotherapists who were present at the research site.

37. Interestingly, during these briefing sessions I was cast into the role of an 'expert in language' who could offer some professional advice on language and communication (cf. Jones and Stubbe 2004).

38. Cicourel (1992) advocates the idea of collaborative interpretation and emphasizes the need for seeking support in the form of data feedback in order to ensure ecological validity.

39. Dörnyei (2007: 70) refers to it as 'active consent' as opposed to a 'passive' one which consists of "not opting out and not objecting to the study". As Dörnyei explains, the latter relates to a situation when, for instance, in the case of educational research, the consent form is sent to the parents of school children and they are asked to return it only when they refuse their consent.

40. The psychotherapist who was conducting the two workshops and personally knew all the participants suggested the oral consent for the participants of the first workshop. The participants of the second workshop signed the written informed consent – this was suggested by one of the co-organizers.
41. The decision to participate was mainly motivated by the scarcity of research into the discourse of psychotherapy from a more linguistic-oriented perspective. The withdrawal decision was related to the highly intimate and personal type of material to be disclosed.
42. These obligations are recognized by the ethical Standards of the American Educational Research Association (AERA 2002) (Dörnyei 2007: 66–67).
43. Hesse-Biber and Leavy (2006) notice that there is a tendency for ethical considerations to remain detached or marginalized from discussions of the 'real' research projects almost as an afterthought (Dörnyei 2007: 64).
44. Sarangi (2002: 123–127) provides succinct answers to these 4 questions: 1. We should look for the data "almost everywhere", 2. We should identify a set of problems of interest to our participants "as far as practicable", 3. The notion of collaborative interpretation "needs to be reassessed on a case-by-case basis", 4. The answer to whether we should tell our participants everything we find "has to be a cautious 'no'".
45. See, for example Schiffrin (1998).
46. Antaki et al. (2003) comment on different approaches to discourse analysis in the areas of social sciences and the humanities, and tensions between their different aims and the styles of work associated with them.
47. In fact, Schiffrin (1998) refers to these as 3 issues that are central to discourse analysis and about which discourse analysts must make assumptions.
48. On the topic of how psychotherapists use talk to socialize their clients into psychotherapy see Friedlander (1984). See also Friedlander (1984) on how therapists behave as 'socializing agents' by limiting the range of possible responses in order to elicit desirable behavior from their clients.
49. As Pea and Russel (1987: 303) explain, the extract was "a result in an experiment in which Garfinkel instructed his class to ask for clarifications of the meaning of everyday statements, thus calling into question common sense taken-for-granted structures shared by co-conversationalists".
50. According to Farber's (2006: 150) review, in deciding whether to self-disclose or not, the therapists "must reconcile the tension among three competing needs: first, to be as helpful as possible to patients, according patients the substantial benefits of disclosure; second, to respect and adhere to firm professional boundaries that afford a sense of safety and reflect an unwavering commitment to attend to the needs of the patient; and third, to express themselves in a genuine and open manner, one reflecting the profound sense of intimacy or potential intimacy in the relationship".
51. Countertransference constitutes an example of such undesirable input from the therapist in interactions with the client. Countertransference is "the

thoughts and feelings of the therapist, left over from old relationships and transferred onto the client" (Moursund and Erskine 2004: 67; cf. also Racker 1968). Countertransference was thought to interfere with the therapist's ability to do his/her job properly. More current views, however, claim that countertransference in fact can be used therapeutically: "while at one point the countertransference may have been viewed primarily as error to be corrected, it has more and more been recognized as a necessary component of the human interaction involved in psychotherapy" (Stone 1996: 29). Transference, as originally used by Freud (1912/1958) refers to "the displacement onto the therapist of feelings and thoughts originally experience[d] in previous relationships" (Moursund and Erskine 2004: 67).

52. Graf (2007) similarly claims that in coaching, instead of an implicit negotiation of meaning between communicative partners, we often find explicit negotiation for meaning as one of the characteristics of this type of discourse.

53. As Schiffrin (1999: 276) states, almost anything one says is a candidate for repair either by the speaker or listener. Speakers are more likely to participate in their own repairs either by initiating (self-initiation) or completing (self-completion) the repair.

54. In fact, Key (1975: 24) says that communication does not have to include words, but "some kind of body stance, movement, facial expression, or some noise is always present".

55. Even though Birdwhistell (1952, 1970) and Hall (1959) as pioneers in the study of non-verbal communication underlined the need to examine both non-verbal and verbal behavior in concert, in the 1960s and 1970s scholars tended to investigate verbal and non-verbal components separately (Streeck and Knapp 1992). Streeck and Knapp state that in the 1980s there was a renewed interest in the examination of verbal and non-verbal behavior in naturalistic conversation (cf. Poyatos 1980; Kendon 1987, 1988).

56. As Streeck and Knapp (1992) explicate, the so-called emblems (quotable gestures) are conceptualized as lexical units and they may be an exception. They are, however, used in situations where speech is not applicable.

57. Some researchers claim that non-verbal decoding skill is at the core of social intelligence, e.g. Archer (1980).

58. The research dedicated to exploring the role of non-verbal communication in psychotherapy has been focused mainly on the therapist's non-verbal behavior and its association with the therapist-client relationship. As Tickle-Degnen and Rosenthal (1992:143) state, "very little is about the client's behavior, or the interaction between the behavior of both the therapist and client". In fact, the same authors say that the purpose of research on client non-verbal behavior is usually to determine non-verbal signs of pathological conditions (cf. Waxer 1976, 1977) or psychodynamic processes (cf. Mahl 1987).

59. Some early researchers on therapeutic discourse (e.g. Gill, Newman, and Redlich 1954; Gottman and Markman 1978; Kiesler 1973; Mahrer 1985;

Russel 1987; Small and Manthei 1986) were aiming at finding the so-called 'moments of movement' in therapy that led to a change of the client's personality and/or behavior.

60. Similarly Key (1982: 10) states the following "it seems that nonverbal modalities carry the heavier weight of expressive and emotive messages. Thus, tone of voice and vocal quality, as seen in paralanguage, contribute to the meaning of the speech act".

61. This strategy is discussed in more detail in the chapter on Self-disclosure.

62. Key (1975: 33) adduces that "psychiatry has long recognized these contradictions".

63. This was one of the workshops organized by the Institute for Integrative Psychotherapy, which the author has attended.

64. Throughout the current discussion the terms self-verbalization and self-disclosure will be considered for practical purposes synonymous concepts and they will be used interchangeably.

65. Jourard's ideas as stated in his 1959 article are referred to as 'ideology of intimacy' (cf. Bochner 1982; Parks 1982, 1995).

66. According to Labov and Fanshel (1977), A-events are those known only to the speaker. A-events represent the speaker's personal experience. A-B-events are known both to the speaker and another participant.

67. Extreme case formulations are likely to occur when attempts are made to defend, justify, or rationalize a description or assessment. These formulations often rely on using such extreme terms as: all, none, most, absolutely, completely (cf. Edwards 2000).

68. Researchers who have begun to investigate issues related to patient disclosure are e.g., Farber (2003), Kelly (1998), Stiles (1995).

69. Yet, as Farber (2006) points out, Freud's 'fundamental rule' according to which the patient must disclose every thought that comes to mind, is almost certainly unfeasible.

70. Besnier (1990) also refers to it as a frequently recognized problem, i.e., the question of multiple keys. He refers to the contradictory signals as disjunction. Bateson (1972) in his pioneering work on schizophrenia documented how 'I love you' can be uttered with an aggressive tone of voice and angry face thus contradicting the literal meaning of the sentence.

71. Interactants in case of conflict or uncomfortable situations tend to subscribe to the position that they do not mean what they have not literally said and do not understand what they have not literally heard. Thus the messages which are not explicitly verbalized can be denied or they are subject to (re)negotiation at all times (Arndt and Janney 1991; cf. also Goffman 1959).

72. In fact, Gaik (1992: 273) states that comments such as "Stop playing pop shrink", "Stop practicing therapy without a license" or "Whattya trying to psychoanalyze me" testify to people's awareness of situations in which a therapeutic activity has been evoked in an ordinary conversation. Addition-

ally, psychotherapy functions as a thematic frame in many popular movies (cf. Farber 2006).

73. Farber and Hill (2002), in discussing their research findings and also the findings of numerous other scholars, state that clients typically withhold the issues of sex and procreation while happily disclosing the matters related to negative affection, intimacy and existential concerns.

74. This section partially reproduces material from an earlier publication, "Expressing the unexpressed: Self disclosure as interactional achievement in the psychotherapy session". *Communication & Medicine* 5/1: 39–48 (2008).

75. In psychotherapeutic terms 'resistance' is referred to as "the universal tendency to be withholding in therapy, to be not entirely open, present, or amenable to change" (Farber 2006: 31).

76. Pomerantz (1984) distinguishes between 2 types of disagreement: strong disagreements occur in turns containing exclusively disagreement components, and are not accompanied by agreement components: weak agreements, on the other hand occur in agreement-plus-disagreement turns.

77. Pittenger, Hockett, and Danehy (1960: 235) observe that if a therapist misses some crucial sign from a patient, the very fact that it is crucial means that it will come again, perhaps in a more intelligible manner.

78. Synchronic repetition refers to recurrence of words and collocations in the same discourse, diachronic repetition, on the other hand, is concerned with the recurrence of words in discourse at a later time (Tannen 1989). Both types of repetition tend to occur in the classical psychoanalytic session (cf. Vehviläinen 2003).

79. Sacks (1992 Vol. I) refers to it as the 'chaining rule'.

80. According to Pomerantz (1980), type 1 knowables comprise the information that one knows intimately, e.g., one's name, what one is doing, "assumed to be available to a competent subject-actor" (1980: 187). Type 2 knowables "are those that subject-actors are assumed to have access to by virtue of the knowings being occasioned. Where your friend is, what she or he did yesterday and the like are accountably available by virtue of the subject actor's having been told, having figured it out, having seen the friend, and so on" (1980: 187–188).

81. Litotes "describes the object to which it refers not directly, but through the negation of the opposite" (Bergmann 1992: 148).

82. Heritage (1985: 100) claims that formulation is "relatively rare in conversation" but it tends to characterize certain forms of institutional interaction. In this particular setting, according to Heritage it is most often undertaken by questioners.

83. Heritage and Watson (1979) divide conversational formulation into two types: gist formulation – primarily constitute clarifications, or demonstrations of comprehension or continuity with the talk so far, while upshot formulations, on the other hand draw out relevant implication from the talk so far (cf.

Antaki, Barnes, and Leudar 2005a). This distinction, according to Antaki and associates (2005a), has been otherwise neglected. According to Antaki and colleagues (2005a), in the wider usage, formulation has come to be referred to as "any commentary by one speaker, in whatever format, which may be taken to propose or imply a reworking of events described or implied by a previous speaker" (2005a: 17).

84. Davis (1986) made a reference to the possibility of a client's resistance to a therapist's claim. Yet, as Madill, Widdicombe, and Barkham (2001) state, this has not been studied in detail.

85. As Kamio (1997: 26) states 'I have a headache' locates the information clearly in the speaker's territory, examples such as 'I hear your German is excellent' locates the information in the hearer's realm of knowledge. Thus, whether the information falls into the speaker's territory or not affects the form of the utterances.

86. Oatley and Jenkins (1996) underline however, that emotions had traditionally been regarded as superfluous in psychology with no serious mental function (cf. also Cacioppo and Gardner 1999). Similarly, Frijda (1988: 349) says that "emotion was an underprivileged area in psychology. It was not regarded as a major area of scientific psychological endeavor that seemed to deserve concerted research efforts or receive them". Emotions have become a serious focus of psychological studies since around the mid 1970's (Frijda 1988).

87. The work on emotional intelligence, for instance is based on the notion that emotion significantly contributes to a fulfilling life: "the heightened ability to monitor one's own and others' emotions, to discriminate among them, and to use the information to guide one's thinking and action has proven to be as important a determinant of life success as traditional measures of intelligence such as IQ" (Cacioppo and Gardner 1999: 192–193). Greenberg (2004b: 3) states that – within his Emotion-focused therapy – emotional intelligence involves "honing the capacity to use emotions as a guide, without being a slave to emotions".

88. This perspective is variously referred to as positivist, essentialist, organismic, and traditional (Lupton 1998).

89. LeDoux, the author of *The Emotional Brain. The Mysterious Underpinnings of Emotional Life* (1998) says that basic emotions are in fact adaptive behaviors crucial to survival. The questions whether there is indeed a set of basic emotions independent of language and culture, or whether emotions have to do with the culturally-grounded labeling of bodily sensations, aspects of the context, and behavior before and after the event have been one of the major controversies within psychology (Gallois 1994).

90. In the words of Fairclough (1992: 64) "discourse is a practice not just representing the world, but of signifying the world, constituting and constructing the world in meaning".

91. In Lambert and Bergin's (1994) view this is what unites all the potentially divergent approaches to psychotherapy (cf. also Czabała 2006).

92. Parkinson (1996) states that 'cultures' function as an evaluative frame of reference as to what there is to get emotional about. Thus cultures to a great extent define and regulate emotional expression, cf. Lutz (1988), Harré (1986), Wierzbicka (1991).

93. Schemas "make up an internal system of categories and procedures that allow us to navigate through and make sense of the confusion of data available to us at any given moment" (Moursund and Erskine 2004: 19). What makes schemas a very important concept in psychology and psychotherapy is that they can form larger patterns, the so-called scripts (Berne 1972; Perls 1973). Scripts then constitute the major object of psychotherapeutic work as they constitute: "the old habits, the familiar ways of relating to people, the unquestioned knee-jerk reactions that prevent us from growing and changing and forming new kinds of relationships" (Moursund and Erskine 2004: 20).

94. Greenberg (2004b) succinctly summarizes this approach by stating that one cannot leave a place (here obviously get rid of an unwanted, negative, painful emotion) until one has arrived at it (thus has acknowledged the existence of this emotion).

95. Primary emotions are "the person's most fundamental direct initial reactions to a situation like being sad at a loss. Secondary emotions are those responses that are secondary to other, more primary, internal processes and may be defenses against these such as feeling hopeless when angry" (Greenberg 2004b: 7).

96. LeDoux (1998: 168–169) compares the amygdala to the hub of a wheel: "It receives low-level inputs from sensory-specific regions of the thalamus, higher level information from sensory-specific cortex, and still higher level (sensory independent) information about the general situation from the hippocampal formation. Through such connections, the amygdala is able to process the emotional significance of individual stimuli as well as complex situations. The amygdala is, in essence, involved in the appraisal of emotional meaning. It is where trigger stimuli do their triggering". The author also explains how the fact that the amygdala has a greater influence on the cortex than the cortex on the amygdala results in emotional arousal dominating and controlling thinking.

97. Sarangi refers to the function of language in the psychotherapeutic setting as externalizing since "for a diagnosis to be made, verbal expressions have to be taken aboard" (2001: 40).

98. Coates (2007: 41) says that "co-construction can involve a second speaker adding just a single word or an entire clause to an utterance, but in all cases of co-constructed utterances, what is achieved is two speakers speaking as if with a single voice".

99. This excerpt has also been discussed in the chapter on Self-disclosure.

100. Lines 15–20 of this extract are also discussed in the chapter on The Transparency of Meaning: Personalizing the Meaning in Psychotherapy.

101. Interestingly, psychotherapists explicate it on the basis of the dictate that clients do not express negative feelings towards significant others in their lives.

102. Psychotherapists, e.g. Bohart and Tallman (1998), suggest specific strategies that will enable clients to actively experience their hidden feelings. Mahrer (1998) discusses how to work with long-buried feelings and beliefs.

103. The context of the psychotherapy session presents an ideal opportunity to study the externalization of inner affect as it not only expects and encourages clients to verbalize any kind of emotion, but more importantly, unlike in other everyday contexts, negative social consequences of such emotional release are minimized to the point of elimination. This is to say that the client does not run the high risk of social ridicule or negative repute (as in everyday social interaction) since whatever transpires in the session is shared by the client and therapist within the protective bounds of the therapeutic alliance.

104. The more qualitatively-oriented psychology studies on silence single out 3 dominant interpretations of the phenomenon under discussion: silence as resistance, silence as regression, and silence as communication (Levitt 2002).

105. Interestingly, however, the theoretical literature is quite contradictory on the advisability of using silence in therapy as well as the effects of silence in therapy (cf. Hill, Thompson, and Ladany 2003). A number of scholars point to methodological flaws in the research on silence (cf. Levitt 2001, 2002).

106. In this type of interview, the interviewer and participant review a taped therapy session and examine recollections of the participant's experiences (Levitt 2002: 228; cf. also Elliott 1986; Kagan 1975).

107. Nelson (2005) states that such a ubiquitous and profound behavior as crying has received disproportionately little attention in the psychological literature and in training programs for psychotherapists.

108. This also addresses the practical problem of numerous therapy publications whose instruction on conveying empathy, genuineness and warmth (thus the so-called therapeutic conditions) are often "disappointingly general and vague" (Burleson 1994: 138).

109. As Bachelor (1988) explicates, cognitive empathy consists in the therapist accurately recognizing the client's ongoing innermost experience, state or motivation; affective empathy is characterized by the psychotherapist partaking of the same feeling the client is personally experiencing at that moment. When a psychotherapist discloses to a patient that they have something in common, this is sharing empathy. Nurturant empathy is expressed by the therapist when being supportive, security-providing, or totally attentive.

110. Cawyer and Smith-Dupré (1995: 255) claim that "a full understanding of supportive communication requires that one considers aspects of it which are mutually managed by the people involved".

111. The client's added third element in the list is particularly interesting in view of Potter's (1996) following Jefferson's (1990) observation that three-part lists tend to indicate the commonality of individual instances. Thus the client's ratification of the therapist's expression of empathy in fact contributed to building the client's typical home circumstances.

112. Burleson (1994: 151) discusses several rules for managing emotional distress as a consequence of being exposed to comforting strategies: "(a) don't suppress or ignore feelings, but rather work to explore, recognize, and articulate them, (b) view feelings as responses to specific situations (rather than as chronic conditions), (c) try to understand how particular features of situations, and their effects on hopes and goals, cause particular feelings, and (d) view distressful situations in the context of broader goals, ambitions, and hopes".

113. Psychologists, counselors and psychotherapists regard active listening as a skill, and this is how it is referred to in numerous handbooks. This skill however, can only be enacted by verbal and/or non-verbal behavior thus in the actual interaction it becomes a practice, and whether a psychotherapist possesses this skill or not becomes evident only in the actual interaction with a client.

114. http://www.swarthmore.edu/SocSci/kgergen1/web/page.phtml?id=manu6&st =manuscripts&hf=1

115. Ochs (1992: 337) refers to her discussion as "exemplary of a more general relation between language and social meaning".

116. In fact ten Have (2001: 3) refers to one of the aspects of applied Conversation Analysis as "efforts to apply CA findings and/or specific studies to advise people and organizations how specific practical problems might be handled in order to facilitate smooth and effective practice".

References

Adler, Ronald, and Neil Towne
    1999   *Looking Out / Looking In*. New York: Harcourt Brace College Publishers.
Agar, Michael
    1985   Institutional discourse. *Text* 5: 147–168.
Ainsworth-Vaughn, Nancy
    2001   The discourse of medical encounters. In *The Handbook of Discourse Analysis*, Deborah Schiffrin, Deborah Tannen, and Heidi Hamilton (eds.), 453–469. Malden, MA: Blackwell.
Albrecht, Terrance L., and Mara B. Adelman
    1987   *Communicating Social Support*. Thousand Oaks, CA: Sage.
Anderson, Harlene
    1997   *Conversation, Language, and Possibilities*. New York: Basic Books.
Angus, Lynne, Levitt Heidi, and Karen Hardtke
    1999   The narrative process coding system: Research applications and implications for psychotherapy practice. *Journal of Clinical Psychology* 55: 1255–1270.
Angus, Lynne, and John McLeod (eds.)
    2004   *Handbook of Narrative and Psychotherapy: Practice, Theory and Research*. Thousand Oaks, CA: Sage.
Antaki, Charles
    2002   Personalized revision of 'failed' questions. *Discourse & Society* 4: 411–428.
Antaki, Charles, Barnes Rebecca, and Ivan Leudar
    2005a   Diagnostic formulations in psychotherapy. *Discourse Studies* 7/6: 1–22.
    2005b   Self-disclosure as a situated interactional practice. *British Journal of Social Psychology* 44: 181–199.
Antaki, Charles, Billig Michael, Edwards Derek, and Jonathan Potter
    2003   Discourse analysis means doing analysis: A critique of six analytic shortcomings. http://extra.shu.ac.uk/daol/articles/open/2002/002/antaki 2002002-paper.html (date of access September 2007).
Archer, Dane
    1980   *Social Intelligence*. New York: M. Evans & Co.
Argyle, Michael, Slater Veronica, Nicholson Hillary, Williams Marylin, and Philip Burgess
    1970   The communication of inferior and superior attitudes by verbal and non-verbal signals. *British Journal of Social and Clinical Psychology* 9: 221–231.

Arminen, Iikka
   1998   Sharing experiences: Doing therapy with the help of mutual references in the meetings of Alcoholics Anonymous. *Sociological Quarterly* 39: 491–515.
Arminen, Iikka, and Anna Leppo
   2000   The dilemma of two cultures in a twelve-step treatment: Professionals' responses to clients who act against their best interests. In *Listening to the Welfare State*, Michael Seltzer, Søren P. Olesen, Iimari Rostila, and Christian Kullberg (eds.), 183–212. Aldershot: Ashgate.
Armon-Jones, Claire
   1986   The thesis of constructionism. In *The Social Construction of Emotions*, Rom Harré (ed.), 32–56. Oxford: Basil Blackwell.
Arndt, Horst, and Richard Janney
   1987   *Intergrammar: Toward an Integrative Model of Verbal, Prosodic, and Kinesic Choices in Speech*. Berlin/New York: Mouton de Gruyter.
   1991   Verbal, prosodic, and kinesic emotive contrasts in speech. *Journal of Pragmatics* 15: 521–549.
Atkinson, John M., and Paul Drew
   1979   *Order in Court: The Organization of Verbal Interaction in Judicial Settings*. London: Macmillan.
Bachelor, Alexandra
   1988   How clients perceive empathy: A content analysis of 'received' empathy. *Psychotherapy* 25: 227–240.
Bakhtin, Mikhail
   1984   *Problems of Dostoevsky's Poetics*. Minneapolis: University of Minnesota Press.
Barrett-Lennard, Godfrey T.
   1981   The empathy cycle: Refinement of a nuclear concept. *Journal of Counseling Psychology* 28/2: 91–100.
Bartesaghi, Mariaelena
   2009   How the therapist does authority: Six strategies for substituting client accounts in the session. *Communication & Medicine* 6/1: 15–25.
Barton, Ellen
   2002   Inductive discourse analysis: Identifying rich features. In *Discourse Studies in Composition*, Ellen Barton, and Gail Stygall (eds.), 19–42. Cresskill, NJ: Hampton Press.
   2004   Linguistic discourse analysis: How the language in text works. In *What Writing Does and How it Does it: An Introduction to Analyzing Text and Textual Practices*, Charles Bazerman, and Paul Prior (eds.), 57–82. Mahwah, NJ: Ablex.
Bateson, Gregory
   1972   *Steps to an Ecology of Mind: Collected Essays in Anthropology, Psychiatry, Evolution, and Epistemology*. Chicago: University of Chicago Press.

Beach, Wayne A., and Christie N. Dixson
    2001   Revealing moments: Formulating understandings of adverse experiences in a health appraisal interview. *Social Science & Medicine* 52: 25–44.
Bechara, Antonine, Damasio Hanna, Tranel Daniel, and Antonio R. Damasio
    1997   Deciding advantageously before knowing the advantageous strategy. *Science* 275: 1293–1295.
Becker, Dana
    2005   *The Myth of Empowerment: Women and the Therapeutic Culture in America*. New York: New York University Press.
Beier, Ernst, and Davis M. Young
    1998   *The Silent Language of Psychotherapy: Social Reinforcement of Unconscious Processes*. 3rd ed. New York: Aldine.
Bercelli, Fabrizio, Rossano Federico, and Maurizio Viaro
    2008   Clients' responses to therapists' re-interpretations. In *Conversation Analysis and Psychotherapy*, Anssi Peräkylä, Charles Antaki, Sanna Vehviläinen, and Ivan Leudar (eds.), 77–109. Cambridge: Cambridge University Press.
Berg, John H., and Valerian J. Derlega
    1987   Themes in the study of self-disclosure. In *Self-Disclosure*, Valerian J. Derlega, and John H. Berg (eds.), 1–8. New York: Plenum.
Berger, Charles
    1979   Beyond initial interactions. In *Personality and Interpersonal Communication*, Howard Giles, and John Daly (eds.), 122–144. Oxford: Blackwell.
Bergmann, Jörg R.
    1992   Veiled morality: Notes on discretion in psychiatry. In *Talk at Work: Interaction in Institutional Settings*, Paul Drew, and John Heritage (eds.), 137–162. Cambridge: Cambridge University Press.
Berne, Eric
    1972   *What Do You Say After You Say Hello?: The Psychology of Human Destiny*. New York: Grove Press.
Berscheid, Ellen
    1987   Emotion and interpersonal communication. In *Interpersonal Processes: New Directions in Communication Research*, Michael E. Roloff, and Gerald R. Miller (eds.), 77–88. Newbury Park, CA: Sage.
Besnier, Nico
    1990   Language and affect. *Annual Review of Anthropology* 19: 419–451.
Birdwhistell, Ray L.
    1952   *Introduction to Kinesics*. Louisville, KY: University of Louisville Press.
    1970   *Kinesics and Context*. Philadelphia, PA: University of Pennsylvania Press.
Blache, Geraldine, Bor Robert, Eleftheriadou Zack, and Margaret Lloyd
    1996   *Communication Skills for Medicine*. New York: Churchill Livingstone.

Bloch, Charlotte
1996   Emotions and discourse. *Human Studies* 16/3: 323–41.
Bloor, Michael
1997   Addressing social problem through qualitative research. In *Qualitative Research: Theory, Method and Practice*, David Silverman (ed.), 221–238. London: Sage.
Bochner, Stephen (ed.)
1982   *International Series in Experimental Psychology* 1: 59–160.
Bohart, Arthur C., and Karen Tallman
1998   The person as active agent in experiential therapy. In *Handbook of Experiential Psychotherapy*, Leslie S. Greenberg, Jeanne C. Watson, and Germain Lietaer (eds.), 178–200. New York: The Guilford Press.
Bolinger, Dwight
1982   Intonation and gesture. *Papers from the Parasession on Non-declaratives*: 1–22. Chicago: Chicago Linguistic Society.
Bongar, Bruce, and Larry E. Beutler
1995   *Comprehensive Textbook of Psychotherapy Theory and Practice.* Oxford/New York: Oxford University Press.
Braun, Virginia, and Victoria Clarke
2006   Using thematic analysis in psychology. *Qualitative Research in Psychology* 3: 77–101.
Breuer, Josef, and Sigmund Freud
1957   *Studies on Hysteria* (first edition 1895). New York: Basic Books.
Brinton, Laurel
1990   The development of discourse markers in English. In *Historical Linguistics and Philology*, Jacek Fisiak (ed.), 45–71. Amsterdam/Philadelphia: John Benjamins.
Brown, Gillian, and George Yule
1983   *Discourse Analysis.* Cambridge: Cambridge University Press.
Bruner, Jerome
1987   *Actual Minds, Possible Worlds.* Cambridge, MA: Harvard University Press.
1990   Autobiography as self. In *Acts of Meaning*, Jerome Bruner (ed.), 33–66. Cambridge, MA: Harvard University Press.
Bucholtz, Mary, and Kira Hall
2005   Identity and interaction: A sociocultural linguistic approach. *Discourse Studies* 7/4–5: 585–614.
Burleson, Brant R.
1984   Age, social-cognitive development, and the use of comforting strategies. *Communication Monographs* 51: 140–153.
1994   Comforting messages: Features, functions, and outcomes. In *Strategic Interpersonal Communication*, John A. Daly, and John M. Wiemann (eds.), 135–161. Hillsdale, NJ: Lawrence Erlbaum.

2003   Emotional support skills. In *Handbook of Communication and Social Interaction Skills*, John O. Greene, and Brant R. Burleson (eds.), 551–594. Mahwah, NJ: Lawrence Erlbaum.

Burleson, Brant R., and Erina L. MacGeorge

2002   Supportive communication. In *Handbook of Interpersonal Communication*, Mark L. Knapp, and John A. Daly (eds.), 374–424. 3rd ed. Thousand Oaks, CA: Sage.

Buttny, Richard

1993   *Social Accountability in Communication*. London: Sage.

2004   *Talking Problems: Studies of Discursive Construction*. New York: State University of New York Press.

Buttny, Richard, and Jodi R. Cohen

1991   The uses of goals in therapy. In *Understanding Face-to-Face Interaction: Issues Linking Goals and Discourse*, Karen Tracy (ed.), 63–78. Hillsdale, NJ: Lawrence Erlbaum.

Cacioppo, John T., and Wendi L. Gardner

1999   Emotion. *Annual Review of Psychology* 50: 191–214.

Caffi, Claudia, and Richard W. Janney

1994   Towards a pragmatics of emotive communication. *Journal of Pragmatics* 22: 325–374.

Cameron, Deborah

2000a   *Good to Talk? Living and Working in a Communication Culture*. London: Sage.

2000b   Styling the worker: Gender and the commodification of language in the globalized service economy. *Journal of Sociolinguistics* 4/3: 323–347.

2001   *Working with Spoken Discourse*. London: Sage.

Cameron, Deborah, Frazer Elizabeth, Harvey Penelope, Rampton Ben, and Kay Richardson

1992   *Researching Language: Issues of Power and Method*. London: Routledge.

Campos, Joseph, Mumme Donna L., Kermoian Rosanne, and Rosemary Campos

1994   A functionalist perspective on the nature of emotion. *Monographs of the Society for Research in Child Development* 59 (2/3): 284–303.

Candlin, Christopher N.

2000   *The Cardiff Lecture 2000: New discourses of the clinic rediscovering the patient in healthcare*. Cardiff. Cardiff University. (March) University of Wales Press. http://www.cf.ac.uk/encap/hcrc/cardlecturepubs.html

Candlin, Sally

2000   New dynamics in the nurse-patient relationship? In *Discourse and Social Life*, Malcolm Coulthard, and Srikant Sarangi (eds.), 230–245. Harlow: Longman/Pearson.

Cawyer, Carol S., and Athena Smith-Dupré

1995   Communicating social support: Identifying supportive episodes in an HIV/AIDS support group. *Communication Quarterly* 43: 243–358.

Cicourel, Aaron V.
1992   The interpenetration of communicative contexts: Examples from medi-
          cal encounters. In *Rethinking Context. Language as an Interactive
          Phenomenon*, Alessandro Duranti, and Charles Goodwin (eds.), 291–
          310. Cambridge: Cambridge University Press.
Clark, Fred C.
1996   The client's uniqueness: A personal discovery of therapeutic relations-
          hip. *Transactional Analysis Journal* 26/4: 312–315.
Clarke, Angus
2000   On being a subject in discourse research. Paper presented at the *Inter-
          national Conference on Text and Talk at Work*, University of Gent,
          16–19 August.
Coates, Jennifer
1997   Competing discourses of femininity. In *Communicating Gender in
          Context*, Helga Kotthoff, and Ruth Wodak (eds.), 285–313. Amster-
          dam/Philadelphia: John Benjamins.
2007   Talk in a play frame: More on laughter and intimacy. *Journal of
          Pragmatics* 39: 29–49.
Cook, John J.
1964   Silence in psychotherapy. *Journal of Counseling Psychology* 11: 42–
          46.
Cosby, Paul C.
1973   Self-disclosure: A literature review. *Psychological Bulletin* 79: 73–91.
Coupland, Justine, Coupland Nikolas, Howard Giles, Henwood Karen, and John M.
          Wiemann
1988   Elderly self-disclosure: Interactional and intergroup issues. *Language
          and Communication* 8/2: 109–133.
Cutrona, Carolyn E.
1996   *Social Support in Couples*. Thousand Oaks, CA: Sage.
Cutrona, Carolyn E., and Daniel Russel
1990   Type of social support and specific stress: Toward a theory of optimal
          matching. In *Social Support: An Interactional View*, Irwin G. Sarason,
          Barbara R. Sarason, and Gregory R. Pierce (eds.), 319–366. New
          York: Wiley.
Cutrona, Carolyn E., and Julie A. Suhr
1994   Social support communication in the context of marriage: An analysis
          of couples' supportive interactions. In *The Communication of Social
          Support: Messages, Interactions, Relationships, and Community*, Burt
          R. Burleson, Terrance Albrecht, and Irwin Sarason (eds.), 113–135.
          Newbury, CA: Sage.
Czabała, Jan C.
2006   *Czynniki Leczące w Psychoterapii* [The Healing Factors in Psychothe-
          rapy]. Warszawa: Wydawnictwo Naukowe PWN.

Damasio, Antonio
1994   *Descartes' Error: Emotions, Reason, and the Human Brain.* New York: Grosset/Putnam.
Darwin, Charles
1872   *The Expression of Emotions in Man and Animals.* London: John Murray.
Davis, Kathy
1986   The process of problem (re)formulation in psychotherapy. *Sociology of Health and Illness* 8: 44–74.
Drew, Paul, and John Heritage
1992   *Talk at Work: Interaction in Institutional Settings.* Cambridge: Cambridge University Press.
Dörnyei, Zoltan
2007   *Research Methods in Applied Linguistics.* Oxford: Oxford University Press.
Duranti, Alessandro
1997   *Linguistic Anthropology.* Cambridge: Cambridge University Press.
Eckert, Penelope, and Sally McConnel-Ginet
1992   Think practically and look locally: Language and gender as community-based practice. *Annual Review of Anthropology* 21: 461–490.
Edwards, Derek
1997   *Discourse and Cognition.* London: Sage.
1999   Emotion discourse. *Culture & Psychology* 5: 271–291.
2000   Extreme case formulations: Softeners, investment, and doing nonliteral. *Research on Language and Social Interaction* 33/4: 347–373.
Ekman, Paul, and Wallace Friesen
1969   Nonverbal leakage and clues to deception. *Psychiatry* 32: 88–106.
Elliott, Robert
1984   A discovery-oriented approach to significant events in psychotherapy: Interpersonal Process Recall and comprehensive process analysis. In *Patterns of Change: An Intensive Analyses of Psychotherapy Process*, Laura Rice, and Leslie S. Greenberg (eds.), 249–286. New York: The Guilford Press.
1986   Interpersonal Process Recall (IPR) as a psychotherapy process research method. In *The Psychotherapeutic Process*, Leslie Greenberg, and William Pinsof (eds.), 503–527. New York: The Guilford Press.
1989   Comprehensive Process Analysis: Understanding the change process in significant therapy events. In *Entering the Circle: Hermeneutic Investigation in Psychology*, Martin Packer, and Richard B. Addison (eds.), 411–420. Albany, NY: SUNY Press.
Erskine, Richard
1989   A relationship therapy: Developmental perspectives. In *Developmental Theories and the Clinical Process: Conference Proceedings of the Eastern Regional Transactional Analysis Conference*, Bruce R. Loria (ed.), 123–135. Madison, WI: Omnipress.

Erskine, Richard, and Janet Moursund
1988   *Integrative Psychotherapy in Action.* Newbury Park, CA: Sage.
Erskine, Richard, Moursund Janet, and Rebecca Trautmann
1999   *Beyond Empathy: A Therapy of Contact in Relationship.* Philadelphia: Brunner/Mazel.
Erskine, Richard, and Rebecca Trautmann
1996   Methods of an Integrative Psychotherapy. *Transactional Analysis Journal* 26/4: 316–328.
Fairclough, Norman
1989   *Language and Power.* London: Longman.
1992   *Discourse and Social Change.* Cambridge: Polity Press.
Farber, Barry A.
2003   Self-disclosure in psychotherapeutic practice and supervision: An introduction. *Journal of Clinical Psychology* 59/5: 525–528.
2006   *Self-Disclosure in Psychotherapy.* New York/London: The Guilford Press.
Farber, Barry A., Berano Kathryn C., and Joseph S. Capobianco
2004   Clients' perceptions of the process and consequences of self-disclosure in psychotherapy. *Journal of Counseling Psychology,* 51/3: 340–346.
Farber, Barry A., and Desnee A. Hall
2002   Disclosure to therapists: What is and is not discussed in psychotherapy. *Journal of Clinical Psychology* 58: 359–370.
Ferrara, Kathleen
1994   *Therapeutic Ways with Words.* New York: Oxford University Press.
Fisher, Sue
1986   *In the Patient's Best Interest: Women and the Politics of Medical Decisions.* New Brunswick, NJ: Rutgers University Press.
Fosha, Diana
2000   *The Transforming Power of Affect: A Model for Accelerated Change.* New York: Basic Books.
Frank, Jerome D.
1961   *Persuasion and Healing. A Comparative Study of Psychotherapy.* New York: Schocken.
1974   Psychotherapy: The restoration of morale. *American Journal of Psychiatry* 131: 271–274.
1977   Jak leczy psychoterapia [How psychotherapy heals]. *Psychoterapia* 20: 3–10.
Frank, Kenneth A.
1991   Action, insight, and working through: Outlines of an integrative approach. *Psychoanalytic Dialogues* 1: 535–577.
Freed, Alice
1996   Language and gender in an experimental setting. In *Rethinking Language and Gender Research: Theory and Practice,* Victoria Bergvall, Janet Bing, and Alice Freed (eds.), 54–76. New York: Longman.

Freed, Alice, and Alice Greenwood
1996   Women, men, and type of talk: What makes the difference? *Language in Society* 25/1: 1–26.

Freemantle, David
1998   *What Customers Like about You: Adding Emotional Value for Service Excellence and Competitive Advantage*. London and Santa Rosa, CA: Nicholas Brealey.

Freud, Sigmund
1912/1958 The dynamics of transference. In *The Standard Edition of the Complete Works of Sigmund Freud*, James Strachey (ed. & trans.), Vol. 12: 97–108. London: Hogarth Press.

Friedlander, Myrna
1984   Psychotherapy talk as social control. *Psychotherapy: Theory, Research, Practice, Training* 21: 335–341.

Frijda, Nico
1988   The laws of emotion. *American Psychologist* 43/5: 349–358.

Fromm-Reichmann, Frieda
1950   *Principles of Intensive Psychotherapy*. Chicago: Chicago University Press.
1959   *Psychoanalysis and Psychotherapy*. Chicago: Chicago University Press.

Frosh, Stephen
1997   Screaming under the bridge: Masculinity, rationality and psychotherapy. In *Body Talk. The Material and Discursive Regulation of Sexuality, Madness and Reproduction*, Jane M. Usher (ed.), 70–84. London/New York: Routledge.

Fuller, Janet M.
1998   Marking common knowledge and negotiating common ground: The use of *y'know* in Pennsylvania German. *Paper Presented at NWAVE 27*, 1–4 October, Athens, Georgia.
2003   The influence of speaker roles on discourse marker use. *Journal of Pragmatics* 35: 23–45.

Furedi, Frank
2004   *Therapy Culture: Cultivating Vulnerability in an Uncertain Age*. London: Routledge.

Gaik, Frank
1992   Radio talk-therapy and the pragmatics of possible worlds. In *Rethinking Context. Language as an Interactive Phenomenon*, Alessandro Duranti, and Charles Goodwin (eds.), 271–289. Cambridge: Cambridge University Press.

Gale, Jerry E.
1991   *Conversation Analysis of Therapeutic Discourse: The Pursuit of a Therapeutic Agenda*. Norwood, NJ: Ablex Publishing Corporation.

Galison, Peter
    1997   *Image and Logic: A Material Culture of Microphysics*. Chicago: Chicago University Press.
Gallois, Cynthia
    1994   Group membership, social rules, and power. A social-psychological perspective on emotional communication. *Journal of Pragmatics* 22: 301–324.
Garfinkel, Harold
    1967   *Studies in Ethnomethodology*. Englewood Cliffs NJ: Prentice-Hall.
Geertz, Clifford
    1973   *The Interpretation of Cultures*. New York: Basic Books.
Gehrie, Mark
    1999   On boundaries and intimacy in psychoanalysis. In *Pluralism in Self-Psychology: Progress in Self-Psychology, vol. 15*, Arnold Goldberg (ed.), 229–232. Hillsdale, NJ: The Analytic Press.
Gergen, Kenneth
    1991   *The Saturated Self: Dilemmas of Identity in Modern Life*. New York/Oxford: Basic Books.
Gerhardt, Julie, and Charles Stinson
    1995   'I don't know': Resistance or groping for words? The construction of analytic subjectivity. *Psychoanalytic Dialogues* 5/4: 619–672.
Giddens, Anthony
    1991   *Modernity and Self-identity. Self and Society in the Late Modern Age*. Cambridge: Polity Press.
Gill, Merton, Newman Richard, and Frederic Redlich
    1954   *The Initial Interview in Psychiatric Practice*. New York: International Universities Press.
Goffman, Ervin
    1959   *Presentation of Self in Everyday Life*. Garden City, NY: Doubleday Anchor.
    1967   *Interaction Ritual*. New York: Anchor Books.
    1978   Response cries. *Language* 54/4: 787–815.
    1981   *Forms of Talk*. Oxford: Blackwell.
Gold, Jerold R.
    1996   *Key Concepts in Psychotherapy Integration*. New York: Plenum.
Goodwin, Charles
    1986   Audience diversity, participation and interpretation. *Text* 6/3: 283–316.
    1994   Professional vision. *American Anthropologist* 96: 606–33.
Gottman, John M., and Howard J. Markman
    1978   Experimental design in psychotherapy research. In *Handbook of Psychotherapy and Behavior Change*, 2nd ed., Sol L. Garfield, and Allen E. Bergin (eds.), 23–62. New York: Wiley.

Graf, Eva
    2007   'I'm not embarrassed' – 'a little ... uncomfortable? Is that nearer?' The negotiation for meaning in the discourse of coaching. In *Current Trends in Pragmatics*, Piotr Cap, and Joanna Nijakowska (eds.), 281–302. Cambridge: Cambridge Scholar Press.

Grant, David, Keenoy Tom, and Cliff Oswick
    1998   Introduction. Organizational discourse: Of diversity, dichotomy and multi-disciplinarity. In *Discourse and Organization*, David Grant, Tom Keenoy, and Cliff Oswick (eds.), 1–17. London: Sage.

Greenberg, Leslie S.
    1984   Task analysis: The general approach. In *Patterns of Change: Intensive Analysis of Psychotherapeutic Process*, Laura N. Rice, and Leslie S. Greenberg (eds.), 124–148. New York: The Guilford Press.
    1991   Research on the process of change. *Psychotherapy Research* 1/1: 3–16.
    1999   Ideal psychotherapy research: A study of significant change processes. *Journal of Clinical Psychology* 55: 1467–1480.
    2004a   Introduction. *Emotion* Special Issue. *Clinical Psychology and Psychotherapy* 11: 1–2.
    2004b   Emotion-focused Therapy. *Clinical Psychology and Psychotherapy* 11: 3–16.

Greenberg, Leslie S., and Lynne Angus
    2004   The contribution of emotion process to narrative change: A dialectical constructivist approach. In *Handbook of Narrative and Psychotherapy: Practice Theory and Research*, Lynne Angus, and John McLeod (eds.), 331–350. Thousand Oaks, CA: Sage.

Greenberg, Leslie S., and Sandra C. Paivio
    1997   *Working with the Emotions in Psychotherapy*. New York: The Guilford Press.

Greenberg, Leslie S., and Juan Pascual-Leone
    1995   A dialectal constructivist approach to experiential change. In *Constructivism in Psychotherapy*, Robert A. Neimeyer, and Michael J. Mahoney (eds.), 169–191. Washington, DC: American Psychological Association.
    2001   A dialectical constructivist view of the creation of personal meaning. *Journal of Constructivist Psychology* 14: 165–168.

Greenberg, Leslie S., Rice Laura N., and Robert Elliott
    1993   *Facilitating Emotional Change*. New York: The Guilford Press.

Greenberg, Leslie S., and Jeremy D. Safran
    1987   *Emotion in Psychotherapy: Affect, Cognition and the Process of Change*. New York: The Guilford Press.
    1989   Emotion in psychotherapy. *American Psychologist* 44: 19–29.

Gunnarsson, Britt
    2009   *Professional Discourse*. London/New York: Continuum.

Gunnarsson, Britt, Linell Per, and Bengt Nordberg
1997   Introduction. In *The Construction of Professional Discourse*, Britt
            Gunnarsson, Per Linell, and Bengt Nordberg (eds.), 1–12. London:
            Longman.
Hak, Tony, and Fijgje de Boer
1996   Formulations in first encounters. *Journal of Pragmatics* 25: 83–99.
Hall, Edward T.
1959   *The Silent Language*. Garden City, NY: Doubleday.
Harré, Rom
1986   An outline of the social constructionist viewpoint. In *The Social Const-
            ruction of Emotions*, Rom Harré (ed.), 2–14. Oxford: Basil Blackwell.
1991   *Physical Being: A Theory for a Corporeal Psychology*. Oxford: Basil
            Blackwell.
He, Agnes W., and Brian Lindsey
1998   You know as an information status enhancing device: Arguments from
            grammar and interaction. *Functions of Languages* 5: 133–155.
Hearn, Jeff
1993   Emotive subjects: Organizational men, organizational masculinities
            and the (de)construction of "emotions". In *Emotion in Organizations*,
            Stephen Fineman (ed.), 142–166. London: Sage.
Hepburn, Alexa
2004   Crying: Notes on description, transcription and interaction. *Research
            on Language and Social Interaction* 37: 251–290.
Heritage, John
1984   A change-of-state token and aspects of its sequential placement. In
            Structures of Social Action, John M. Atkinson, and John Heritage
            (eds.), 299–345. Cambridge: Cambridge University Press.
1985   Analyzing news interviews: Aspects of the production of talk for an
            overhearing audience. In *Handbook of Discourse Analysis: Volume* 3,
            Teun van Dijk (ed.), 95–117. London: Academic Press.
Heritage, John, and Rod Watson
1979   Formulations as conversational objects. In *Everyday Language*,
            George Psathas (ed.), 123–162. Mahwah NJ: Lawrence Erlbaum.
Hermans, Hubert
2004   The dialogical self: Between exchange and power. In *The Dialogical
            Self in Psychotherapy*, Hubert Hermans, and Giancarlo Dimaggio
            (eds.), 13–28. New York: Brunner/Routledge.
Hermans, Hubert, and Giancarlo Dimaggio (eds.)
2004   *The Dialogical Self in Psychotherapy*. New York: Brunner/Routledge.
Hesse-Biber, Sharlene N., and Patricia Leavy
2006   *The Practice of Qualitative Research*. Thousand Oaks, CA: Sage.
Hill, Clara E., Thompson Barbara J., and Nicholas Ladany
2003   Therapist use of silence in therapy: A survey. *Journal of Clinical Psy-
            chology* 59/4: 513–524.

Hochschild, Arlie
  1983   *The Managed Heart: Commercialization of Human Feeling*. Berkley, CA: University of California Press.
Holmes, Janet
  1986   Functions of 'you know' in women and men's speech. *Language in Society* 15/1: 1–21.
Hornberger, Nancy
  1994   Ethnography. *TESOL Quarterly* 28/4: 688–90.
Horvath, Adam O.
  2001   The alliance. *Psychotherapy* 38: 365–372.
Horvath, Adam O., and Leslie S. Greenberg
  1994   *The Working Alliance: Theory, Research and Practice*. New York: Wiley.
Hustvedt, Siri
  2008   *The Sorrows of an American*. New York: Henry Holt and Company.
Hutchby, Ian
  2002   Resisting the incitement to talk in child counseling: Aspects of the utterance 'I don't know'. *Discourse Studies* 4/2: 147–168.
  2004   Conversation analysis and the study of broadcast talk. In *Handbook of Language and Social Interaction*, Robert E. Sanders, and Kristine Fitch (eds.), 437–460. Mahwah. NJ: Lawrence Erlbaum.
  2005   Active listening: Formulations and the elicitation of feelings-talk in child counseling. *Research on Language and Social Interaction* 38/3: 303–329.
  2007   *The Discourse of Child Counselling*. Amsterdam/Philadelphia: John Benjamins.
Irvine, Judith T.
  1990   Registering affect: Heteroglossia in the linguistic expression of emotion. In *Language and the Politics of Emotion*, Catherine A. Lutz, and Lila Abu-Lughod (eds.), 126–161. Cambridge: Cambridge University Press.
Jamison, Kay
  2004   *Exuberance. The Passion for Life*. New York: Vintage Books.
Jaworski, Adam
  1993   *The Power of Silence: Social and Pragmatic Perspectives*. Newbury Park, CA: Sage.
Jefferson, Gail
  1988   On the sequential organization of troubles-talk in ordinary conversation. *Social Problems* 35: 418–441.
  1990   List construction as a task and resource. In *Interaction Competence*, George Psathas (ed.), 63–92. Lanham, MD: University Press of America.
  2004   Glossary of transcript symbols with an introduction. In *Conversation Analysis: Studies From the First Generation*, Gene H. Lerner (ed.), 13–23. Amsterdam/Philadephia: John Benjamins.

Johnstone, Barbara
    2000   *Qualitative Methods in Sociolinguistics.* New York: Oxford University Press.
Jones, Alan, and Christopher N. Candlin
    2007   Interprofessional contact zones: Building on members' reflexivity. Paper given at the 4th Conference on *Discourse, Identity and the Enterprise.* Nottingham 2007.
Jones, Deborah, and Maria Stubbe
    2004   Communication and the reflective practitioner: A shared perspective from sociolinguistics and organizational communication. *International Journal of Applied Linguistics* 14/2: 185–211.
Jorgensen, Danny L.
    1989   *Participant Observation: Methodology for Human Studies.* Newbury, CA: Sage.
Jourard, Sidney M.
    1959   Self-disclosure and other cathexis. *Journal of Abnormal and Social Psychology* 59: 428–431.
    1968   *Disclosing Man to Himself.* New York: Van Nostrand.
    1971   *Self-Disclosure: An Experimental Analysis of the Transparent Self.* New York: Wiley.
Jourard, Sidney M., and Paul Lasakow
    1958   Some factors in self-disclosure. *Journal of Abnormal and Social Psychology* 56: 91–98.
Jucker, Andreas H., and Sarah W. Smith
    1998   And people just you know like 'wow': Discourse markers as negotiating strategies. In *Discourse Markers: Descriptions and Theory. Pragmatics and Beyond Series* 57, Andreas H. Jucker, and Yeal Ziv (eds.), 171–120. Amsterdam/Philadelphia: John Benjamins.
Kagan, Norman
    1975   *Influencing Human Interaction.* Washington DC: American Personnel and Guidance Association.
Kahn, Michael
    1991   *Between Therapist and Client. The New Relationship.* W.H. Freeman/Owl Books: New York.
Kamio, Akio
    1997   *Territory of Information.* Amsterdam: John Benjamins.
Kelly, Anita E.
    1998   Clients' secret keeping in outpatient therapy. *Journal of Counseling Psychology* 45: 50–57.
Kendon, Adam
    1980   Gesticulation and speech: Two aspects of the process of utterance. In *The Relationship of Verbal and Nonverbal Communication,* Mary R. Key (ed.), 207–228. The Hague: Mouton de Gruyter.

1983   Gesture and speech: How they interact. In *Nonverbal Interaction*, John M. Wiemann, and Randall P. Harrison (eds.), 13–43. Beverly Hills: Sage.

1985   Uses of gesture. In *Perspectives on Silence*, Deborah Tannen, and Muriel Saville-Troike (eds.), 215–234. Norwood, NJ: Ablex.

1987   On gesture: Its complementary relationship with speech. In *Nonverbal Behavior and Communication*, 2nd ed., Aron W. Siegman, and Stanley Feldstein (eds.), 65–97. Hillsdale, NJ: Lawrence Erlbaum.

1988   How gestures become like words. In *Cross-Cultural Perspectives in Nonverbal Communication*, Fernando Poyatos (ed.), 131–141. Toronto: Hogrefe.

Key, Mary R.
1975   *Paralanguage and Kinesics: Nonverbal Communication.* Metuchen, NJ: The Scarecrow Press.

1982   Overall considerations of human beings interacting in their world. In *Nonverbal Communication Today*, Mary R. Key (ed.), 3–13. New York: Mouton de Gruyter.

Kiełkiewicz-Janowiak, Agnieszka, and Joanna Pawelczyk
2004   Globalization and customer service communication at Polish call centres. In *Speaking from the Margin: Global English from a European Perspective*, Anna Duszak, and Urszula Okulska (eds.), 225–238. Frankfurt/Main: Peter Lang Verlag.

Kiesler, Donald J.
1973   *The Process of Psychotherapy: Empirical Foundations and Systems of Analysis.* Chicago: Aldine King.

Labov, William
1972   Some principles of linguistic methodology. *Language in Society* 1: 97–120.

1982   Objectivity and commitment in linguistic science: The case of the Black English trial in Ann Arbor. *Language in Society* 11/2: 165–201.

1984   Field methods of the project on linguistic change and variation. In *Language in Use: Readings in Sociolinguistics*, John Baugh, and Joel Sherzer (eds.), 28–53.Englewood Cliffs: Prentice Hall.

Labov, William, and David Fanshel
1977   *Therapeutic Discourse: Psychotherapy as Conversation.* New York: Academic Press.

Ladany, Nicholas, Hill Clara E., Thompson Barbara J., and Karen M. O'Brien
2004   Therapist perspectives on using silence in therapy: A qualitative study. *Counselling and Psychotherapy Research* 4/1: 80–89.

Lakoff, Robin
1973   The logic of politeness, or minding your p's and q's. *Papers from the Ninth Regional Meeting of the Chicago Linguistics Society*, 292–305.

1982   The rationale of psychotherapeutic discourse. In *Handbook of Inter-personal Psychotherapy*, Jack Anchin, and Donald Kiesler (eds.), 132–146. New York /Frankfurt: Pergamon Press.

1989   The limits of politeness: Therapeutic and courtroom discourse. *Multilingua* 8–2/3: 101–129.

1990   *Talking Power: The Politics of Language in Our Lives.* New York: Basic Books.

Lambert, Michael J., and Dean E. Barley
2001   Research summary on the therapeutic relationship and psychotherapy outcome. *Psychotherapy* 38: 357–361

Lambert, Michael J., and Allen E. Bergin
1994   The effectiveness of psychotherapy. In *Handbook of Psychotherapy and Behavior Change*, 4th ed., Allen E. Bergin, and Sol L. Garfield (eds.), 143–190. New York: Wiley.

Lambert, Michael J., Bergin Allen E., and Sol L. Garfield
2004   Introduction and historical overview. In *Bergin and Garfield's Handbook of Psychotherapy and Behavior Change*, Michael J. Lambert (ed.), 3–15. New York: John Wiley.

Lambert, Michael J., and Clara E. Hill
1994   Assessing psychotherapy outcomes and processes. In *Handbook of Psychotherapy and Behavior Change*, Michael J. Lambert, and Sol L. Garfield (eds.), 72–113. New York: Wiley.

Lambert, Michael J., and Benjamin M. Ogles
2004   The efficacy and effectiveness of psychotherapy. In *Bergin and Garfield's Handbook of Psychotherapy and Behavior Change*, Michael J. Lambert (ed.), 139–193. New York: Wiley.

Lasch, Christopher
1979   *The Culture of Narcissism: American Life in an Age of Diminishing Expectations.* New York: Norton.

Lave, Jean, and Etienne Wenger
1991   *Situated Learning: Legitimate Peripheral Participation.* Cambridge: Cambridge University Press.

Lazarus, Richard S.
1989   *Emotion and Adaptation.* New York: Oxford University Press.

LeDoux, Joseph
1998   *The Emotional Brain. The Mysterious Underpinnings of Emotional Life.* New York/London: Phoenix.

Leudar, Ivan, Antaki Charles, and Rebecca Barnes
2006   When psychotherapists disclose personal information about themselves to their clients. *Communication & Medicine* 3/1: 27–41.

Levinson, Stephen
1979   Activity types and language. *Linguistics* 17(5/6): 356–399.

Levitt, Heidi M.
2001   Sounds of silence in psychotherapy: The categorization of clients' pauses. *Psychotherapy Research* 11/3: 295–309.
2002   Clients' experiences of obstructive silences: Integrating conscious reports and analytic theories. *Journal of Contemporary Psychotherapy* 31/4: 221–244.

Linde, Charlotte
1993   *Life Stories: The Creation of Coherence.* New York: Oxford University Press.

Luhmann, Niklas
1986   *Love as Passion: The Codification of Intimacy.* Cambridge: Polity.
1990   *Essays on Self-Reference.* New York: Columbia University Press.

Lupton, Deborah
1998   *The Emotional Self.* London: Sage.

Lutz, Catherine
1988   *Unnatural Emotions: Everyday Sentiments on a Micronesian Atoll and Their Challenge to Western Theory.* Chicago: Chicago University Press.

Lutz, Catherine, and Lila Abu-Lughod
1990   Introduction: Emotion, discourse, and the politics of everyday life. In *Language and the Politics of Emotion*, Catherine Lutz, and Lila Abu-Lughod (eds.), 1–23. Cambridge: Cambridge University Press.

Madill, Anna, Widdicombe Sue, and Michael Barkham
2001   The potential of Conversation Analysis for psychotherapy research. *The Counseling Psychologist* 29: 413–434.

Madonik, Barbara G.
2001   *I Hear What You Say, but What Are You Telling Me?: The Strategic Use of Nonverbal Communication in Mediation.* San Francisco, CA: Jossey-Bass.

Mahl, George F.
1987   *Explorations in Nonverbal and Vocal Behavior.* Hillsdale, NJ: Lawrence Erlbaum.

Mahrer, Alvin R.
1985   *Psychotherapeutic Change.* New York: W. W. Norton.
1998   How can impressive in-session changes become impressive postsession changes? In *Handbook of Experiential Psychotherapy*, Leslie S. Greenberg, Jeanne C. Watson, and Germain Lietaer (eds.), 201–223. New York: The Guilford Press.

Mahrer, Alvin R., and Wayne P. Nadler
1986   Good moments in psychotherapy: A preliminary review, a list, and some promising research avenues. *Journal of Consulting and Clinical Psychology* 54: 10–15.

McLeod, John, and Sophia Balamoutsou
2001   A method for qualitative narrative analysis of psychotherapy transcripts. In *Qualitative Psychotherapy Research: Methods and Methodol-*

ogy, Jörg Frommer, and David Rennie (eds.), 128–152. Lengerich, Germany: Pabst.

McLeod, Julie, and Kate Wright

2003   Shaping the self through psychotherapeutic means: Gender and cross-generational perspectives. In *NZARE/AARE 2003: Educational Research, Risks and Dilemmas: New Zealand Association for Research in Education and the Australian Association for Research in Education*, Eddy van Til (ed.), 1–13. Coldstream, Victoria: Australian Association for Research in Education.

2009   The talking cure in everyday life: Gender, generations and friendship. *Sociology* 43/1: 122–139.

Mercer, Neil

2000   *Words and Minds*. London: Routledge.

Milroy, James, and Lesley Milroy

1978   Belfast: Change and variation in an urban vernacular. In *Sociolinguistic Patterns in British English*, Peter Trudgill (ed.), 19-36. London: Arnold.

Milroy, Lesley, and Matthew Gordon

2003   *Sociolinguistics. Method and Interpretation*. Oxford: Blackwell.

Mishler, Elliot G.

1984   *The Discourse of Medicine: Dialectics of Medical Interviews*. Norwood, NJ: Ablex.

Mitchell, Stephen A.

2002   *Can Love Last?: The Fate of Romance over Time*. New York: Norton.

Moerman, Michael

1990   *Ethnography and Conversation Analysis*. Philadelphia: University of Pennsylvania Press.

Morse, Janice M., and Lyn Richards

2002   *Readme First For a User's Guide to Qualitative Methods*. Thousand Oaks, CA: Sage.

Moursund, Janet, and Richard Erskine

2004   *Integrative Psychotherapy. The Art and Science of Relationship*. Thompson & Brooks/Cole.

Mullany, Louise

2007   *Gendered Discourse in the Professional Workplace*. Basingstoke: Palgrave Macmillan.

Nelson, Judith K.

2005   *Seeing through Tears. Crying and Attachment*. New York: Brunner/Routledge.

Norcross, John C., and Donald K. Freedheim

1992   Into the future: Retrospect and prospect in psychotherapy. In *History of Psychotherapy. A Century of Change*, Donald K. Freedheim (ed.), 881–900. Washington: American Psychological Association.

Oatley, Keith, and Jennifer Jenkins
  1996   *Understanding Emotions.* Cambridge, MA: Blackwell.
Ochs, Elinor (ed.)
  1989   Introduction. *Text* 9/1. Special issue on *The pragmatics of affect*, 1–5.
Ochs, Elinor
  1992   Indexing gender. In *Rethinking Context. Language as an Interactive Phenomenon*, Alessandro Duranti, and Charles Goodwin (eds.), 335–359. Cambridge: Cambridge University Press.
Ochs, Elinor, and Bambi Schieffelin
  1989   Language has a heart. *Text* 9/1: 7–25.
O'Hanlon, Bill, and James Wilk
  1987   *Shifting Contexts: The Generation of Effective Psychotherapy.* New York: The Guilford Press.
Orlinsky, David E.
  1989   Researchers' images of psychotherapy: Their origins and influence on research. *Clinical Psychology Review* 9: 413–441.
Orlinsky, David E., and Kenneth I. Howard
  1986   Process and outcome in psychotherapy. In *Handbook of Psychotherapy and Behavior Change*, 3rd ed., Sol L. Garfield, and Allen E. Bergin (eds.), 311–381. New York: Wiley.
Östman, Jan O.
  1981   *You know: A Discourse Functional Approach.* Amsterdam: John Benjamins.
Parkinson, Brian
  1996   Emotions are social. *British Journal of Psychology* 87: 663–683.
Parks, Malcolm R.
  1982   Ideology in interpersonal communication: Off the couch and into the world. In *Communication Yearbook 5*, Michael Burgoon (ed.), 79–107. New Brunswick, NJ: Transaction Books.
  1995   Ideology in interpersonal communication: Beyond the couches, talk-shows, and bunkers. In *Communication Yearbook 18*, Brant R. Burleson (ed.), 480–497. Newbury Park, CA: Sage.
Pavlenko, Anita
  2005   *Emotions and Multilingualism.* Cambridge: Cambridge University Press.
Pawelczyk, Joanna, and Richard Erskine
  2008   Expressing the unexpressed: Self-disclosure as interactional achievement in the psychotherapy session. *Communication & Medicine* 5/1: 39–48.
Pea, Roy D., and Robert L. Russel
  1987   Ethnography and the vicissitudes of talk in psychotherapy. In *Spoken Language in Psychotherapy: Strategies of Discovery*, Robert L. Russell (ed.), 303–338. New York: Plenum.

Peräkylä, Anssi
1995   *AIDS Counselling: Institutional Interaction and Clinical Practice.*
        Cambridge: Cambridge University Press.
Peräkylä, Anssi, Antaki Charles, Vehvilläinen Sanna, and Ivan Leudar, I. (eds.)
2008   *Conversation Analysis and Psychotherapy.* Cambridge: Cambridge
        University Press.
Peräkylä, Anssi, and Sanna Vehviläinen
2003   Conversation analysis and the professional stocks of interactional
        knowledge. *Discourse & Society* 14/6: 727–750.
2007   Conversational practices of psychotherapy – an overview. *Paper given
        at the 4th International Conference: Conversation Analysis of Psy-
        chotherapy.* 20–22 September, 2007, Bologna, Italy.
Perls, Fritz
1973   *The Gestalt Approach and Eyewitness to Therapy.* Palo Alto, CA: Sci-
        ence & Behavior Books.
Petronio, Sandra (ed.)
2000   *Balancing the Secrets of Private Disclosure.* Mahwah, NJ: Lawrence
        Erlbaum.
Philippot, Pierre, Feldman Robert S., and Erik J. Coates
2003   The role of nonverbal behavior in clinical settings: Introduction and
        overview. In *Nonverbal Behavior in Clinical* Setting, Pierre Philippot,
        Robert S. Feldman, and Erik J. Coats (eds.), 3–16 Oxford/New York:
        Oxford University Press.
Pittenger, Robert E., Hockett Charles F., and John J. Danehy
1960   *The First Five Minutes. A Sample of Microscopic Interview Analysis.*
        Ithaca, NY: Paul Martineau.
Planlap, Sally, and Karen Knie
2002   Integrating verbal and nonverbal emotion(al) messages. In *The Verbal
        Communication of Emotions: Interdisciplinary Perspectives*, Susan R.
        Fussell (ed.), 55–78. New Jersey: Lawrence Erlbaum.
Plutchik, Robert
1982   A psychoevolutionary theory of emotions. *Social Science Information*
        21 (4/5): 529–53.
Pomerantz, Anita
1980   Telling my side: 'Limited access' as a fishing device. *Sociological
        Inquiry* 50: 186–98.
1984   Agreeing and disagreeing with assessments: Some features of prefer-
        red/dispreferred turn-shapes. In *Structures of Social Action: Studies in
        Conversation Analysis*, John M. Atkinson, and John Heritage (eds.),
        57–101. Cambridge: Cambridge University Press.
1986   Extreme case formulations: A way of legitimizing claims. *Human Stu-
        dies* 9: 219–30.

Pomerantz, Anita, and John M. Atkinson
  1984   Ethnomethodology, conversation analysis and the study of courtroom interaction. In *Topics in Psychology and Law*, Dave J. Muller, Derek E. Blackman, and Antony J. Chapman (eds.), 283–294. Chichester: Wiley.
Potter, Jonathan
  1996   *Representing Reality. Discourse, Rhetoric and Social Construction.* London/New Delhi: Sage.
Potter, Jonathan, and Alexa Hepburn
  2005   Qualitative interviews in psychology: Problems and possibilities. *Qualitative Research in Psychology* 2: 281–307.
Poyatos, Fernando
  1980   Interactive functions and limitations of verbal and nonverbal behaviors in natural conversation. *Semiotica* 30 (3/4): 211–244.
  1982   New perspectives for an integrative research of nonverbal systems. In *Nonverbal Communication Today: Current Research*, Mary R. Key (ed.), 121–138. New York: Mouton de Gruyter.
Pudlinski, Christopher
  2005   Doing empathy and sympathy: Caring responses to troubles tellings on a peer support line. *Discourse Studies* 7/3: 267–288.
Racker, Heinrich
  1968   *Transference and Countertransference.* New York: International Universities Press.
Ragan, Sandy L.
  2000   Social talk in women's health care contexts: Two forms of nonmedical talk. In *Small Talk*, Justine Coupland (ed.), 269–287. Harlow: Longman.
Rawlins, William K.
  1998   Theorizing public and private domains and practices of communication: Introductory Concerns. *Communication Theory* 8: 369–380.
Redeker, Gisela
  1990   Identical and pragmatic markers of discourse structure. *Journal of Pragmatics* 14: 367–381.
Reusch, Jurgen, and Gregory Bateson
  1951   *Communication: The Social Matrix of Psychiatry.* New York: Norton & Co.
Richmond, Virginia P., and James C. McCroskey
  2000   *Nonverbal Behavior in Interpersonal Relations.* 4th ed. Needham Heights, MA: Allyn & Bacon.
Rieff, Philip
  1966   *The Triumph of the Therapeutic: Uses of Faith after Freud.* New York: Harper & Row.
Riggio, Ronald E.
  1986   Assessment of basic social skills. *Journal of Personality and Social Psychology* 51: 649–660.

1989   *Manual for the Social Skills Inventory.* Palo Alto, CA: Consulting Psychologists Press.
1992   Social interaction skills and nonverbal behavior. In *Applications of Nonverbal Behavioral Theories and Research,* Robert S. Feldman (ed.), 3–30. Hillsdale, NJ: Lawrence Erlbaum.

Riggio, Ronald E., Tucker Joan S., and David Coffaro
1989   Social skills and empathy. *Personality and Individual Differences* 10: 93–99.

Roberts, Celia, and Sarah Campbell
2006   *Talk on Trial. Job Interviews, Language and Ethnicity.* Retrieved October 20, 2007 from Department for Work and Pensions, http://www.dwp.gov.uk/asd/asd5/rrs2006.asp#talkontrial.

Roberts, Celia, and Srikant Sarangi
1999   Hybridity in gatekeeping discourse: Issues of practical relevance for the researcher. In *Talk, Work and Institutional Order: Discourse in Medical, Mediation and Management Settings,* Srikant Sarangi, and Celia Roberts (eds.), 473–503. Berlin: Mouton de Gruyter.
2002   Mapping and assessing medical students' interactional involvement styles with patients. In *Unity and Diversity in Language Use,* Kristyan Spellman-Miller, and Paul Thompson (eds.), 99–117. London: Continuum.
2003   Uptake of discourse research in interprofessional settings: Reporting from medical consultancy. *Applied Linguistics* 24/3: 338–359.
2005   Theme-oriented discourse analysis of medical encounters. *Medical Education* 39: 632–640.

Rogers, Carl R.
1942   *Counselling and Psychotherapy. Newer Concepts in Practice.* Houghton Mifflin Company.
1951   *Client-Centered Therapy.* Boston: Houghton Mifflin.

Rose, Nikolas
1990   *Governing the Soul: The Shaping of the Private Self.* London: Routledge.

Russel, Robert L.
1987   *Language in Psychotherapy. Strategies of Discovery.* New York/London: Plenum Press.

Ruusuvuori, Johanna
2000   Control in medical interaction. Practices of giving and receiving the reason for the visit in primary health care. Ph. D. diss., Department of Sociology and Social Psychology, University of Tampere. *Acta Electronica Universitatis Tamperensis* 16. http://acta.uta.fi

Ryle, Gilbert
1949   *The Concept of Mind.* London: Penguin.

Sabbadini, Andrea
1991   Listening to silence. *British Journal of Psychotherapy* 7: 406–415.

Sacks, Harvey
1992   *Lectures on Conversation.* Vol. 1 & Vol. 2. Oxford: Blackwell.
Sacks, Harvey, Schegloff Emanuel A., and Gail Jefferson
1974   A simplest systematics for the organization of turn-taking for conversation. *Language* 50: 696–735.
Sarangi, Srikant
2000   Activity types, discourse types and interactional hybridity: The case of genetic counseling. In *Discourse and Social Life*, Srikant Sarangi, and Malcolm Coulthard (eds.), 1–27. London: Longman.
2001   A comparative perspective on social-theoretical accounts of language-action relationship. In *Sociolinguistics and Social Theory*, Nikolas Coupland, Srikant Sarangi, and Christopher N. Candlin (eds.), 29–60. London: Longman.
2002   Discourse practitioners as a community of interprofessional practice: Some insights from health communication research. In *Research and Practice in Professional Discourse*, Christopher N. Candlin (ed.), 95–135. Hong Kong: City University of Hong Kong Press.
2004   Language/activity: Observing and interpreting ritualistic institutional discourse. *Cahiers de Linguistique Française* 26: 136–150. http://clf.unige.ch/files/26/12-Burger.pdf
Sarangi, Srikant, Bennert Kristina, Howell Lucy, Clarke Angus, Harper Peter, and Jonathon Gray
2004   Initiation of reflective frames in counseling for Huntington's disease predictive testing. *Journal of Genetic Counseling* 13/2: 135–155.
Sarangi, Srikant, and Christopher N. Candlin
2001   Motivational relevancies: Some methodological reflections on sociolinguistic and social theoretical practices. In *Sociolinguistics and Social Theory*, Nikolas Coupland, Srikant Sarangi, and Christopher N. Candlin (eds.), 350–388. London: Longman.
2003   Trading between reflexivity and relevance: New challenges for applied linguistics. *Applied Linguistics* 24/3: 271–285.
Sarangi, Srikant, and Christopher Hall
1997   Bringing off 'applied' research in inter-professional discourse studies. Paper presented at the *BAAL/CUP Seminar on Urban Culture, Discourse and Ethnography*. Thames Valley University, 24–25 March.
Sarangi, Srikant, and Celia Roberts (eds.)
1999   *Talk, Work and Institutional Order: Discourse in Medical, Mediation and Management Settings.* Berlin: Mouton de Gruyter.
Schafer, Roy
1992   *Retelling a Life: Narration and Dialogue in Psychoanalysis.* New York: Basic Books.
Scheflen, Albert E.
1973   *Communicational Structure: Analysis of Psychotherapy Transaction.* Bloomington: Indiana University Press.

Schegloff, Emanuel A.
  1981   Discourse as an interactional achievement: Some uses of uh-huh and other things that come between sentences. In *Analyzing Discourse: Text and Talk. Georgetown University Roundtable on Languages and Linguistics*, Deborah Tannen (ed.), 71–93. Washington, DC: Georgetown University Press.
  2001   Discourse as an interactional achievement III: The omnirelevance of action. In *The Handbook of Discourse Analysis*, Deborah Schiffrin, Deborah Tannen, and Heidi Hamilton (eds.), 229–249. Malden, MA: Blackwell.
  2007   *Sequence Organization in Interaction: A Primer in Conversation Analysis.* Cambridge: Cambridge University Press.
Scherer, Klaus R.
  1986   Vocal affect expression: A review and a model for future research. *Psychological Bulletin,* 99/2, 143–165.
Schiffrin, Deborah
  1985   Conversational coherence: The role of *well. Language* 61: 640–667.
  1987   *Discourse Markers. Studies in Interactional Sociolinguistics 5.* Cambridge: Cambridge University Press.
  1996   Narrative as self-portrait: Sociolinguistic constructions of identity. *Language in Society* 25: 167–203.
  1998   *Approaches to Discourse.* Cambridge, MA: Blackwell.
  1999   OH as a marker of information management. In *The Discourse Reader*, Adam Jaworski, and Nikolas Coupland (eds.), 275–288. London: Routledge.
Schiffrin, Deborah, Tannen Deborah, and Heidi Hamilton (eds.)
  2001   *The Handbook of Discourse Analysis.* Malden, MA: Blackwell.
Schourup, Lawrence
  1985   *Common Discourse Particles in English Conversation.* New York: Garland Publishing, Inc.
  1999   Discourse markers: Tutorial overview. *Lingua* 107: 227–265.
Scollon, Ronald
  1998   *Mediated Discourse as Social Interaction. A Study of News Discourse.* New York: Longman.
Sennet, Richard
  1974   *The Fall of Public Man.* New York: Random House.
Silverman, David
  1987   *Communication and Medical Practice.* London: Sage.
  1996   *Discourses of Counselling.* London: Sage.
  2000   *Doing Qualitative Research: A Practical Guide.* London: Sage.
  2001   *Interpreting Qualitative Data: Methods for Analysing Talk, Text and Interaction.* 2nd ed. London: Sage.
  2005   *Doing Qualitative Research.* 2nd ed. London: Sage.

Silverstein, Michael
1985   Language and the culture of gender: At the intersection of structure, usage, and ideology. In *Semiotic Mediation: Sociocultural and Psychological Perspectives*, Elizabeth Mertz, and Richard J. Parmentier (eds.), 219–259. Orlando: Academic Press.

Small, John J., and Robert J. Manthei
1986   The language of therapy. *Psychotherapy* 23/3: 395–404.

Spinelli, Ernesto
2006   *Tales of Unknowing: Therapeutic Encounters from an Existential Perspective*. Ross-on-Wye: PCCS Books.

Staemmler, Frank M.
2004   Dialogue and interpretation in Gestalt Therapy: Making sense together. *International Gestalt Journal* 27/2: 33–57.

Stiles, William B.
1995   Disclosure as a speech act: It is psychotherapeutic to disclose. In *Emotion, Disclosure and Health*, James W. Pennebaker (ed.), 71–91. Washington DC: American Psychological Association.

Stiles, William B., Elliott Robert, Llewelyn Susan P., Firth-Cozens Jenny A., Margison Frank R., Shapiro David A., and Gilian Hardy
1990   Assimilation of problematic experiences by clients in psychotherapy. *Psychotherapy* 27: 411–420.

Stolorow, Robert D.
1992   Closing the gap between theory and practice with better psychoanalytic theory. *Psychotherapy* 29: 159–166.

Stone, Andrew
1996   Clinical assessment of affect. In *Knowing Feeling*, Donald L. Nathanson (ed.), 22–36. New York: W. W. Norton,.

Streeck, Jürgen, and Mark L. Knapp
1992   The interaction of visual and verbal features in human communication. In *Advances in Nonverbal Communication. Sociocultural, Clinical, Esthetic and Literary Perspectives*, Fernando Poyatos (ed.), 3–23. Amsterdam/Philadelphia: John Benjamins.

Stubbs, Michael
1997   Language and the mediation of experience: Linguistic representation and cognitive orientation. In *The Handbook of Sociolinguistics*, Florian Coulmas (ed.), 358–373. Oxford: Blackwell.

Szasz, Thomas
1978   *The Myth of Psychotherapy: Mental Healing as Religion, Rhetoric, and Repression*. Syracuse: Syracuse University Press.

Tannen, Deborah
1986   *That's Not What I Meant!: How Conversational Style Makes or Breaks Relationships*. New York: Ballantine.
1989   *Talking Voices: Repetition, Dialogue, and Imagery in Conversational Discourse*. Cambridge: Cambridge University Press.

Tannen, Deborah, and Cynthia Wallat
    1987   Interactive frames and knowledge schemas in interaction: Examples from a medical examination/interview. *Social Psychology Quarterly* 50/2: 205–216.

Tashakkori, Abbas, and Charles Teddlie
    1998   *Mixed Methodology: Combining Qualitative and Quantitative Approaches.* Thousand Oaks, CA: Sage.

Taylor, Charles
    1992   *Sources of the Self: The Making of the Modern Identity.* Cambridge: Cambridge University Press.

Taylor, Steve, and Melissa Tyler
    2000   Emotional labour and sexual difference in the airline industry. *Work, Employment and Society* 14/1: 77–96.

Ten Have, Paul
    2001   Applied conversation analysis. In *How to Analyse Talk in Institutional Settings: A Casebook of Methods*, Alec McHoul, and Mark Rapley (eds.), 3–11. London/New York: Continuum.

Thomas, Jenny
    1995   *Meaning in Interaction. An Introduction to Pragmatics.* London: Longman.

Tickle-Degnen, Linda, and Robert Rosenthal
    1992   Nonverbal aspects of therapeutic rapport. In *Applications of Nonverbal Behavioral Theories and Research*, Robert S. Feldman (ed.), 143–164. Hillsdale, NJ: Lawrence Erlbaum.

Todd, Alexandra
    1989   *Intimate Adversaries: Cultural Conflict between Doctors and Women Patients.* Philadelphia: University of Pennsylvania Press.

Trad, Paul V.
    1993   Silence: The resounding experience. *American Journal of Psychotherapy* 47: 167–170.

Trömel-Plötz, Senta
    1981   'I'd come to you for therapy': Interpretation, redefinition and paradox in Rogerian therapy. *Journal of Pragmatics* 5/2–3: 243–260.

Tsui, Amy
    1991   The pragmatic functions of 'I don't know'. *Text* 11/4: 607–622.

Turner, Roy
    1972   Some formal properties of therapy talk. In *Studies in Social Interaction*, David Sudnow (ed.), 367–396. New York: Free Press.

Tusting, Karin, and Janet Maybin
    2007   Linguistic ethnography and interdisciplinarity: Opening the discussion. *Journal of Sociolinguistics* 11/5: 575–583.

Van Leeuwen, Theo
    2005   Three models of interdisciplinarity. In *New Agendas in Critical Discourse Analysis*, Ruth Wodak (ed.), 3–18. Amsterdam: John Benjamins.

Vehviläinen, Sanna
   1999   *Structures of Counselling Interaction. A Conversation Analytic Study on Counselling in Career Guidance Training.* Helsinki: University of Helsinki: Department of Education.
   2003   Preparing and delivering interpretations in psychoanalytic interaction. *Text* 23/4: 573–606.
Verhofstadt-Dillen, Leni, Dillen Let, Helskens Denis, and Mariska Siongers
   2004   The psychodramatical 'social method' with children: A developing dialogical self in dialectic action. In *The Dialogical Self in Psychotherapy*, Hubert J. M. Hermans, and Giancarlo Dimaggio (eds.), 152–170. Hove East Sussex/New York: Brunner/Routledge.
Wachtel, Paul L.
   1990   Psychotherapy from an integrative psychodynamic perspective. In *What is Psychotherapy? Contemporary Perspectives*, Jeffrey K. Zeig, and W. Michael Munion (eds.), 234–238. San Francisco: Jossey-Bass.
Wardhaugh, Ronald
   1985   *How Conversation Works.* Oxford: Blackwell.
Watzlawick, Paul, Hemlick-Beavin Janet H., and Don D. Jackson
   1967   *Pragmatics of Human Communication: A Study of Interactional Patterns, Pathologies, and Paradoxes.* New York: Norton.
Waxer, Peter
   1976   Nonverbal cues for depth of depression: Set versus no set. *Journal of Consulting & Clinical Psychology* 44: 493.
   1977   Nonverbal cues for anxiety: An examination of emotional leakage. *Journal of Abnormal Psychology* 86: 306–314.
Whalen, Jack, and Don Zimmerman
   1998   Observations on the display and management of emotion in naturally occurring activities: The case of 'hysteria' in calls to 9-1-1. *Social Psychology Quarterly* 61: 141–159.
White, Michael
   1992   Deconstruction and therapy. In *Experience, Contradiction, Narrative, and Imagination-Selected Papers of David Epston and Michael White, 1989–1991*, David Epston, and Michael White (eds.), 109–152. Adelaide, Australia: Dulwich Centre Publications.
Wierzbicka, Anna
   1991   *Cross-Cultural Pragmatics. The Semantics of Human Interaction.* Berlin/New York: Mouton de Gruyter.
Wolfram, Walt
   1993   Ethical considerations in language awareness programs. *Issues in Applied Linguistics* 4: 225–255.
Wong, Jean
   2000   Repetition in conversation: A look at first and second sayings. *Research on Language and Social Interaction* 33/4: 407–424.

Wynn, Rolf, and Michael Wynn
    2006   Empathy as an interactionally achieved phenomenon. Characteristics of some conversational resources. *Journal of Pragmatics* 38: 1385–1397.
Yalom, Irvin
    1989   *Love's Executioner and Other Tales of Psychotherapy.* Penguin Books.
Yalom, Irvin, and Ginny Elkin
    1974   *Every Day Gets a Little Closer. A Twice-Told Therapy.* Basic Books.
Yeh, Christine J., and Arpana G. Inman
    2007   Qualitative data analysis and interpretation in counseling psychology: Strategies for best practices. *The Counseling Psychologist* 35/3: 369–403.
Zimmerman, Don
    1992   The interactional organization of calls for emergency assistance. In *Talk at Work: Interaction in Institutional Settings*, Paul Drew, and John Heritage (eds.), 418–469. Cambridge: Cambridge University Press.
    1998   Identity, context and interaction. In *Identities in Talk*, Charles Antaki, and Sue Widdicombe (eds.), 87–106. London: Sage.
Zimmerman, Stephanie, and James L. Applegate
    1992   Person-centered comforting in the hospice interdisciplinary team. *Communication Research* 19: 240–263.
Zuckerman, Miron, DePaulo Bella M., and Robert Rosenthal
    1986   Humans as deceivers and lie-detectors. In *Nonverbal Communication in the Clinical Context*, Peter D. Blanck, Ross Buck, and Robert Rosenthal (eds.), 13–35. University Park: Pennsylvania State University Press.

Index